The Word of The Day

365 Daily Devotional

Rev. Lettie Moses Carr, Esq.

DEDICATION

I dedicate this to my mother, Sweet Marie Robinson
Moses, who planted the seeds of faith in my life that
continue to bear fruit impacting the lives of others. She
taught me to trust God to always make a way somehow.
In addition, I dedicate this to my children, Nelson and
Gabrielle, and my husband Neal. I pray this inspires you
and millions of others to read the Word of God daily.

The Word of the Day

Forward

As I prepared to send this to the publisher, I am reflecting on how we got here and how long it took. I was a young child when I told my mother I wanted to be a writer. Her response to me was in essence that I should go get a real job, have a career doing something else. Then I could always write on the side. But as I write the Word of the Day each weekday for my website WhosoeverBelieves.org I find it is a passion I have had all my life. I love to write. I realize I am not the world's best but still it's something I believe the Lord created me to do.

This 365-day devotional has been years in the making. I started posting the WOD a few years ago in the heart of the Covid-19 pandemic to encourage people who were very anxious about the state of the world. But really it has been in the making long before then. My little girl self always wanted to write. Some of the readers of the daily devotional began asking when I would publish a devotional. People have asked me when I would write a book for years. Once while I was a chaplain at the Maryland Correctional Institution for Women, one of the residents had a vision from the Lord. He told her to tell me to write the book. Shamefully, even all these prompts still did not result in me writing a book. It was only when I started posting daily that it began to evolve and take shape in spite of myself!

I want to thank God for allowing me to share His Word. I pray you find this encouraging, enlightening, and captivating enough to cause you to read your Bible more. And, hopefully, you will buy copies to share with your family and friends.

May God be both please and glorified.

Blessings,

Rev. Lettie Moses Carr, Esq.

ACKNOWLEDGMENTS

I want to thank Diane Hill Taylor and others who read the Word of the Day daily on WhosoeverBelieves.org and inspired me to believe these messages were worth compiling into a book. Most of all, I thank my Heavenly Father and the Lord Jesus Christ whose Word serves as the basis for this devotional. To God be the Glory!

January 1
God Will Make a Way

There have been many times in my life when things looked hopeless. It seemed as though I did not have enough help, money, time or other things I thought I needed. Sometimes bills were due, and I could not see how I could pay them. Other times the demands on my job were so numerous I did not see how I could get it all done and take care of my other responsibilities. Yet God has never failed to be faithful. There have been some instances when He changed my circumstances; but often, He has changed my view of my circumstances to allow me to see things were not as bad as they seemed. I have come to realize the way I *view* my experiences is often more important than the situations themselves. As a man thinks, so is he. Once I learned to recognize God will show up in unexpected ways, I shifted from seeing things as hopeless to recognizing as long as I have life, I have a reason to hope. Be like David, remember the way God has taken care of you in the past. No matter how bad a situation seems, God will make a way where there seems to be no way. Look up to change your outlook.

Today's Reading:
Joshua 3:7-17; Psalm 42:5-11; Romans 8:24

1

January 2
Led To A Hard Place

Sometimes God leads or allows us to go into places that will challenge us. They can seem frightening. Like when Moses and the Israelites were at the Red Sea things looked bleak, but God had a plan to bring His Name glory. Had they not been facing the Red Sea; we would not know God can move a sea! Knowing God has allowed a hardship in our life can cause some to question God's love or feel discouraged. It was this way when Lazarus died. His sister immediately went to Jesus when He arrived to say, "if you had been here, my brother would not have died." John 11:21. She looked at what she believed to be a horrible ending for her brother, not knowing that Jesus would call him from the grave to be glorified as the Son of God. Maybe He has allowed a circumstance in your life that seems hard to bear. Rather than be overtaken by your emotions, remind yourself He is in control and is well able to resurrect any dead relationships, finances, health condition or anything else that looks desolate in your life. Maintaining a spiritually mature viewpoint allows you to anticipate seeing how He may move in your situation to show He is God Almighty.

Today's Reading:
Exodus 6:2-5, 7:3, 14:5-14; Matthew 4:1
John 11:1-4; Acts 21:10-14

2

January 3
Knowing Your Position and Purpose

When you know who you are and what you are purposed to do, you can walk in God's will for your life. You can focus on the things God leads you to do, instead of trying to do what you think will please others. Jesus gave us the perfect example. He got up each day and spent time with our Father before He did anything else. By the time people started clamoring for His attention, He had already determined His agenda for the day. He did not change it even to pray for the sick who were nearby. How could this be? Because He knew His purpose. He did not let people deter Him from going to the next town as He had predetermined to do. Knowing your purpose and position also keeps you from feeling a need to defend yourself. When King David encountered a man who disrespected him, he did not need to prove he was powerful by punishing him. He was secure in his position as king. He knew who he was. Likewise, when you spend time in God's Word, you will become more aware of who you are as His child. You don't have to spend time trying to convince anyone of your significance, nor defend yourself, when you know God is pleased with you.

Today's Reading:
2 Samuel 19:21-22; Mark 1:32-38; Acts 27:23

January 4
Saving The Best For Last

Have you ever prayed for God to heal someone, and they passed away? Maybe you have jokingly shared your gratitude about knowing you are going to heaven, but also noted you are not in a hurry to get there. It is as though we think this side of natural death is better than the other. For a believer in the Lord Jesus Christ, nothing could be further from the truth. To be absent from your body means you will be present with the Lord. There will be no more sickness, heartache, or pain in heaven. God will wipe away every tear. You can rest assured; because Jesus rose from the grave, you too shall rise and be with Him forever! If you've accepted Jesus as your Savior, no matter how good your life is here on earth, nor how much money or prestige you attain, what lies ahead is far better. Certainly, it can be painful to let go of your loved ones who die in the Lord. You can feel as though the Lord did not hear your prayers. But He said in the Holy Bible, He loves you with an everlasting love. Rejoice in knowing that nothing on earth compares to being with the Lord in glory. Always remember, the best is yet to come!

Today's Reading:
Job 19:26; Matthew 22:32; John 11:25,26
1 Corinthians 15:54,55; 2 Corinthians 5:1-8
Revelations 7:16, 17

January 5
Rewards In The Secret Place

If someone loaned you money and went around boasting about it, you might be offended. You might not want everyone to know what they had done for you. Likewise, when you give to the poor, refrain from boasting or telling everyone about it. According to scripture, when you give to the poor you are not only giving to the person, but you are also lending to the Lord. He said do acts of charity in the secret place and He will reward you openly. Similarly, you can pray just to be heard by others or you can commune with God in the secret place. Go into your room, shut the door and pray, and then watch how God will reward you. Even when some people fast, they walk around looking somber so others will know. Instead, God said anoint your head and go about as normal. When we do these things in secret, He will bless you out in the open. The choice is yours. Either receive rewards from men by practicing your righteousness as a show or go into the secret place where only God will see. The latter pleases God. Give, pray and fast unto God in secret. Then others will see the many blessings He will bestow on you for honoring Him.

Today's Reading:
Psalm 91:1; Proverbs 19:17; Matthew 6:1-6, 16-21

January 6
Commissioned

Being a witness is not for a select few. Witnessing is part of the evidence of your faith. It is not optional if you are a follower of Christ. As His ambassador you represent Him in the earth. Everywhere you go you can bear witness to what He has done for you. Jesus gave us the Great Commission to go out and tell others about Him, teaching them to obey His word, and baptizing them in His Name. A commission is an instruction; a command that is given by a superior. In this instance it has been given to us by the highest-ranking person to ever walk the earth. Jesus has commanded us to tell others about His virgin birth, death on a cross, burial and resurrection from the dead for your sins and mine. You are called to let others know God has commanded everyone everywhere to repent. You are to let them know that those who believe and put their faith in Jesus Christ are forgiven of all their sins. Like a test that comes at the end of a semester, a day is coming when we will stand before God to give an account for all our actions while in the body. Will you have a good report?

Today's Reading:
Matthew 25:31-46, 28:18-20
Acts 1:8, 10:42-43, 17:30

January 7
When The Ungodly Prosper

Why does God allow people who do not obey the law to prosper? They seem to have no problems and lots of money. It may seem unfair to you, especially if you are struggling while trying to live a life that pleases God. Well, a few things come to mind. First off, God is not mocked. Whatever a man sows he will reap. If you sow to your flesh, you will reap destruction. If you sow to please God, you will reap eternal blessings. God honors His Word. So, no one will be able to avoid giving an account to Him. The other thing to consider is we all sin and fall short of God's will. So, you should never judge another. You may not know their full story. No sin is justified. Still, you might view their actions differently if you knew their motives, pain, struggles or even all their actions. Even the worst person you know has some good in them. Plus, God is patient. He wants everyone to have an opportunity to repent. Pray for the people you see as ungodly and trust God to be God.

Today's Reading:
Numbers 23:19; Job 21:7-33; Matthew 7:1-6
Romans 3:23, 14:4; 2 Peter 3:9

January 8
Can You Hear Me Now?

A cell phone service provider had a commercial wherein the actor would ask, "Can you hear me now?" It made fun of other carriers' connections being so poor you couldn't hear the caller unless you stood in the right spot to get the signal. One of the key factors to hearing God's voice is to be positioned to do so. You must get in the right spot: God's Word. It is the conduit to knowing His will for your life. It connects you to His voice. As you meditate on His Word daily your mind is renewed, and you are able to hear Him. Just like you wash your body daily to remove the germs and grime of being out in society, your mind needs to be cleansed and refreshed. Your mind gets bogged down with the world's pattern of thinking and negativity. However, by meditating on His Word every day your mind is renewed, and your thoughts start aligning with God's. It gets you to the right "spot" where you can "hear" Him and know His perfect will for your life. Then to fully walk that perfect will of God out, you cannot merely hear the Word, you must do what it says.

Today's Reading:
Psalm 119:15, 105; Colossians 3:16
Romans 12:1-2; James 1:22

January 9
Sudden Blessings

I love the way God demonstrates His Sovereignty. You can find yourself going through all kinds of challenges. Your circumstances may last for months or even years. Perhaps you have been struggling. Maybe, you have been trying to find a way out. Perhaps you have tried all you know to do. Yet, you feel like nothing is changing. Be encouraged. There is an old saying, "it's not over until the fat lady sings." Well, I want to suggest to you it's not over until God says it's over. The God we serve is able. Right in the middle of your situation God can step in and bless you suddenly. The God we serve is not limited to time nor space. It doesn't matter how long you have been dealing with whatever you are facing. No matter what remember, God is Almighty and bigger than any problem you may be facing or ever will face! Never count Him out. Never think your situation cannot be overcome. Never give up hope no matter how dire your circumstances may seem. God can step into your life to bless you and demonstrate His glory suddenly! Do Not Be Afraid!

Today's Reading:
Numbers 16:42; 2 Kings 2:11; Psalm 6:10,64:7
Isaiah 29:5,48:3; Luke 2:13; Acts 9:3,10:30

January 10
There's A Word For That!

A commercial became popular when the iPhone was emerging, and apps were introduced to cell phones. The saying was, "there's an app for that." It was intended to encourage you to download an app for whatever you might want to accomplish from figuring out a math problem to getting help with grammar. The Bible is an even greater resource. Whatever issue or challenge arises in your life, there is a Word for that. As a physician knows which prescription to give her patient, God's word has an appropriate response to address any issue that may arise in your life. It may not have the exact same circumstances, but it will have a principle that is applicable to every circumstance. So next time you need direction, rather than run to a fortune teller or even a friend, open your Bible to see what God has to say about anything you may encounter. He has a word for that!

Today's Reading:
Joshua 1:8; Psalm 119:11; John 8:31,32
2 Timothy 3:15,16; 2 Peter 1:3

January 11
Your Final Answer

How you respond to people who offend you is a sure sign of your spiritual maturity. You demonstrate whether Jesus is truly your Lord or whether you still call the shots or worst, someone else does. You can allow others to become your "gods" by allowing their behavior to determine yours. If you are only kind when others are kind to you, you are allowing them to rule you. In other words, you get to choose to follow the pattern set by the Lord or to follow the example of others. If you repay evil for evil, then you are following another voice. God's way is to overcome evil with good. Good always trumps evil. God challenges you to love your enemies. He says to still be kind even when others are unkind to you. Don't respond to evil with evil. Respond in love. As His disciple, you demonstrate His way to the world by treating others better than they treat. Not only does He say you should love your enemies, but He also says you should pray for those who persecute you. Through this you glorify your heavenly Father.

Today's Reading:
Psalm 38:20; Matthew 5:16,44
Romans 12:17,21; 1 Peter 3:9

January 12
Be Prepared

My son was a fan of the original Lion King movie. So was I! One memorable scene was when the antagonist was plotting the murder of the king. He was telling his co-conspirators to be ready when the moment came to execute their treasonous plans. He sang a song, "Be Prepared." That's good advice for all of us. Life can come at you very fast. Pharaoh found this out when he had a dream with two sets of images that turned out to represent the same thing. God showed him what the world was about to experience. Joseph, who was imprisoned, was summoned to interpret the Pharaoh's dream. He determined it to mean a famine was coming. He discerned there would be 7 years of plenty, followed by 7 years of famine. God forewarned them. Consequently, Joesph led the nation's efforts to plan for the lean years by saving while things were plentiful. When the famine came, they were able to live on the saved-up grain. Like then, God's message to you is to store up. Prepare for lean days ahead because things can shift quickly. Be prepared.

Today's Reading:
Exodus 16:5; Genesis 41:33-36; Ezra 10:4
Proverbs 16:9; Ezekiel 38:7; John 14:2

January 13
Even In A Famine

Over the history of the world there have been many famines. During the times they have occurred, God has always sustained His people. In Abraham's lifetime there was a great famine, but God was with him and ensured he survived. When a famine covered the region of Egypt and the Middle East during Joseph's lifetime, God had already made a way for his people to be sustained. God foreknew and forewarned of a 7-year famine that was to come. He had already sent Joseph ahead of his family, albeit in an unorthodox way, so that they were postured and prepared for the famine. He was able to feed his family during that difficult time. Remember God is always with you no matter what happens. He is the same today, yesterday, and forever. He is faithful. He will be with you in times of trouble. He will deliver you when you call upon Him. Famines may come but they are no match for our God. You don't have to worry as you see what is happening in the world because you can rest assuring knowing nothing can separate you from the love of God, not even a famine.

Today's Reading:
Genesis 12:10, 50:20; Job 5:20,22
Psalm 33:18-20; Philippians 4:16-19; Romans 8:35

January 14
God Is Not Surprised

God is omniscient. This means He knows everything. Nothing surprises Him. He knows your thoughts and what you will say before you say it. Nothing is hidden from His sight. He knows the end of a thing before the beginning. He does nothing without first forewarning His servants. Just like God forewarned Pharaoh through a dream when He was about to bring a famine, the Holy Spirit will reveal things to us that is yet to come. He shows us what you need to know in order for you to prepare for what lies ahead. If He chooses not to give you a revelation of what is to come, then it means you don't need to know. The important thing is He knows. He is your refuge and strength. He is an ever-present help in times of trouble. You may not know what tomorrow holds, but you know who holds tomorrow. Since He knows, there is no reason to fear. You can rest knowing He has you in the palm of His hands. He loves you with an everlasting love and nothing is kept from His sight.

Today's Reading:
Genesis 41:28; Psalm 46:1, 139:2-4
Isaiah 46:10, 49:16; Matthew 24:7
Luke 21:1; Hebrews 4:13

January 15
Another Famine Is Coming

We are living in an unprecedented time. It sounds cliché yet it is true. One of the things that makes this time so unique, is the ability for nearly anyone on the planet earth to hear the Word of God. No matter where you are on the globe, with little exception, you can read, be taught, or hear the Bible preached. Many take it for granted that ministries will always be around to share the gospel. They see a preacher on television and flip the channel. A radio station broadcasting faith related content will be avoided by many. Yet, when crisis hits their lives, they come to church or seek someone to pray for them. When 9-11 brought terrorist attacks, churches around the country were brimming with people who hadn't attended a service for many days or even years, absent a funeral or a wedding. Yet, the Lord has said to seek His face while He may be found because a day is coming when we will want to hear a Word but not be able to do so. "The days are coming," declares the Sovereign Lord, "when I will send a famine through the land— not a famine of food or a thirst for water, but a famine of hearing the words of the Lord."

Today's Reading:
2 Chronicles 7:14; Isaiah 55:6; Amos 8:11 NIV

January 16
Not The End Yet

There are several things that have occurred in our lifetime that have caused people to say the end of time is near. Yet, Jesus forewarned us not to get ahead of God. He said we would hear of wars and rumors of wars. Nation will rise against nation. And kingdoms will rise against kingdoms. He told us we would experience famines, pestilences (epidemics), and earthquakes in various places. We surely have seen all of this and then some but there is still more to happen before His return. He said many will come in His name, claiming to be Him. We have seen this, too. Christians being delivered up for tribulation is one huge thing that we have seen but I believe will grow worse before He returns. In fact, Jesus said some will be delivered up to be killed, many will be offended, and Christians will betray one another and will hate one another. Sadly, although we have seen these things, the worst is still to come. The things we have witnessed so far is just a prelude to the things to come. Consequently, it is not the end yet.

Today's Reading:
Matthew 24:4-26; Mark 13:5-23
Luke 21:5-24; Acts 1:6,7

January 17
Seeds Produce More

When a seed is planted, it produces a crop far more than its original size. One apple seed can produce an entire tree. This holds true in the natural and in the spiritual realm. Scripture says you shall reap what you sow. You should expect a harvest from the seeds you plant. If you sow love, you can expect to reap love in greater abundance. When you show grace to others, God will let even more grace flow to you. When you bless others financially you will reap a harvest pressed down, shaken together, and running over. Pouring into a ministry will lead to God supplying all your needs according to His glorious riches. God loves a cheerful giver. He said He will not only bless you, but He will also give you even more seed to sow. Even in prayer, expect your prayers to yield even more than you have asked. Like those prayed for Peter when he was in jail, many don't expect God to do exceedingly more than they ask. Though they prayed for Peter, they did not expect him to show up at their door after being set free by an angel. God's Word is true. Expect an abundant harvest from whatever seeds you plant.

Today's Reading:
Mark 4:31,32; Luke 6:38; Acts 12:12-15
Galatians 6:7-10; Ephesians 4:32

January 18
Like A Scrimmage

When you play in a scrimmage and lose the game, it doesn't count against your record. Hence you can lose multiple times before the regular season starts but still be undefeated. Your record remains unblemished as long as you win in the real game. Jesus died for every one of your sins. So even if you "lose" a scrimmage with your flesh by messing up again and again, your sins are not counted against you. In the real game you will be victorious. You will win the final battle in the game of life and death. Jesus paid the penalty for your sins. Though the wages of sin is death, it won't impact you because Jesus already paid the penalty. You are free from the sting of sin and death. You have the blessing of receiving eternal life in Christ Jesus. So, the next time you feel like you've lost again by not getting everything perfect, don't beat yourself up. Get up and try again. God is working in you to overcome the habits of sin just as He helped you overcome the penalty of sin. You are not condemned. You are loved. Hallelujah! Even when you fall short you win because He has won the victory!

Today's Reading:
Psalm 32:1,2; Romans 8:1; 1 Corinthians 15:55,56
Philippians 2:13; 3:12-14

January 19
Covered

Many people have anxiety about things going on in their lives. Many have lost loved ones, jobs or their good health. In times like these, you need a place to take cover. God is your refuge, strength and shelter. He has promised to never forsake you. He is committed to being with you in trouble. This means whenever and wherever there is trouble in your life, God is there with you. Though weapons may be forged against you, they will not prosper. Notice scripture doesn't suggest you won't be attacked. You may have obstacles and challenges, but you will overcome them all. I was watching a football game with Tom Brady playing against his former team. He was having a tough time throughout the game. The coach of the former team knew his weaknesses, so he created defensive schemes to hinder his ability to be successful. Yet, in the end the score reflected him as the winner. The challenges he faced were real, but they did not stop him from getting the victory. So too, in your life, obstacles will come. Yet, in the end you shall triumph because you are covered by the Almighty.

Today's Reading:
Psalm 9:9-10; Psalm 46:1-4
Isaiah 43:2, 54:27; John 16:33

January 20
Kept

God uses angels. They are spirit-beings created to do His will. The Lord sent an angel ahead of the Israelites in their exodus from Egypt. Jacob wrestled with an angel all night long until he was blessed. Daniel received the answer to his prayers by an angel sent to him from heaven. Zechariah was visited by an angel to forewarn him of what was about to happen in Jerusalem. Angels ministered to Jesus in the wilderness after He was tempted by Satan. The one who visited Paul gave him directions to save him in a shipwreck. Peter was released from prison by an angel. Like those who appeared in scripture, God has also sent angels to you. They watch over you as your supernatural keepers. You can activate them every time you profess the promises of God in prayer or conversation; you stir up their actions because they were created to perform God's Word. That means they will watch over everything concerning you. Whenever you face a trial or simply go throughout your day, remember you have 10,000 guardian angels at your disposal to keep you in all your ways.

Today's Reading:
Psalm 91:11; 103:20; Matthew 26:53; Acts 12:8, 27:23
Hebrews 1:14, 13:2

January 21
A Pretty Good Deal

Have you ever thought about God owing you something? I mean, it may sound like a crazy thing to say, but I didn't say it. God did. God has committed Himself to repay you for what you give to the poor. You, hopefully, feel a desire to help others as you are blessed just because it is the right thing to do. Yet, God has said in Proverbs 19:17 when you lend to the poor you lend to the Lord and He will repay you. God cares about the oppressed, orphaned, poor, and widowed. Those who are marginalized by their circumstances are important to God. It is easy to look the other way when you see a person in need. Yet, God is clear in His Word that if you truly have faith in Him, you will be compelled to help those you can. Faith without works is dead. Our faith is the impetus for our actions to bless others. So, whenever you have an opportunity to be a blessing, do it with thanksgiving and without grumbling. You not only have the satisfaction of being a blessing, but you will also create an invoice God is willing to pay.

Today's Reading:
Psalm 68:5; Proverbs 19:17; Isaiah 1:17
James 1:27; 2:14-26

January 22
Feeling Me

In today's vernacular it is not uncommon for someone to say, "I feel you". This gesture is intended to relay the fact that the person can relate to what you are going through. It communicates empathy for your circumstances. There is One who can also feel all your pain and relate to your daily life. Just like you, He walked as a man and was tempted in every way; only He never sinned. When Lazarus died and his sisters were mourning over his passing, the shortest verse in the Bible depicts His ability to feel your pain. It says, "Jesus wept." Even in the Old Testament when the Israelites were oppressed by their enemies the Lord related to their plight. In all their affliction, the Word tells us, He too was afflicted. Now Jesus sits at the right hand of the Father making intercession for you day and night. And He can do so effectively because He did walk as a man. He knows what it is like. He can feel you. He is the most excellent High Priest because He is able to empathize with your struggles. Because He understands He knows exactly how to pray for you. He invites you to come boldly to the throne of grace to receive mercy and find grace in your time of need.

Today's Reading:
Isaiah 53:3-9,63:9; John 11:35; Hebrews 4:14-16

January 23
Stay Focused

It is so easy to get distracted by the ungodliness in the world. If you're not very intentional you can easily get caught up in circumstances that lead you away from God's best. It's not usually the big and obviously wrong things that will trip you up, but rather it's the little things that seem like no big deal at first. Be careful! One wrong decision to do something here or there, and you may find yourself having drifted far away from where you once were in Christ. Like being in a small boat on water, if you aren't paying attention you can look up and find yourself far away from the shore. Stay focused on choosing what pleases God in each decision, big or small. Be intentional about seeking what He would have you to do. That is the way to prosper and stay on course. In the words of the commander in the *Return of the Jedi*, to those assigned to destroy the Death Star when they were being attacked on every side: "Stay on target."

Today's Reading:
Matthew 24:12-13; Colossians 3:2; Romans 8:5-6

January 24
Dis Too Much!

All of us experience days and seasons where life can seem like "Dis too much!" How you handle those seasons is important. You can become a big complainer, or you can choose to see it as another part of life's flow. It is not a good time to make major life-changing decisions. You will do better to settle your soul into a peaceful place by meditating on the Word of God. You can also remind yourself of the many times you have faced difficulties in the past. The same way you were able to persevere in other challenging seasons and circumstances, you can be triumphant again. Your past challenges make you stronger and wiser. If you've ever done something you were afraid to do, you were likely feeling anxious. Yet, once you completed it, you were able to acknowledge the accomplishment. Likewise, when you face trials, they equip you to face even greater tests in the future. You have the capacity to know if God bought you through it once, He can do it again. Stand firm in your faith. God knows exactly how much you can bear. Press forward and you will see the hand of the Lord working things out in your favor!

Today's Reading:
John 16:33; James 1:2-3; 1 Peter 4:12-16,5:7

January 25
Take Off The Blinders

The more we've learned about the behind-the-scenes efforts to manipulate people on social media the more we've seen how the devil operates. He has blinded the eyes of unbelievers. He is not carrying a pitchfork. He uses everyday situations and people to control your thinking. Watch a commercial for food and next thing you know you're buying what you've just seen. Likewise, the enemy of our souls has subtly seduced the world to believe God's Word is not true. While the enemy wants you to believe that God will not follow through on His promises, nothing could be further from the truth! God cannot lie, whereas Satan is known as the father of lies. Guard your heart with all diligence. Be careful what you watch on television or listen to on the radio. Don' be fooled by the ways of the world. Renew your mind daily so you won't conform to what the world has deemed acceptable. Develop a personal relationship with God so that you know the truth and won't fall for the manipulation tactics of the devil.

Today's Reading:
Proverbs 4:4-6; Romans 12:1-2; 2 Corinthians 4:3,4

January 26
Practice Makes Perfect

The challenge to becoming a mature Christian is your flesh's resistance to change. You become comfortable in your ways. You, like many, may give your life to Christ after you have lived a lifestyle contrary to biblical standards. Consequently, you likely learned habits that must be replaced with new ones in order to develop a godly lifestyle. You will need to develop new patterns and new behaviors. The way to achieve this goal is through practicing the use of God's Word as a blueprint for making choices. Your daily choices develop your habits. When you use the Word as the basis for your behavior, you learn to discern good from evil and right from wrong. The same way you developed your habits which led to you operating outside of His will, you can mature as a child of God by letting the Bible be your greatest influence. Pay attention to who and what impacts your worldview the most. Make sure those things and people agree with God's worldview. Bad company corrupts good character. The more you put into practice what you read in your Bible; the more Christ will be formed in you.

Today's Reading:
Deuteronomy 12:8; 1 Corinthians 15:33
Galatians 6:7-9; Hebrews 5:14; 1 John 1:6

January 27
Got Rocks?

I was recently on a beach and the waves began crashing around me. Other people on the beach were literally being smashed into a huge rock embedded in the sand. Had the rock not stopped them, they would have been sucked out into the water. The rock acted as a barrier. Who knows what would have happened had it not been in their path. But the rock hurt. It banged their knees and cut their skin. Still, they were grateful the rock stopped them from being swept away. Perhaps in your life you've encountered some obstacle which caused you discomfort. Yet, looking back you could see how it was good that you were afflicted. Paul's encounter with the Lord on the road to Damascus led to him experiencing temporary blindness. He had been persecuting the church, but his affliction led him to know Jesus as his Savior. Without difficulties in your life, you might never experience the depth of God's love for you. In truth, the momentary afflictions you experience pale by comparison to the glory which will be revealed in your life. Praise God for the rocks in your life and the purpose they serve.

Today's Reading:
2 Kings 22:18; Psalm 110:17,75; Isaiah 38:17; Hosea 5:16
Acts 9:1-9; 2 Corinthians 4:17; Galatians 4:13

January 28
Covered By The Blood

Most know Christ's Blood delivered us from the penalty of our sins. Did you know it also cleansed your guilty conscience, took away the condemnation of your past and gave you peace with God? It did all of those things so that you can have a clear conscience before Him. Also, when you are experiencing spiritual warfare, you can plead the Blood of Jesus. Demons tremble at the Name of Jesus and they are petrified by the mention of His Blood as it is a reminder of the devil's defeat at Calvary. Don't beat yourself up over past mistakes. It is inevitable in life that mistakes and bad decisions will happen. Let go of the guilt. Jesus made a way for you to live free from all condemnation and guilt. Accept it and walk in Remember also to plead the Blood of Jesus over your life and circumstances. When the enemy comes to attack, call on the name of Jesus and know that that there is power in His Blood that covers you.

Today's Reading:
Matthews 26:28; Romans 5:9; Colossians 1:19,20,2:15
Hebrews 9:11-14; James 2:19

January 29
Your Way Or His

The way to have God's perfect will be done in your life is to walk by faith and be led by the Spirit. When the Holy Spirit guides you, obedience is required in order to achieve all that God has for you. Walk in faith. Jesus gave us the directions to have our best life when He said, "Follow Me." Sometimes you find yourself choosing your own path based on our own desires and feelings. Your way can seem right, yet still lead you astray. Doing things His way leads to life. You will not always understand why He is leading a certain way, but we can be certain that He wants what is best for us. He will lead us in ways that will bring about blessings. The opposite is also true. Following the way of the flesh leads to death. It's just that simple. In order to follow the Spirit, you must learn to deny yourself. It requires keeping yourself in alignment with His will even when it means turning away from something you might really enjoy. God has great things in store for you. Follow Him to experience the abundant life He wants you to enjoy.

Today's Reading:
Proverbs 16:25; Luke 9:23; John 21:19; Romans 8:12-14
Colossians 2:6

January 30
Remember Them

There are people God wants you to always remember. This was made clear when Jesus shared a parable about those who were commended for visiting Him when He was sick and imprisoned. They questioned when that had occurred. He replied and said what you do to the least of those in society you do to Him. Remember those that are in need and attend to them. God also wants you to remember the leaders He has placed in your life. They serve as examples of how to live. Their lives show what happens when you apply your faith. The blessing of obedience will be yours if you do. Likewise, the opposite is equally important to remember. For example, Lot's wife disobeyed God when she looked back. She and Lot were instructed to not look back just before God destroyed Sodom and Gomorrah. The cost of her disobedience has made her the poster child for the consequences of the failure to obey God's warning. Because of her disobedience, she became a pillar of salt. The cost of rebellion is high, just as the blessings of obedience are abundant.

Today's Reading:
Genesis 19:12-26; Ecclesiastes 12:1; Matthew 25:26-48
Luke 17:32; Hebrews 13:1-3,7; James 1:27

January 31
Can't Nobody Do You Like Jesus!

He is Alpha and Omega, the Beginning and the End! He is the Everlasting Father and the Prince of Peace. He is your peace, your way maker, your provider and your friend. All of the fullness of the Godhead is in Him. Nothing was made without Him. He is the Great Physician. Call upon Him and be healed. He knows your end from the beginning. He is the Way, the Truth, and the Life. He is the Light of the world. Ask Him to guide you when you're unsure. His is the only Name by which you can be saved. He sticks closer than a brother. He is an ever-present help in times of trouble. He will heal your broken heart and bind up your wounds. Call on Him when your heart is heavy. He is the Great I Am! He is the One that began a good work in you. Rest assured He will see it through to completion. The world has a way of bringing you down, but when your eyes are on Jesus and you soak in His presence, there is joy to be found regardless of what life throws at you. It is a joy that the world cannot take away. Jesus loves you with an unconditional love. No one can love you like Jesus.

Today's Reading:
Isaiah 9:6; Acts 4:11,12; Philippians 1:6, 2:9-11
Colossians 1:9,17; Revelation 22:13

February 1
Your Blessed Life

God has made it clear how to live a blessed life. It's so simple even a child could grasp it. He promised to bless us in the city and in the country, bless our comings and goings and prosper us. We tend to complicate matters because we choose not to follow His clear directions on how to live a blessed life. It is easy to get caught up in the ways of the world. The world offers us quick fixes and quick highs, but it is not the way of Jesus. In order to have a blessed life beyond measure, we must follow Him. Leard His ways and allow the Holy Spirit to guide you. When you seek Him and walk the path He has preordained for you, the blessings will follow. Meditate on God's Word to gain understanding. Apply it to your life. Do not depart from it. Seek Him daily so that your relationship with Him is cultivated. Let His Word be a light unto your path and be blessed when you follow it.

Today's Reading:
Deuteronomy 28:1-14; Psalm 1:1-3; Psalm 119:105
John 13:17

February 2
Your Soul Mate

More than anything else He wants from you; God wants you to be with Him. From the beginning He has sought out a relationship with mankind. Before sending the disciples out, Jesus called them to be with Him. It is mind boggling to think that the Maker of heaven and earth wants to know you. In reality, He has known you since before you were in your mother's womb. Now He wants you to get to know Him. He wants you to be His friend and to share things with Him. Nothing about you is insignificant to Him. He wants to hear all about the things that bring you joy as well as the things that break your heart. He wants a personal relationship with you. That won't happen by chance. You must be intentional about investing time into your relationship with God. It is not only the sole relationship you will have with eternal consequences, but it's also the *soul* relationship that will make you whole. He completes you. No other relationship can do that, only your Heavenly Father, your Creator. Invest in the relationship and see for yourself the blessings it brings with it.

Today's Reading:
Genesis 3:8,9; Psalm 144:3; Jeremiah 1:5
Mark 3:14; John 15:15

February 3
Mind Your Mind

The way you think will determine the way you live because as a man thinks so is he. If I think I'm a loser so it shall be. God wants you to think like Him. Let the mind be in you that is also in Christ Jesus. How can you have the mind of Christ? Quite simply, you gain the mind of Christ by washing your mind daily in the Word of God, putting to practice what you read in it, and asking God to help you where you struggle. When you do these things, your thoughts and perspectives will begin to align with His. When you meditate upon His Word, He will not only change your mindset, but He will also transform your life. Remember actions start with a thought and are nurtured into reality. That's why every success story started out with a vision that someone watered until it became a reality. Reject negative thinking. Take thoughts captive - don't let them roam freely in your mind – when they don't align with God's Word. Whatever is pure, whatever is noble, whatever is praiseworthy, think on these things.

Today's Reading:
Proverbs 23:7; Romans 12:1,2; 2 Corinthians 10:4-6
Ephesians 5:26; Philippians 2:2,4:8

February 4
Because of His Mercy

Simply stated, mercy is the reflection of God's forgiveness of your sins. It results in God withholding the consequences you rightly deserve for your sins. The wages of sin is death. Yet God shows you brand new mercies every single day. When you honestly access your actions and soberly acknowledge where you've messed up in various ways, you can't help but thank God for sustaining you and for not treating you as your sins deserve. You could be dead, locked up, homeless, starving, unemployed, rejected, broke, or ostracized because of the choices you have made. But praise be to God that He loves us enough to gives us new mercies each day. God's grace gives you what you don't deserve. But it is His mercy that keeps you from getting what you do. Likewise, we are called to do the same for others. We are to model the ways of Jesus. Extend grace and mercy to others when they do something that offends you, just as God does for you.

Today's Reading:
Lamentations 3:22,23; Micah 6:8; Luke 6:36
Hebrews 4:16; James 2:13

February 5
Whatever It Takes

One of the tools God uses to get your attention is the difficulties in your life. He loves you too much to watch you live in such a way that is contrary to His will for you. He will allow circumstances that are unpleasant to help you avoid making a wrong choice and to turn your heart back to Him. He will let you go through whatever it takes for you to look up to Him. Sometimes in your stubbornness you can prolong your difficulties unnecessarily. Yet, when you repent and turn your heart to Him you can receive His all-surpassing peace to sustain you and His infinite wisdom to guide you through your challenges. The next time you face a hardship, don't be so quick to blame the devil. While it is true that the devil comes to steal, kill, and destroy, the hardship may be God trying to steer you back to the right path. Ask God to show you His intention for allowing the situation to happen. Then, like Mary told the servants at the wedding in Cana, do whatever He tells you to do.

Today's Reading:
Judges 3:7-9; 1 Kings 8:46-50; Proverbs 13:15, 18:12

February 6
God's Doorway

When we reach a point of brokenness and despair, we are postured for an encounter with God. Our sorrow over our sinful ways or those of others, can result in reaching a greater depth in our relationship with God or lead to unhealthy self-depreciation and even depression. A broken spirit is a doorway for God to enter and help you if you are willing to let Him. Unfortunately, for many great despair can be the tipping point that leads you to give up. Cry out to God and turn to Him in times like this, knowing that as His child He had an unfailing love and desire to see you walking in the fullness of joy that comes from Him. God will refresh your spirit and draw you closer to Him. So the next time you experience feelings of brokenness, cry out to Him and consider it an opportunity for you to receive God's grace in your greatest times of need.

Today's Reading:
Psalm 51:17; Isaiah 6:5; Acts 3:18-19; 2 Corinthians 7:10

February 7
Do What You Hear

The fact that faith comes from hearing the Word of God should encourage you to hear it as much as possible. Whether it be sitting down with your Bible for some one-on-one time with your Father, attending a church service to hear the Word preached, or listening to a good biblically sound message on the radio, hearing the Word of God increases your faith. Faith is needed to receive many of the blessings God has for you. The scripture also states that without faith, you can't please God. Still, while hearing the Word is important for building up faith, more is required in order to live a life that is pleasing to God. To walk in the promises of God you must not only hear the Word, but you must do what it says! When Jesus spoke, He said you will be blessed if you do these things. Don't be a hearer only. Do what you hear. Faith without works is dead.

Today's Reading:
John 13:17; Romans 10:16; Hebrews 11:6: James 1:22-25

February 8
What Do You Believe?

The Bible says in 1 Timothy 3:16 that all scripture is given by inspiration from God. Our Heavenly Father, the Creator of heaven and earth and all that is within it, inspired the writings of the scripture. Do you believe it? The real answer is not whether you say you do. The real answer is reflected in what you do. If you believe the Bible is true, you live by its principles. You put up an umbrella in the rain because you know it will keep you from the rain. You make decisions based on what the Bible says because you know it will protect you from making choices you will later regret. If you truly believe the Bible is God's wisdom for you, then follow the principles laid out in it. Don't make a single decision, no matter how small, without making sure it agrees with the Word of God. The Word will always steer you to the ways that are Holy and pleasing to Him. Obedience to His Word will put you in a posture to receive blessings. Read the Word. Hear the Word. Believe the Word. It will direct your path until our Lord Jesus Christ comes again in all His glory!

Today's Reading:
Luke 1:37; 2 Timothy 3:16,17
1 Thessalonians 5:23,24 NLT

February 9
An Appointment You Must Keep

Some of us are known for being late for our appointments. Others, habitually miss theirs. However, there is one appointment you will not be late for or miss. The time you're appointed to transition to your eternal resting place is established by God. You won't be able to delay it. As we heard the sobering news of over one million people having passed in the United States alone due to the Covid19 virus, I was reminded of how swiftly life can change. Make sure you're ready for your appointed time. Learn about Jesus Christ and know that He died for all your sins. He made a way for you to have eternal life once your appointment arrives. Share the good news of the Gospel with your family, friends, co-workers and even strangers so that they too can be ready for their appointment. There is no reason to fear when you know God has saved you. Whenever the time comes for you to be absent from your body, you will be present with the Lord where you will be at peace forever. There is no better place you can be.

Today's Reading:
Romans 14:12; 2 Corinthians 5:8-10; Hebrews 9:27

February 10
Out Of The Closet

Are you undercover? Or, as my father would say back in the day, are you on the QT? Are you only a Christian when you're in church or with other Christians? Sometimes people hesitate to talk about Jesus because they are fearful of what others will think, or they want to please others. Jesus made it clear If you are ashamed of Him before men, He will be ashamed of you before His Father. It is far more important to please God. He is the One from Whom all blessings flow. You are not called to be undercover. You are called to be His ambassador. Tell the world about His saving grace and what He has done for you. Similar to the teacher having you come to the board to work a math problem, or have you repeat your multiplication table, God calls us to share our faith over and over. And the more you tell it the more confident you will be in what you believe.

Today's Reading:
Luke 9:26; John 12:42-43; Romans 10:17
2 Corinthians 5:20

February 11
Don't Believe Your Own Press

Self-awareness is a good thing. We should know ourselves. Self-aggrandizement, on the other hand, is not so wise. We should always maintain a humble attitude. We are all blessed with gifts and talents. They are gifts from God. If your abilities are from God why pump yourself up as though you accomplish it all on your own? God enabled you. Let Him get the glory for it. If your accomplishments move others to talk about what you've done, that's great. Let them boast about you, but guard against promoting yourself. Remember people can be kind and generous with their accolades one moment and then tear you down the next. On the Sunday before his death, they waved palm branches at Jesus and cried Hosanna! Before the end of the same week, they yelled "crucify Him!" Don't get caught up in basking in the things people say about you - good or bad. Simply live your life in obedience to God as best you know how. Play to an audience of One, so He can give you the greatest accolade of all: "well done my good and faithful servant."

Today's Reading:
Proverbs 27:2; Matthew 25:21; Romans 12:3
1 Corinthians 4:6-7; Philippians 2:2,8

February 12
You Have Something To Offer

Everyone is born with innate talents and abilities. Everyone born again is gifted by the Holy Spirit with spiritual attributes. As you lean into your gifts and talents you begin to see what God has in mind for you. Your gifts and talents align with God's purpose for your life. And those gifts will make room for you. All too often people focus on what they think they cannot do to the detriment of their maximizing what they can do. When the coach of the Chinese ping pong multiple-year Olympic gold medal winning team was asked why his team dominated the US team – even though the sport initially began in the US - he said it was because they focused on what they do well while Americans focused on trying to improve on their weaknesses. Focus on perfecting the abilities God has given you and they will open doors of opportunity for you beyond your imagination.

Today's Reading:
Proverbs 18:16; Romans 12:4-8; 1 Corinthians 12:7
2 Corinthians 8:12

February 13
Follow The Lord's Leading

In every decision you make you will have to weigh out various opinions and options. Your opinion may be based on your desires. You want what you want. You may have visions of tall dark and handsome, but you meet a wonderful short guy. You think she should be 36/24/36 but she is an inwardly beautiful person who captures your heart. You don't want kids until after college, but you discover you are with-child. Then there is public opinion which will be based on what's popular with everyone else. It too is usually based on selfishness, wanting to look good, having a lot of possessions and impressing others. We usually lean towards what we want. But there is another opinion that deserves the utmost attention: God's opinion. He sets forth principles in His Word that can be applied to every situation in your life. If you choose the option that you believe would most please God, you can't go wrong. And therein lies the blessings. He blesses your obedience and honor of His Word. But you always have a choice. Choose this day whom you will serve: you, popularity or God.

Today's Reading:
Deuteronomy 28; 1 John 2:16

February 14
Remember These

Some are like Janet Jackson. They operate under the mindset of what have you done for me lately. But God wants you to remember His works. Don't be like the children of Israel who forgot how the Lord had delivered them. Take the time to remember where God bought you from and the many blessings you have. Don't allow anything or anyone to cause you to be bitter. He wants you to remember how He has made a way for you in the past. He wants you to tell others about His mighty works. He wants you to live a sanctified lifestyle that will set you apart from the in-crowd. In keeping His commands, you will experience favor over your family. Remember His name and know that He is mighty. Remember what the apostles have taught in the Holy Word so you can live victoriously. Hide His Word in your heart so you won't sin against Him. Lastly, especially when things are going on in your life that make it challenging, remember that Jesus Christ died, was buried, and was raised from the dead to bring you to God. In Him you are declared as righteous. Rejoice because you are His child!

Today's Reading:
Exodus 20:8; Numbers 15:40; Judges 8:34; Job 36:24
Isaiah 46:9-10; 2 Timothy 2:8; Jude 1:17

February 15
Do The Next Best Thing

We all know when you make choices you should do your best to do the right thing. However, you live in a fallen world, and no one is perfect except Jesus Christ. You will make mistakes, but it is what you do next that is important. Do you cover it up? Tell a little white lie? Or do you fess up and acknowledge you missed it? Your best next move is to own it and try to do what is right. Trust God to cover and protect you even if it means you must adjust your own plans. For example, if you got pregnant unexpectedly, don't abort the baby. Do the next best thing and let God provide for you. Or, if you messed up at work don't let someone else take the brunt of it, own what you did and trust God to favor you. We are all going to miss it sometimes. The most important thing to do is to do what's right afterwards and trust God; because anything we do that is not motivated by faith is sin. Following one bad move with another is not wise. Trust God He will always have your back when you choose to do things His way.

Today's Reading:
Romans 3:23, 14:23; 2 Corinthians 5:7

February 16
Keep Standing

The Apostle Paul gave us such inspiring testimonies. You can't help but feel like a spiritual superhero as you imagine God using you the way He used Paul. When Paul was bitten by a poisonous snake, the natives of the island were waiting for him to drop dead. Instead, he shook it off and continued with the mission. It was Paul who taught us to put on the full armor of God. He helped us understand our weapons aren't carnal but mighty for pulling down strongholds. However, Paul also understood the purpose of hardships when God allowed them. Paul said he takes pleasure in his "infirmities, in reproaches, in needs, in persecutions, in distresses, for Christ' sake." In other words, Paul's thorn in the flesh was tormenting him. Yet through it, he unpacked a weapon far more powerful than any other in his spiritual tool belt. He learned to rely on God's strength. When you encounter hardships that God allows you to endure, remember it is in your weakness that His strength is made perfect. When you are weak, He is strong. What's your pleasure?

Today's Reading:
Judges 16:28-30; Mark 16:17-18; Luke 10:19
Acts 28:1-5; 2 Corinthians 12:7-10

February 17
Restoration And Strength To The Weary

When you are exhausted you can grow weary. You can feel spent as though you have no more to give. Instead of staying this way, find the strength you need in the Lord. He never gets tired or grows weary. He never runs out of strength. He is an in-exhaustible source of power. A power plant can provide electricity when you turn on a light switch. Once the connection is made to the source, it will continue to provide power for the appliance. God is the same to you. Once you plug into His presence, He will outpour the strength you need. The prophet Isaiah said even young people can get tired. The weariness is not merely physical. Your mind can get drained. Your spirit can feel depleted. Like your iron can stay hot for as long as it is plugged into the source of electricity, you can stay refreshed if you continuously seek after the Lord. Drinking from the brook of His word can keep you refreshed. He is all wise. He can provide you with wisdom to accomplish any task if you ask. Sometimes that which you are seeking is not obvious to you or revealed right away. Wait on Him. He will provide all that you need to be refreshed and renewed.

Today's Reading:
Psalm 27:14,46:1,55:22,130:6
Isaiah 40:28-31; James 1:5

February 18
Let Peace Rule

Peace is the umpire God has given you to guide you in life. When you make a decision about anything, be led by peace within your soul. Pray before you make a decision. When you find yourself feeling uneasy in any situation stop and pray before you proceed. God will guide you with His peace. If you are on a path that is not the one God has for you, a sense of uneasiness will likely be present. The opposite is also true. When you are in alignment with His will, there is peace within your soul. Countless people have taken jobs, joined groups, entered relationships, or made other life altering decisions they have lived to regret because they ignored the warning sign from God. If you don't have peace about something pray about it some more and ask Him to show you which way to go. It is also important to make every effort to live at peace with everyone in your sphere of influence. Jesus Himself is not merely peaceful, He is your peace. He gave you His peace when you gave Him your heart, and consequently He is the one that helps you to have peace with those around you. Let peace rule.

Today's Reading:
John 14:27; Rom 12:18; Ephesians 2:14
Philippians 4:6-7; Colossians 3:15
Hebrews 12:14; James 3:18

February 19
He Hears

God hears you when you call to Him. This is critical to remember. There have been many high-profile deaths by suicide. In addition, there has been a number committed by people who may not be famous, but whose lives are precious to God and those who love them. People who become suicidal reach a place where they believe there is no way out. That is a lie from the pit of hell. When you reach a place of intense frustration and feel like all hope is gone, remember to call out to the Lord. He will always hear you. Jesus said in this life you will have troubles. Life may not be trouble-free but do not fall for the trap of believing something is wrong with you. Difficult seasons may come, but God is always with you. Never give up. Wait for Him to guide you. Not only will He hear you, but He will also hear those who try to plot evil against you. The psalmists tell us, He will hear them and humble them, because they have no fear of God. Never let your opposition cause you to believe you can't be victorious. God will hear your cries and will answer. Be encouraged. He will see you through everything that happens in your life. God hears you.

Today's Reading:
2 Kings 6:8-12; Psalm4:3; 55:16-19

February 20
Your Way And Why

God is not merely interested in what you do. His greater concern is your character. Your motivation for how and what you do is reflected in your character. Like when the prophet Samuel was led by the Lord to go to Jesse's house to anoint the next king. Jesse paraded all his sins before the prophet except for his youngest, David. Yet, it was David who the Lord wanted. Perhaps his father saw him as a scrawny kid, but God viewed him as an up-and-coming king. Don't let anyone else define your potential. People are inclined to look at outward appearances, but God looks at your heart. For example, you can give money to a cause just so you can boast about it, or you can do it purely to be a blessing to someone in need. You can say, "thank you", because it seems appropriate, or you can express sincere gratitude from your heart. God sees and knows the truth about your character. He wants you to be truthful, honor others, and engage in kind deeds from a pure heart. Conduct yourself with integrity and you will establish a good name with both men and God.

Today's Reading:
1 Samuel 16:7; Proverbs 20:14.17; 24:12
1 Thessalonians 5:18; 1 Timothy 5:18

February 21
Fall Forward

No matter who we are or how much we love God we will sin. Make no mistake about it, you will mess up sometimes. While the devil looks for opportunities to make you stumble, God will lift you and allow you to feel sorrow. This leads to repentance. to lead you to repent. Repenting means not only acknowledging you have messed up; it also about turning away from it and doing it no more. When you repent, God will refresh you and forgive you. He won't condemn you, rather He will continue loving you with His everlasting love. Guard against allowing shame to set into your heart. God does not want you to feel any kind of rejection. Even when others reject you, He doesn't. You are His child, and nothing can change that fact. Also remember Jesus continues to pray for you all day and night. He knows what you're up against in this world full of temptations. So be encouraged if you fail in some way. God loves you and will uphold you with His righteous right hand.

Today's Reading:
Proverbs 24:16; Luke 21:31,32; Acts 3:19.
Romans 3:23,8:12; 2 Corinthians 7:9-10

February 22
Promise Keeper

Every promise God made about the past was fulfilled. Likewise, His promises about the future will come to be. God kept His promise to bring the Israelites out of bondage and His promise to Abraham to make him the father of many nations. Some promises are personal, like when He promised Heman, one of the Old Testament ministers of music, that He would elevate him. You can trust whatever God speaks to you. My father was a non-church attending alcoholic, but God gave my mother a vision of my father asking to be filled with the Spirit. Over 20 years later, he woke up early one Sunday morning expressing a strong desire to be filled with the Spirit. I had the privilege of leading him in prayer so he could be filled. Sometimes it may take a while, but His promises are true. Some promises apply come after a condition has been met. The greatest example is in John 3:16. God so loved the world He gave his only begotten Son the whoever believes in Him would not perish but have everlasting life. Have you met the condition? Believe in Jesus and you have God's promise of eternal life.

Today's Reading:
Joshua 23:14; 1 Kings 8:56; 1 Chronicles 25:5
Romans 4:18,9:8; 2 Corinthians 1:20; Galatians 3:29

February 23
Foolishness

You do not want to be a fool unless you are a fool for Christ. A fool despises wisdom and instruction. Foolish people reject God. A foolish person shows everyone their lack of wisdom. The choices a fool makes can cause their troubles. They leave a legacy of shame rather than glory. They will not follow the directions which often leads to their own failures. It is foolish people who spread slander (untruths) about others. For the fool, doing evil is like a sport. They do it for their pleasure or just to see if they can "win" by getting away with it. They have no filter. Those behaving foolishly will pour out their unwise thoughts without reservation. Contrast this with one who is wise. They know the fear of the Lord is the beginning of wisdom. They honor God. Prudent people welcome correction. They are slow to speak and quick to listen. They heed instruction and, thereby, avoid setting themselves up to fail. When you do what is pleasing in God's sight you may look like a fool to the world. But it is far better to look like a fool to unwise people than to be one in the eyes of the Lord.

Today's Reading:
Psalm 92:6,107:17; Proverbs 1:7,3:35,10:10,18,23,12:23
Ecclesiastes 10;3; 1 Corinthians 3:18,4:10

February 24
Love For God

Gary Chapman's book about the 5 love languages has been read all over the world. It helps you to understand your primary way of feeling loved. The options are: acts of service, physical touch, quality time, receiving gifts and words of affirmation. You may enjoy more than one of these, but one makes you feel loved more than all the others. In a personal human relationship, you may have to study the other person to figure out which is their primary love language. But when it comes to showing God you love Him, you don't have to guess His love language. He says in His Word if you love Him, keep His commandments. No matter how much you serve in ministry or give of yourself or of your treasures, there is no substitute for obedience to God's Word. Not only should you follow His example of telling others what makes you feel loved, your ultimate goal should always be to show God some love by obeying His will.

Today's Reading:
1 Samuel 15:22,23; John 8:28,29, 14:15

February 25
How We Fight

Christian's fight. When you fight, don't fight against people. Your war is against the spiritual powers of darkness that operate in the heavenly realms and through people. Your weapons are prayer, praise, and obedience to God's word. You can break the bondage of unclean spirits when you war in the Spirit. When you fall on your knees in prayer and lift your voice in praise, you posture yourself for war. When you mediate on God's Word, you can demolish strongholds in your mind and take captive the thoughts that stand up against truth in your patterns of thinking. You can uproot lies and distortions of truth with the truth, thereby winning the battle for your mind. Fight against evil by praying God's will be done on earth. Bind every spirit that is not of the Spirit of God. Loose those who are held captive by unclean spirits by praying God's Word and taking authority over them. Fight for truth to prevail in the highways and byways of your influence in life by speaking and doing what the Lord says. As you do these things, God will empower you by His Spirit, and He will even fight for you.

Today's Reading:
Deuteronomy 20:11;2 Chronicles 20:17
Matthew 18:18-19; Ephesians 6:12;2 Corinthians 10:4

February 26
Omnipotent

When the Israelites left Egypt, they were pursued by the Egyptians. They found themselves trapped with their enemies behind them and the Red Sea before them. They were panicked, but God simply parted the sea. What seemed like an impossible situation to them was nothing for God. It's the same in your life. As He did for them, He will do for you. After they disobeyed and questioned His plans, they wandered in the wilderness for 40 years. When they finally reached the Jordan river, they saw it was flowing to capacity. Once again, God moved the water so that they could walk on dry land, but this time He did it differently. He commanded Joshua to tell the priests to step into the flooding water. They had to trust Him and take that first step of faith. When they did, the water receded. There is nothing too hard for God. Even the winds and waves obey Him. Jesus spoke to the storm that was raging when He told the disciples to cross over it. He said, "Peace, be still" and it ceased. When He directs you, what may seem untenable to you is a small thing to Him. Trust Him.

Today's Reading:
Deuteronomy 3:24; Joshua 3; Jeremiah 32:7
Jonah 4:8; Mark 4:35-41

February 27
He Sees

When Sarah had the bright idea to have Abraham sleep with their slave Hagar, it was a recipe for disaster. Hagar bore his son and much turmoil arose between the two women. Eventually the whole situation grew toxic, and Hagar ran away. She felt alone and rejected. Like many who go through difficulties she likely felt no one cared. She thought she and her son were going to die. Perhaps you've had times when it seemed no one cared. Perhaps you have been lonely, wondering if God is paying you any attention. In the midst of Hagar's despair, God spoke to her and assured her He would not forsake her or her son. He saw her! Likewise, God sees you. No matter what kind of turmoil you may be facing, He will not forget about you. He has plans to prosper you. Your best days are still ahead. There is nothing hidden from God's sight. Yes, He even sees your secret sins. He knows Your foolishness. He also sees your acts of obedience. He sees your kindness towards His children. Do not become discouraged or dismayed. You are never alone. He has great things in store for you.

Today's Reading:
Genesis 16:13; Isaiah 40:27-28; Jeremiah 29:11
2 Corinthians 4:5; Hebrews 6:10

February 28
Servant Of All

One of the factors that distinguishes the Kingdom of God from the world's system is how leaders lead. In the world, the leader looks out for his own interest or perhaps the interest of an enterprise. In the Kingdom, leaders are called to look out for the interest of those they lead. This is what Jesus did. He did not come to be served. Rather, He came to serve the lost and to present Himself as a ransom for all mankind. He willingly made the ultimate sacrifice. He laid down His Deity for you to have a life free from the bondage of sin and death. Even now He continues to serve as He makes intercession for you. The world says leaders are to be served. God says a true leader is a servant. You have been given the invaluable gift of salvation. Now you are called to serve others even as He serves you. You are called to lay down your life for others' sake. John 3:16 tells why God sent His only Begotten Son. And 1 John 3:16 tells why He sent you. A mature Christian understands the calling to look out for the well-being of others. Thank God for the Greatest Servant of all time. Seek to walk as He did.

Today's Reading:
Matthew 20:25-28,23:11; Mark 10:43-45; Luke 22:26;
Galatians 5:13; Philippians 2:6-7; Hebrews7:25
1 Peter 4:10; 1 John 3:16

March 1

Your Peace

Jesus is not only the Lord of peace, but He is also your peace. Through the suffering He endured on the Cross, He purchased your peace by satisfying the law's demand for the payment of sin: death. Because of His sacrifice, you are now justified. God views you as holy. He treats you just as if you had never sinned. God sent Jesus to be the propitiation for your transgressions, which is the payment for the wages of sin. Therefore, you have peace with God. Jesus had a forerunner. His first cousin, John, was sent before Him to guide people into the way of peace. He told them to prepare their hearts for repentance. He prepared the people's heart, making the way for the Lord's arrival. The Lord will command your peace. He even makes your enemies live at peace with you as you walk in ways that are pleasing to Him. God's ability to give you peace is not limited to times when there is a lack of trouble. Rather, He can grant you His supernatural, incomprehensible peace that supersedes your understanding in the midst of your trials and tribulations, as you keep your mind focused on Him.

Today's Reading:
Isaiah 26:3,12, 53:5; Proverbs 16:7; Luke 1:79
Ephesians 2:14; 1 Thessalonians 5:23
2 Thessalonians 3:16; Hebrews 12:14, 13:20

March 2
Love On

In relationships, inevitably there will be conflicts. We all have our own perspectives and opinions. When conflict comes, rather than shrink back you can choose to love the person anyway. Seek to understand before being understood. Make sure you have "heard" the other person. Ask clarifying questions. Be quick to listen, slow to speak and slow to become angry. Instead of truly listening, you can find yourself just bearing with the person until there is a pause giving you the ability to state your opinion. That's not fruitful. Be intentional. Hear the person's heart. Everyone wants to be heard and know their viewpoint is valued by you, even if you don't agree with it. We can all become too argumentative and defensive. Love overlooks an offense; not goes looking for one. You can choose not to be offended even when you do hear correctly and don't like what is being said. Like our fingerprints, we are unique. You can choose to hear the other person's perspective as just that - their perspective - and choose to love them as they are. This is how men will know we are truly His disciples. Love on!

Today's Reading:
Proverbs 19:11; John 13:35; Ephesians 4:32
Colossians 3:13; James 1:19

March 3
Looking To Become

When Moses went up on Mount Sinai to meet with God, he spoke with Him as close to face to face as any man had ever come. Consequently, when he returned to the camp of the Israelites, his face shone so brightly they couldn't handle its brilliance. They asked him to put a veil over his face. And he did. Today, you too can experience God's radiance as you look into His Word. As you mediate on the truths, allowing it to permeate your thinking, you behold that which you are destined to become. Paul suggests it is like looking in a mirror and being transformed into what you see. You go from glory to glory as you are elevated spiritually. You take on His likeness. Many will respond to you as the children of God responded to Moses. Your light will be starkly juxtaposed to any darkness in the world and in others. In Him there is no darkness at all. Some will avoid you to avoid His light in you. As they rejected Jesus so some will reject you. Nevertheless, keep shining. Keep looking deeply into the Word of God so He can be formed in you.

Today's Reading:
Exodus 35:29-35; 2 Corinthians 3:16-18; 1 Peter 5:10

March 4
It's About Your Character

What is the ultimate goal God has for you? It is to have a relationship with you forever. Along the way He takes you through the transformative process called sanctification. It begins the moment you accept Christ. From that instant you are being set apart for God. He said, "be holy as I am holy". This process continues until Christ returns. Most can recite Romans 8:28. What you may not know is the reason God works all things together for good. It is so you can be conformed into the image of His Son. He wants your character to look just like His. God's desire is that you will become like Him. He may choose to let you go through difficulties like He did when He allowed Paul's flesh to be buffeted by a messenger from the devil himself. Being buffeted means he was repeatedly experiencing pain, like a stabbing pain in his body. All of this was so Paul would not become conceited. Paul's character mattered to God even more than his comfort. The same is true for you. God will work all things together for your good so Christ's character can be formed in you.

Today's Reading:
Leviticus 11:45; Romans 1:28-29; 1 Corinthians 1:30
2 Corinthian 12:7; Philippians 1:6,2:13; Galatians 4:19
Colossians 1:28; 1 Thessalonians 4:3

March 5
Let This Mind Be In You

You must be intentional about developing a healthy thought life. Your thoughts turn into behaviors and attitudes. A mind set on pleasing your flesh will be carnal. A mind set on pleasing God will be filled with life and peace. Basically, how you think plays a huge role in how you will live. Think of your mind like the CPU in a computer. You program it to do what you want it to do. As the saying goes: garbage in, garbage out. Consequently, you should guard your ear gates and your eye gates. Be particular about what you focus on and listen too. The world is full of things that will try to grab your attention but are not pleasing to God. To lead a blessed life, fill up instead on the Word of God and music that edifies Him because what you feast on will determine who and what you become. Let the mind of Christ - one rooted and grounded in the Word of God - be in you.

Today's Reading:
Proverbs 23:7; Philippians 2:1-5
Romans 8:5-8,12:1,2,15:2,3; 1 Corinthians 2:16

March 6
Small And Powerful

Your tongue is a small portion of your body, yet it does more than any other part to reflect who you really are because what you speak expresses what's in the core of your being. Your tongue is like a magnifying glass that makes it easier to see who you are inside. It has the power of life and death in it. By it you can build up another's confidence or crush their spirit. It is a potent instrument; a tool you must master. By it Jesus cursed a fig tree causing it to wither and die in one instance and called Lazarus from the grave - back to life - in another. God spoke the world into existence; so it came to be. You were created in His image. You too can speak over dead things to bring them to life. You too can call things that are not, as though they were. Your tongue is powerful. Use it wisely. Yield it to God.

Today's Reading:
Psalm 34:3, 37:30, Proverbs 15:4, 18:20,21
Matthew 12:34; Romans 4:17; James 3:2-12

March 7
Talkers Talk

My uncle liked to say, "whoever will bring a bone will take a bone". It had to do with gossiping. The person who will bring you some gossip about someone else, will also say something to them about you. That's why scripture tells us not to be caught up in people who like to flatter you. They may, for example, yell your praises one minute and talk about you the next. God's Word is true we should not gossip. And sometimes, though you may have accurate information, you need to keep it to yourself; when you do you demonstrate you are a disciple of Jesus, by covering a transgression rather than conceal it. You show love. But when you repeat what you know you can cause close friends to end up in conflict at best and enemies at worst. You are admonished by Solomon's wisdom in a Proverbs to not associate with those who flatter excessively. They are likely people who are talebearers who go around revealing other's secrets. Instead of gossiping let your words be like those of the Lord's. Choose to speak words which edify and encourage your hearers.

Today's Reading:
Exodus 23:1; Leviticus 19:16; Ephesians 4:29; James 4:11

March 8
Spy Wednesday

Imagine you had been planning for something all your life and as the day finally grew near to accomplish it you discovered a spy (a person who secretly collects and reports information on the activities, movements, and plans of an enemy or competitor) in your inner circle. On the Wednesday before His death, known as "Spy Wednesday," Jesus had such an experience. If something like this were to happen and you weren't aware, having someone close to you to betray you could destroy what you had been working for your entire life. However, the opposite was true for Jesus because He already knew ahead of time what Judas would do. Not only did He know, but He had also planned for it. It was a part of His story of our redemption. Take away Judas and there is no crucifixion. Without it, there is no Resurrection. And without it, our souls would perish. God knew the end before the beginning. And He used Judas' betrayal for His Divine purposes.

Today's Reading:
Matthew 26:14-26; Luke 23:3-6
John 6:64, 13:10,11

March 9
When It All Looks Bad, It's All Good

Do not think it strange or worry when the enemy uses people close to you to try to destroy your destiny and purpose. He cannot stop you from fulfilling God's will for your life. Or as the prophet MC would say, "he can't touch this!" And if you seek His face, God will also guide you in handling those working against you. He will even bless you in their presence. God is not surprised by those who oppose you, neither should you be. In fact, they are a part of your story - they often are used to help you draw closer to the Lord and pray more! Like that Good Friday that appeared to be so bad, you may have moments that look like you're defeated. But don't get caught up fretting over them. You're more than a conqueror. Just as death could not hold Jesus down, you too shall rise above every situation, including death! And God works all things together for the good - including those being used by the devil knowingly or unknowingly in your life and every situation that looks like you won't make it - to bring about His Divine purpose for you.

Today's Reading:
1 Samuel 23:9-12; Psalm 23:5; Jeremiah 29:11
Romans 8:28

March 10
A refuge

When the Israelites prepared to enter the promised land, the Lord provided instructions on how they should live. One of the things was to build cities of refuge. If a person committed a crime, they could flee to the city of refuge and live. He gave specific examples like of a person who unintentionally killed another. they could normally be punished by death. A refuge is a condition of being safe or sheltered from pursuit or trouble: God provided a way of escape where the person could flee. I am grateful we too have a refuge, a strong tower, where we can run in times of trouble. The wages of sin is death. All have sinned and fall short of the glory of God so all deserve to die. We could be put to death daily. But God has chosen to instead provide a way to be forgiven of every one of our sins. He has provided a way of escape from death, as well. Jesus is our refuge. When the weight of the world seems too hard to bear you can run to Him and be safe. When you know you have messed up again, others may choose to shun you, but He will never leave you nor forsake you. He is always available as a hiding place, a refuge for your soul.

Today's readings:
Deuteronomy 19:1-7; Psalm 9:9,28:8,46:1,91:2,9-15,94:22; Romans 3:23,6:23; 2 Thessalonians 3:3

March 11
Beyond Your Understanding

You can seek the Lord for wisdom. Yet, there may be times when you sense His guidance even though you do not understand why. In those moments, it is better to do what He says without hesitation. Do not move against His direction. Do not follow your own plans, even if you do not understand. Allow Him to guide you. You are always free to ask Him to clarify why He is guiding you in a certain direction, but obedience is still of utmost importance. I was listening to a minister's testimony about his invitation to preach in an African nation. The host pastor came to meet him before he was to speak. He had never met him. He asked the pastor why he invited him if he did not know him. The pastor responded, "the Holy Spirit told me your name. I called my friend, and he knew you." The pastor demonstrated a keen awareness of the Lord's voice. More importantly, he did what the Spirit said. It is important to heed the check in your spirit. The Holy Spirit may gently whisper to you. You will not necessarily hear an audible voice, rather you will have a strong urgence inside. Learn to heed His guidance and you will walk in His perfect will for your life.

Today's readings:
Proverbs 3:3-5

March 12
First Things First

When king Hezekiah found out his nation was surrounded by his enemies, note what he did ***not*** do. He did not gather around his friends to complain. He did not call anyone to spew it all out to them. He did not seek prayer from anyone else before he tore off his clothes and sought the face of God for himself. You may be inclined to go to your best friend and tell them all about what is bothering you, but it should not be before you've spoken to the Lord. He sticks closer than a brother. He is a very present help in times of trouble. It was only after he prayed for himself that the king sought out his counselors and sent them to the prophet Isaiah to beseech him to also pray for their country. God spoke to him through the prophet to let him know everything was going to be alright. It is fine to seek others to touch and agree with you in prayer. You should. The key is to keep first things first. First, talk to God. You may find it unnecessary to get anyone else to pray because the Lord can choose to move so quickly no further prayer is needed. This is a key to cultivating your faith in God and your friendship with Him.

Today's readings:
Psalm 34:6; Isaiah 37:1-4,38:1-8; Luke 22:39-44
2 Corinthians 12:7-9

March 13
Monday On His Way To The Cross

Jesus had a date with destiny. On the day following what we traditionally know as Palm Sunday, He left Bethany. Bethany was the city where Lazarus lived, along with his sisters Mary and Martha. This was the same Lazarus who had died earlier during Jesus' earthly ministry. Jesus had been in another town and waited until Lazarus had been in the grave 4 days before he arrived to call him from the grave. He declared Himself as the God of the living, not the dead. His act of resurrecting Lazarus was foretaste of what the Father would do for Him and all of us who believe in Him. He called the Pharisees whitewashed tombs. They appeared to be clean on the outside but were filled with dead men's bones on the inside. As that fateful day was nearing its end, before He departed and returned to Bethany, He went on to weep over Jerusalem and its coming destruction. He cleansed the temple for a second time because the people were using the house of God as a mere marketplace. His Father, and our Father, wants His house to be called a house of prayer for all nations.

Today's readings:
Matthew 21:1-13; Mark 11:15-21; Luke 19:41-46

March 14
On His Way To Calvary

Jesus rose early on that Tuesday and left Bethany, where He stayed with Lazarus, Mary and Martha. When the disciples saw the fig tree Jesus had cursed the day before, He used it as a teachable moment on the power of your faith. He taught them the importance of believing. When you have faith, you can speak to a mountain, and it will be moved. As you encounter mountains of debt, fear, or even humans, you can pray and decree they must move in Jesus' name. He went into the temple to teach for the last time. He observed the widow and others giving offerings and noted her 2 mites were more than all the rich people had offered because she gave out of her livelihood. He taught on what we are now seeing manifested in our world, at least in part, on way His back to Bethany when He stopped in the Garden of Gethsemane. This is when He gave much detail about the end of times before His return, including the wars and rumors of wars, false prophets who will rise and the destruction of the temple. Rather than be afraid, He exhorted you to look up! Know your redemption draws near.

Today's readings:
Matthew 24:1:3-25:46; Mark 11:20-24,13:3-35
Luke 6:38; 20:1-21:37

March 15
Preparation For Destiny

Sometime between late Tuesday and Wednesday of the week of Jesus' crucifixion Judas was used by the devil to cut a deal with the religious leaders to betray Jesus. For 30 silver coins he agreed to deliver Jesus to them to be crucified. Though the devil was using him to plot against Jesus, God was working to turn it around for our good. For about this same time, Jesus was anointed by a woman with an alabaster flask of very costly oil. She poured the oil on His head. When the disciples complained of the waste Jesus said she was preparing Him for His burial. They did not understand God was readying Him for His death and burial. In your own life there are things you are going to go through and may not understand. Yet, God is preparing you for the things you will encounter in the future, including transitioning into glory. God is preparing great thing for you. Though the enemy of your soul may come against you, he cannot thwart your destiny. Do not despise any experience you may have. All things are working together for the good of those who love God.

Today's readings:
Jeremiah 29:11; Matthew 26:14-26:7,27:9
Mark 14:3; Luke 7:37

March 16
What Others Don't Know

It is amazing how much others do not know about you. They know what schools you attended. They may know your family's history. They might know where you live or work. Yet, none of these facts display what God has in store for you. Jesus walked with His disciples for 3 years preparing them for the day He would be leaving them. Yet, they did not have a clue as it all unfolded around them. On Maundy Thursday, Jesus directed Peter and John to go to an upper room to prepare for the Passover meal. On this Passover occurring about 2000 years ago, Jesus ate with his 12 disciples. He washed the feet of His disciples, and He told them to go do likewise for one another, symbolizing the new commandment to love one another, as He has loved us. Then He instituted what we now call communion, symbolizing the New Covenant established with His Blood. He directed them to take and eat the bread, then to drink from the shared cup of wine. These represented His Body and His Blood. As often as you take the bread and drink the cup, you should do it in remembrance of Him.

Today's readings:
Matthew 26:1,17-30; Mark 14:1,12-26; Luke 22:1,7-23
John 13:1-35; 1 Corinthians 11:23-32

March 17
An awful good Friday

Imagine yourself on Good Friday over 2000 years ago. While you were settling in for the evening, in the quiet of the night, Jesus would have been in the Garden of Gethsemane crying out in agony for the impending events about to unfold. He asked His disciples to watch and pray with Him. Instead, they slept. They were tired, but Jesus couldn't sleep. As sweat like drops of blood dripped from His head, He prayed earnestly that the cup of suffering would pass Him by until finally He resolved, in agreement with the Father, His time had come. Throughout the night they held 6 trials against Him. The same crowd who had cried Hosanna just a few days before now cried, "Crucify Him or we will tell Rome!" They whipped Him with cattails, spat on Him, mocked Him with a crown of thorns, and cast lots for His clothing. They made Him carry the heavy wooden implement of His own execution: His cross. As He hung on that cross, before they pierced Him in His side with a sword and He gave up His Spirit, He uttered the profound words of grace upon which you can stake your soul's salvation today, "Father, forgive them..."

Today's readings:
Matthew 26:1l; Mark 14:53; Luke 22:1-23:43; John 18:13

March 18
The Son Came Up And Lifted Up!

Historically speaking, Friday was good for those who follow Jesus. He died that you might live forever free of accusation. Yet, for those close to Him at the time of His crucifixion, it was sheer agony. They went from walking with the King of kings to hiding out in fear of being persecuted by those who had crucified Him. Alhough His closest disciples had walked with Him, and multitudes in crowds had followed Him for 3 years, when He died, they all scattered like sheep without a Shepherd. But early Sunday morning the Son came up! Just as He had said He would, Jesus rose from the dead. Death could not hold Him down! In the wee hours of that morning Mary Magdalene went to the sepulcher where He had been buried. She was astonished to find the huge stone they had sealed it with had been moved. When she reached the tomb, she saw two beings in radiant clothing. They asked her why she was seeking the living among the dead. Jesus' resurrection gave you victory over death and the grave. Because He rose, you who believe in Him shall also rise! Hallelujah!

Today's readings:
Matthew 28:1,5-7; Mark 16:1; Luke 24:1
John 20:1,11-16; 1 Corinthians 15:54-55

March 19
He Lifted Others

Jesus not only defeated death He crushed the lie that women were somehow inferior beings. Because He honored Mary to be the first to see Him, and He spoke to her, and He gave her the first "sermon" (message after His resurrection), He established the fact that women can hear from God. Women can carry a message. Women are valued by God. Even to this day there are those (male and female) who don't believe women should preach or teach. Still others believe women are less significant. Some would say this is not so, just as some deny racism exists in America. Yet, in the USA, women make on average 82 cents to every dollar men make, while African American women make 62 cents for every dollar men make. But God demonstrated His value for women over 2000 years ago in a garden. Just like He rose, He also lifted women. Because in Christ Jesus there is neither male nor female. He is no respecter of persons. He will use whosoever diligently seeks Him.

Today's readings:
Matthew 28:1,5-7; Mark 16:1; Luke 24:1
John 20:1,11-16; Galatians 3:28

March 20
You Don't Have To Understand

It would be a mistake for you to obey God only when you understand the reason for His directions. In other words, there will be times when you will know what God wants you to do, although you may not fully comprehend why He wants you to do it. You must choose obedience to Him over your understanding if you want to be blessed and walk in His perfect will. I can imagine, for example, Abraham didn't understand why God told him to sacrifice his only son. Yet, out of obedience, he was about to do it when God told him to stop. God realized Abraham feared (reverenced) Him more than he loved Isaac. Abraham, on the other hand, trusted God and believed He was able to raise Isaac from the dead. God blessed Abraham abundantly - and you through him - because of his obedience. So, if at times you don't understand God's will, obey Him anyway. As the saints of old would sing, you will understand it better by and by.

Today's Reading:
Genesis 22:2-18; Proverbs 3:3-5, Isaiah 58:8
Romans 4:16,11:33, Hebrews 11:17-19

March 21
He Still Loves You

Gods knows your good, your bad and your ugly. He even knows your thoughts before you think them. He saw what you did and who you were with when you did it. He heard everything you said. Nothing is hidden from His sight. And He still loves you! You cannot out-sin the love or the grace of God. Because the more you sin, the more grace abounds toward you. Your sins (past, present, and future) were covered, are covered and will be covered by the blood of Jesus. No matter what you do God will never stop loving you. You can create brokenness in your fellowship with Him by continuing to purposely disobey His will. But like the father watching for his prodigal son to return ran to meet him as soon as he saw him, God's arms are always open to embrace you.

Today's Reading:
Psalm 139:1-3; Romans 5:20, 8:38-39
Hebrews 4:13; 1 John 4:19

March 22
Live Righteously

Let justice roll down like water and righteousness like a mighty stream through your life. Do the right thing while holding others accountable to do the same. Living justly with mercy is what God requires of you. It's amazing just how easily you can treat one person one way then turn to another person and treat them a totally different way. As a chaplain at the state prison, I remember being around correctional officers who would treat me with dignity and respect. But then I would see some of the ways they treated the inmates and it was horrendous. It was as though they were a totally different person. You are like Dr. Jekyll and Mr. Hyde if you treat one group of people honorably but turn into an evil person to another group of people. Many Klansman are viewed as respectable citizens because of their position in a church or for their support with various charities. Yet there is another side to them that is steeped in hatred and evil. Let's all examine ourselves. You must live righteously towards all to please God.

Today's Reading:
Amos 5:24; Micah 6:8

March 23
Make The Best Use Of Your Time

For each of the 24 hours in a day we get to choose how to spend our time. Once a day is over you can never get it back. Don't meander through the precious moments of your life. Invest time doing what pleases God. A great use of time is to envision what you want to see manifest in your life and ask God to guide you. Pray about everything in your life. Pray in the Spirit. The Holy Spirit in you communicates with the Father. Speak God's will into the atmosphere and bring heaven to earth through your prayers. When you pray in unknown tongues, the Spirit prays. Though God understands completely, your mind is unable to comprehend the meaning. Next time when you're standing in line, running errands, traveling to work or - even better – when you set aside time to pray, take time to envision and invite God's perfect will into your life. Remember, that is exactly what Jesus is doing.

Today's Reading:
Romans 8:34; 1 Corinthians 14:5a,14,15,18
Ephesians 5:15-16; Hebrews 7:25

March 24
Your Real Mojo

To redeem means to pay a ransom to purchase freedom for one who is bound, or to recover the power of another. You have been redeemed by Christ Jesus with His precious Blood. You got your power back! You were powerless but now you're powerful. You once were in darkness but now you're walking in the light. You have your real mojo back. The power you have is His power. His Holy, wonder-working, magnificent power! Walk in the magnitude of the power He has given you. You are no longer bound by sin. You are free to be who God created you to be. Live in the freedom He has given you. Who Christ has set free, is free indeed! Don't go back to the bondage from which He delivered you. You have been chosen by Him to be His earthly representative. Live this way. Trust God. You can do all things through Him who strengthens you.

Today's Reading:
Romans 8:5; Ephesians 5:8,16z
Philippians 4:19; 1 Peter 2:9

March 25
A Strong Tower

In the days of old people living in cities would build walls around the perimeter of their jurisdictions to serve as protection. It was not uncommon to build a tower inside of the wall from which watchmen could keep watch over the city. The towers were sometimes large enough for all of the city's inhabitants to use as a hiding place when the city was under attack. The people would run to the tower to be out of the reach of their enemies. God's Name is a strong tower for every believer. He is our stronghold, a place where we can hide. You are shielded beneath the banner of His love and are saved. Anytime you feel anxious or afraid, call on His Name and remind yourself He is your strong tower and fortress. He will protect you. You are safe in Him.

Today's Reading:
Judges 9:51; 2 Samuel 22:3; Psalm 18:2, 61:3, 144:2
Proverbs 18:10; Micah 4:8

March 26
Listen To Your Gifts

Our gifts are a major clue to our purpose. As you pay attention your gifts will help you to understand what you're created to do. The abilities you have along with your passions can direct you to your destiny. People will usually look to you for your God given abilities that others value. The key is to pay attention. Be aware of what others affirm in you. When combined with the awareness of what you enjoy doing, you're likely to be drawn towards the opportunities that allow you to use your gifts. If a person is a great painter, for example, others will likely reach out to them to have them paint. They in turn will likely be open to opportunities to paint. In essence, your gifts will make room for you. People will seek you out to operate in the gifts they see in you. Recognize the things you are most noted for, and you will learn how God can best use you for His Kingdom.

Today's Reading:
Proverbs 18:16; 1 Corinthians 12:7; Ephesians 4:16

March 27
Love Builds Up

God is love. Anyone claiming to be in Him must walk in an attitude of love towards everyone, especially fellow believers in the Lord Jesus Christ. It is God's plan that you build others up with love. If you cannot love your brother who you see every day, how can you claim to love God who you've never seen? Walking in love towards others means recognizing they will fall short of your expectations. Likewise, you will fall short of theirs. Be forgiving. God overlooks your faults every day and chooses to love you unconditionally. If you are going to love others, you must follow His example. Love keeps no records of wrongs. I'm reminded of the debtor who was forgiven for a great sum of money, but then went off to threaten to throw someone else in jail who owed him far less. It's amazing how some are quick to seek and expect to be forgiven but so very slow to be forgiving. Yet, God has called you to love even those who have chosen to be unloving towards you just as much as those that adore you. It's not optional. God commands us to love one another in order to demonstrate our love for Him.

Today's Reading:
Matthew 18:21-35; 1 Corinthians 8:1, 13:1-end
1 John 4:7-21

March 28
Renounce

Renounce means to turn away from or give up on an agreement or relationship. All of us have at some point in our lives engaged in things that are not pleasing to God. Many have dabbled in things that unknowingly have had a negative spiritual impact. Reading horoscopes, going to palm readers, engaging in sex outside of marriage, watching movies influenced by demonic themes, or seeking psychics are just a few of the things that opens your soul to unclean spirits. They are all based on divination and witchcraft which God hates. And over time your spirit is impacted. You may struggle with different things in life, experiencing depression or oppression or anxiety. You may find it difficult to believe in God or pray. You may never read a Bible or gain understanding of it. All these things can be tied to the impact of actions you've taken not realizing they were harmful. The best response once you've realized how harmful these things are is to state out loud you renounce them. Pray and ask God to forgive you and to fill you with the Holy Spirit in every place left empty by whatever space these things occupied in you.

Today's Reading:
Proverbs 3:7, 28:13; 2 Corinthians 4:2
Galatians 5:16-21; James 4:7; 2 Peter 1:4

March 29
Having Friends

You get siblings by birth and friends by choice. A friend sticks closer than a brother. To have friends you need be friendly in return. One great example of friendship is found in the Bible. There was a paralyzed man who wanted to be healed. Jesus was in a house teaching nearby. His friends carried him to Jesus. So many people were crowded around Him they couldn't get the paralyzed man to Jesus. They did not give up easily, though. They took their friend up on the roof and lowered him down into the house on his mat. When He saw their faith, Jesus declared the man's sins were forgiven. He told the man to arise and walk; and he did! Notice "their" faith moved God. You can become a good friend by serving others and interceding on their behalf. Be the type of friend who believes and prays for the best for others. As you do, you'll gain friends and reap what you sow.

Today's Reading:
Proverbs 17:17, 18:24; Luke 5:17-26; John 4:46-54
Galatians 6:7-10

March 30
Don't Resist Change

One of the buzz words commonly used during the last few years is pivot. When the Covid-19 pandemic hit the United States of America, many people, companies, organizations and even churches had to pivot into a new normal, seemingly overnight. Change is an inevitable part of your life. Some changes are painful, and some bring great happiness. Regardless of what type of change may come, you will have to adjust to it. Set your heart to not only expect a new normal but embrace it. Don't be like Peter who resisted change because he didn't understand it. When Jesus went to wash his feet, he tried to hinder Him from doing so. Once The Lord explained it to him, Peter relented and enthusiastically accepted. Sometimes you won't receive an explanation or an understanding of why a change occurs. And sometimes, what starts out looking undesirable can be a blessing in disguise. Like with sisters who were furloughed but launched a bakery that has proven to be a phenomenal success, God can take what starts out being difficult to elevate you, in His Kingdom. Change is like the dawning of a new day. It is simply a part of life.

Today's Reading:
Psalm 37:23; Ecclesiastes 3:1; John 13:5-9
Romans 12:1,2

March 31
One Thing Will Never Change

In an ever-changing world there is one thing that will never change. God is immutable. He never changes. He is the solid Rock upon which we can build our lives. Everything else must change. You start out as a baby, grow to an adult and ease into your elderly age. The seasons never stay the same. Winter, spring, summer, and fall are the inevitable part of every year. The temperature outside changes according to every season. You can be supportive of whatever the current hot item is. As soon as that item is no longer in highlighted in a magazine, you move on to something else. Even your friends will change, either because you grow older together or you grow apart. In the midst of all this change there is one thing you can depend on for sure. Heaven and earth will pass away but God's Word will last forever. You can trust that when God says something, He will fulfill it. Jesus is the same today, yesterday, and forever. You can depend on Him.

Today's Reading:
Numbers 23:19; Psalm 18:2; Malachi 3:6
Matthew 24:35; Hebrews 13:8; James 1:17

April 1
All Means All

In a world filled with relatives instead of absolutes it can be challenging to embrace the fact that Jesus died for all your sins. It's probably easier to accept He died for most of your sins. The weight of sin and guilt and condemnation you place on yourself makes it hard to believe, but the fact is Jesus died for every one of your transgressions. Every. Single. One. Jesus is either Lord of all or not Lord at all. While God really does love all of you, all of the time, He also wants all of you to live righteously, all of the time. That's why He sent His only begotten Son to pay the penalty for all your sins. You live in a fallen world and there will be times that you fall short. But there is not a sin you can commit for which Jesus hasn't already died and covered it with His Blood. God has already forgiven you. He made a way through His Son, Jesus. Likewise, there's not one area of your life that He doesn't want you to surrender. He's forgiven all of your sins, and in return He wants all of you to surrender to Him. All means all.

Today's Reading:
Isaiah 43:25,26; Romans 5;8,12, 6:23; Philippians 2:8-11

April 2
Thinking Too Much

God has given us the capacity to reason through problems and seek out understanding. Yet, He wants us to yield our thinking to the principles of scripture. He gives us His Spirit - if we give Him our hearts - to guide us. He always guides us in agreement with biblical wisdom. Sometimes you may sense the Spirit leading you in ways that don't agree. You may think there is a better way. When you use your intellect to override what you hear in your spirit, you determine your own will is best. You become your own little god. You can also resort to following common sense, going along with what most people do. The way of the Kingdom of God is usually contrary to the view of the world. In fact, the road to eternal life is narrow, and many will miss it. You can choose to live by your own understanding or yield to God. Those who belong to God are led by His Spirit.

Today's Reading:
Psalm 25:8; Proverbs 3:3-5, 14:12; Matthew 7:13,14
Romans 8:14; Ephesians 1:13,14; James 3:17

April 3
Protected

What do you do when problems and people are coming against you, and everything seems to be headed toward doom? I recommend you do what Jehoshaphat did when three armies rose up in an attempt to destroy the people of God. He knew he was outnumbered and didn't have the strength, nor the strategy to fight. Do you have anything going on in your life where you just don't know what to do? Jehoshaphat realized he needed wisdom, so he humbled himself and cried out to God. You also have the ability to seek God and obtain His wisdom when you face circumstances you don't know how to handle. When you don't know how to respond to situations, seek the Lord for answers. God has promised He will give wisdom liberally to those who ask Him. Fix your eyes on Jesus, who is the author and finisher of your faith. He will show you the way. Once Jehoshaphat turned his eyes to the Lord, God spoke through a Levite to let him know he was protected. He did not need to be afraid because the battle was not his, it belonged to the Lord! The same is true for you; don't fret or be dismayed for the Lord your God is with you. This battle is not yours, it's the Lord's!

Today's Reading:
2 Chronicles 20:1,12,15; Isaiah 30:19-2
Hebrews 12:2; James 1:5

April 4
Timing Is Everything

Once you know the right thing to do and fail to do it, you are walking outside of God's will. You actually are committing a sin. It may seem strange. Yet, a sin of omission can be just as impactful as a sin of commission. Sometimes you determine to do what you know is best but only after hesitating. When you delay your obedience, you can miss God's perfect will not only for yourself, but also for others or even the world. Imagine if Jesus hadn't died at just the right time. Delayed obedience can be devastating. Sadly, for example, Dorothy Dandridge chose to try and wait for her husband to return before going to the hospital when it was time for her child to be born. Her daughter was born with mental deficiencies and never spoke or recognized her mother and ended up living in an institution. When you know what God is prompting you to do, be obedient without delay.

Today's Reading:
Ecclesiastes 3:1-3; John 13:27; Romans 5:5; James 4:17

April 5
Snatched From The Power Of The Grave

Praise God Who has never, nor will He ever abandon you, not even in death. He will not allow you to perish. He will redeem your soul. He will snatch you from the power of the grave. Because you have been saved from death, you are no longer bound by darkness. Walk in God's marvelous light by keeping your focus on the things of the Spirit. Then you won't walk according to your flesh. Be mindful of the evil times we live in. Don't get caught up in worldly affairs. It's easy to get distracted. Talking about people or focusing on negativity can easily pull you off course. Stop and think about whether what you are saying and doing throughout the day aligns with your godly position and adjust yourself as needed. Let God use you to save others by being an example to guide those who are still lost. Live in such a manner that they too will be drawn to the Light. Pull them out of the enemy's grip by sharing love and the Word of God whenever you can.

Today's Reading:
Psalm 49:15 NLT; Romans 8:5; Ephesians 5:8,16
Jude 1:23

April 6
A Thing Shall Be Established

God's Word is confirmed by others. It tells us a thing shall be established by 2 or more witnesses. That's why when God is speaking you may hear the same message from your devotional that you hear from a sermon. Or a friend may share with you something which confirms what God has spoken to you. Sometimes He will send someone to you specifically to speak His will for your life. Still, some only believe it if science says it. Believe it whether science has affirmed it or not. Scientists announce the "discovery" of some artifact or truth which affirms what the Word has already expressed. Like the studies showing prayer works, science is only stating what has already been established in God's Word. You should expect and look for God to confirm His Word through others. The Word is true, and it proves itself over and over again in various ways.

Today's Reading:
Deuteronomy 17:6; 2 Samuel 12:1-7; Matthew 18:16
1 Timothy 5:19

April 7
You're Rich

Did you know that you are rich? If you have given your life to Christ, you have blessings upon blessings coming your way. Jesus emptied Himself. He became poor so you could be filled and become rich. In Him, you are blessed with the abundance of God's Kingdom if you recognize Jesus Christ as your Lord and Savior. God will fill you with His Spirit, grace, and love. As you surrender to His Spirit and allow Him to work through you, the blessings will be returned. Show grace and love to others and receive it in return. In addition, peace is yours in abundance. Joy – unspeakable joy - is available to you. God will make provision for your needs as you trust Him and walk in obedience to His ways and His will. He gives us all things. I'm reminded of an old Daffy Duck cartoon when he said, "I'm rich! Rich, I tell you!" Isn't it great to know that in Christ Jesus you too are made rich!

Today's Reading:
Proverbs 28:20; Matthew 5:3; Luke 1:53; Romans 8:3
2 Corinthians 6:10, 8:9

April 8
Submission Is Not A Curse Word

It is easier to be submissive to those in authority in our lives is when we realize who really has the ultimate authority. God is sovereign in all the earth. As you come up under those He has placed in your life to lead you in different spheres, you ultimately surrender your will to God's. Conflicts arise when you want to do things your way. It makes it challenging to follow someone else. When you become independent minded and assume you know what's best for you, it can be difficult to fully commit to the leadership of others. God has the ultimate authority though, and with Him it is different. You can trust that even if it isn't the way you wanted, He knows what is best. You are created in His image. He knows far better what you were created for and what you can accomplish. And He sent Jesus to die for your sins. You are not your own. He has purchased you with His precious Blood. When you follow Him through submission to others, He honors your humility. The more you're willing to humble yourself the higher you will be lifted up by the Lord.

Today's Reading:
Psalm 24:1; Romans 13:1; 1 Corinthians 6:20
Ephesians 5:20,21; Philippians 2:5-8; 1Peter 5:6

April 9
Ask Him First

I wonder how much time you have wasted figuring out what to do. Reading and researching are good ways to obtain information. Even having gained valuable knowledge, you should still pray before you act. I had a situation that exemplified this truth. I started driving before I put the address in the GPS. By the time I hit the beltway and finished entering the address I realized it was better for me to go in another direction. The GPS guided me off the beltway to another route that would have been more easily reached if I had never gotten on the beltway at all. Had I programmed the GPS first I would have saved a lot of time. I'm sure following my own way would have gotten me there eventually even though it would have been a longer journey, but I preferred to take the most efficient route. Pray for wisdom before you make a decision, no matter how small the decision may be. God promised to give you wisdom generously if you take the time to ask.

Today's Reading:
Proverbs 3:3-5,7; Matthew 7:7; James 1:5-7

April 10
Enter Into His Rest

There is rest for the people of God who choose to enter it. Sadly, some never take advantage of it. God desires for you to cease from your own labors to rest in Him. He wants you to be set free from the burdens of religious rules and be led by the Spirit. He invites you to enter into His Sabbath. Some never enter God's rest because of their disobedience to the Word. Choose to have regard for the way of the Lord. Let the Spirit lead you. Instead of continuing to do things your own way, rest in the confidence of being in Christ. Although you hear and may even know the scripture, you must combine the Word with faith. You can continue to operate in your own strength and lean to your own understanding. Or you can choose to trust in God, follow His will and live in His rest. The choice is yours. Will you go about trying to do everything in your own power or will you make the choice to rest in the Lord? It is His desire that you come and leave all your burdens with Him. He wants you to rest in Him while you journey through your time on earth.

Today's Reading:
Matthew 11:28-30; Hebrews 4:1-11

April 11
Love is the Key To Your Success

The way society is geared you would think it takes money or position to get people to do what you want them to do, or to get them to be cooperative with you. Yet God's ideal suggests the key to having successful relationships is to walk in love. When you are loving, people want to cooperate. Love is like a magnet. We love God because He first loved us. You too can reap what you love as you sow it into your relationships. Even a person who is not born of the Spirit has an emotional mind that is wired to respond to love with cooperation. When you love someone who is unloving, you can love the "hell" out of them. Most important of all, you are commanded by the Lord to love others. Indeed, according to the Lord Himself, it is the mark of a true disciple. According to scripture, if you can't love those you see every day, you can't love Him who you've never seen. Love disarms dissension and builds others up. The next time you are tempted to give someone a piece of your mind, show them love instead. By loving others, you can develop prosperous relationships and demonstrate to the world that you are truly of God.

Today's Reading:
John 13:35; 1 Corinthians 13; 1 John 4:7-11,20,21

April 12
Hide His Words In Your Heart

In a season where truth is believed to be relative, God's word clearly states the contrary. And God cannot lie. God's Word is the truth. Memorizing the truth is a fundamental part of being a disciple of Jesus Christ. Every word in the Holy Bible is inspired by God. It lights your path to keep you moving in the right direction, helps you to know God's will, and brings conviction when your choices are contrary to its precepts, as it distinguishes between the things of the flesh and the things of the Spirit. Each of today's recommended verses are rubrics in the life of a follower of Christ. Memorize them all and they will bear fruit in your life for the rest of your life.

Today's Reading:
Numbers 22:19; Psalm 119:11, 105; John 17:17
Timothy 2:15, 3:16,17; Hebrews 4:12

April 13
God Of The Breakthrough

Things can seem like you're not moving forward. You may be working hard, praying faithfully and seeking God intently and yet feel like nothing is happening in your favor. Be encouraged. God is going to move in your favor. Breakthrough is coming. God may allow a season of what looks like inactivity only for you to later realize how much you grew through the process. You cannot have a message without going through the mess. You don't get a testimony without a test. Like David witnessed when he had to fight against his enemies, you will come to know God is the God of breakthrough. He broke through David's enemies like a breakthrough of water. Trust the God you serve. He sees and He knows. You will experience the manifestation of what you have labored for in the Spirit and pursue in the natural. You will reap from your efforts if you persevere. Hold on; help is on the way. Greater is coming!

Today's Reading:
2 Samuel 5:20; Psalm 46:1; 1 Corinthians 9:11
Galatians 6:7-9; Hebrews 4:13

April 14
God Is Speaking To You

God has been speaking to mankind since the beginning of time. He has provided wisdom and instructions through the Holy Bible; His inspired Word. He has used priests and prophets, as well as signs and wonders to help His peoples know His will. The Lord uses His Spirit, poured out on the day of Pentecost, to guide you. He uses family, friends, and acquaintances to show you wisdom. He provides apostles, prophets, evangelists, pastors, and teachers to train you in righteousness. He orchestrates circumstances to get your attention. He uses similitudes as markers to guide you along the path to know His plans for your life. His Spirit brings conviction to show you right from wrong. Today He continues to speak to us and show His love for us by way of an event that happened well over 2,000 years ago: the death, burial and resurrection of Jesus, His only begotten Son. That was the greatest statement of all. It happened because God loves you and wants you to have eternal life. He is speaking. Are you listening?

Today's Reading:
Genesis 1:28,29; 2 Samuel 2:1,12:7
Ephesians 4:11-16; Hebrews 1:1,2

April 15
Your Praise Is A Weapon

One of the greatest and most under-utilized weapons you have to overcome the attacks of the enemy of your soul is praise. Praising God not only gives Him glory, but it will also give you strength. You will begin to be invigorated as you focus on the Lord and declare His works. Just think on the things God has done for you. He blessed you to see a brand-new day. He provided for your needs. He protected you from dangers seen and unseen. There are many reasons to praise Him, but the enemy will try to stop you. The spirits of darkness will try to oppress you, make you afraid of the future, and remind you of your failures. Instead of giving into those thoughts that are whispered in your ear, start praising God instead! The devil is a liar. He is the accuser of the Saints of God. He wants to steal your peace, kill your joy, and destroy your life. But greater is He who is in you than any devil. You are empowered by God because He lives in you. Every time you praise Him, you stir up that power. Praise silences the enemy's voice. You can't listen to his lies and focus on the goodness of the Lord at the same time. Lift up a praise!

Today's Reading:
Psalm 8:3, 61:8; John 8:44, 10:10; 2 Corinthians 10:4
2 Timothy 1:6; 1 John 4:4

April 16
You Don't Know My Story

The woman was ostracized. She was smelling because of her hemorrhaging for so many years. She was bleeding and broke. She was alone. ~ The guy was shunned by everyone. He couldn't get himself together. He was crying out and cutting himself. He lived in the tombs. ~He was a leader in the synagogue. He had some resources, no doubt. Yet neither his position nor his personal wealth was enough. His baby girl laid in bed dying. ~ Lacking money, caught up in a health issue, tormented by demons, living alone, and even doing well in life . . . they all had a story. And at first glance you might be tempted to judge them or even shun them. Be careful with your hasty response to people who seem to be in a place you don't understand. Likewise, don't assume you do know how things are for someone who seems to be living a good life. Everyone has a past in which they needed Jesus to come and turn the circumstances around. You are often not privy to a person's complete story. Be careful, therefore, with assumptions.

Today's Reading:
Matthew 7:1; Mark 8:1-7, 21-23, 25-30; John 7:24

April 17
How To Increase Your Longevity

People look for ways to live longer. By exercising and eating right they hope to prolong their lives. God has given you a way to expand the length of your days in His Word. If you fear Him, God is a shelter in the time of a storm. He will keep His eye upon you and feed you during times of famine. He will be your help and shield you from the enemy. He will provide for you, so you do not want. He will bless you. The fear of the Lord will prolong your days. It will cause you to walk in righteousness, keeping you from evil. It will instruct you in wisdom. Indeed, it is the beginning of wisdom. To fear God means to reverence and respect Him. It is not to be terrified by Him. When you fear Him, you consider Him before you speak or act. You make every effort to do what pleases Him. If you want to do what you can to have a long, prosperous life and walk in wisdom, start by fearing the Lord.

Today's Reading:
Psalm 33:18-19, 34:9, 61:3, 115:11, 13
Proverbs 9:10, 10:27, 14:2, 27, 25:12

April 18
What He Said

You are given a choice for each moment of every day. Whose report will you believe? You can listen to naysayers and your own negative thoughts, or you can believe what God said about you. You are a new creation in Christ Jesus. The old has passed. All things have been made new. You are the righteousness of God in Christ Jesus. Your sins are forgiven. You are a minister who has been given the ministry of reconciliation, called to let others know their sins are no longer counted against them when they accept Jesus as their Savior. You are able to do all things through Christ who strengthens you. God shall supply all your needs as you sow into His kingdom. Because you choose to obey Him, the Lord will command the blessing upon you and your belongings. He will bless everything you touch. He will bless you wherever you are. You are the head and not the tail. You are set above in Him. As you face each circumstance that comes your way, remember who God says you are and that you are His child.

Today's Reading:
Deuteronomy 28:8,13; 2 Corinthians 5:17-21
Philippians 4:13,19

April 19
Your Account Is Credited

You were put in right standing with God the moment you accepted Jesus as your Savior. Your position in Him gave you freedom from the bondage of sin. You were made to be justified - fully acquitted of all your sins - in His sight. Now God sees you just as if you had never sinned. You have peace with God. How can this be so? It is because your spiritual account was credited with Jesus' righteousness. He took your sin so you could take His righteousness. Therefore, your sins are no longer counted against you. What a deal! Who wouldn't serve a God like Him? Actually, many don't know the deal they've been offered in Him. If they knew, I'm sure they would gladly accept. Tell someone who you encounter today about the great gift of salvation. Let them know they won't have to work for it. Their account will be credited based upon their faith.

Today's Reading:
Acts 13:39; Romans 3:24-28; 5:1, 8:30; Galatians 2:16
Ephesians 2:8-10; 2 Corinthians 5:19

April 20
Dress For Success

When you belong to God you are to clothe yourself in the full armor of God - the breastplate of righteousness, helmet of salvation, shield of faith, belt of truth and the sword of the Spirit which is the Word of God. Your shoes are the gospel of peace. You are clothed in salvation, wearing a robe of righteousness. You also need to put on tender mercies, kindness, humility, meekness, and longsuffering. Dress in strength and honor. Your justice, being fair in your judgements and interface with others, should be like a robe. Above all else, clothe yourself in love because God is love. In essence, you are to be clothed in Jesus Christ so the world may know whose you are and the power and protection that comes with being a child of the Most High. In order for you to look like your Father in heaven, make every effort to be dressed for success in His Kingdom every day.

Today's Reading:
Job 29:14; Proverbs 31:25; Isaiah 61:10; Matthew 6:30
Mark 5:15; Romans 13:14; 2 Corinthians 5:2
Colossians 3:12-14

April 21
Your "if" or His

It is interesting how we put conditions on God's ability to heal or deliver us. Various people who encountered Jesus had their own "if", a condition they created in order for them or their loved one to be healed. The condition they set for receiving answered prayers were not from the Lord, though. He only gave one condition for our prayers to be answered. Some who begged Him determined they could be healed if they could just touch the hem of His garment. Another said to Jesus if He could do anything, He could heal his son. Still another told Him if He would come to his house, He could heal his daughter. A leper told Jesus if He was willing, He could make him whole. Still another said told Him if He would only speak a word his servant would be healed. Each of them received based upon God's grace. Yet, each of the conditions they set to receive His grace, far exceeded God's requirement for us to receive what we ask for in prayer. His "if" is simple. If you believe, you will receive what you ask for in prayer.

Today's Reading:
Matthew 8:2,8; 14:36, 21:22; Mark 9:22,23
Luke 8:41,50

April 22
It Ain't About You

Let's face it. Your natural inclination is to think about yourself. But you were created to glorify God by serving others. When you were born, you were given talents that enabled you to do some things well. Maybe your physical talents made you a fast runner, a good singer, a good artist or perhaps you had a strong capacity to reason through math problems. Every good thing comes from God. And if you gave your life to Christ, you inherited His supernatural gifts. Each one of us is empowered by God to use His gifts to serve others and bring Him praise. Jesus exemplified this truth. He came to serve; not to be served. So, whatever you do, do it with Him in mind. Never accept mediocrity as your standard. Always give Him your best. And never think it's all about you because whatever abilities you have were given by Him to enhance the world and bless the body of Christ.

Today's Reading:
Deuteronomy 8:18; Isaiah 12:5,43:7; Daniel 2:23
1 Corinthians 4:7,13:7; Ephesians 3:2; James 1:17

April 23
When A Coverup Is A Setup

You would think the best way to be prosperous is to hide all your flaws and cover up your sins. But just the opposite is true. When you try to hide your sins, instead of confessing them to God, you end up shipwrecking your blessings. On the contrary when you confess and forsake your sins you receive mercy from God. Admit to God that you have fallen short. He will not only wipe out the record of your sins, but you will also feel like the weight of the world has fallen off your shoulders. He will grant you His supernatural peace. Sin is a trap that keeps you bound. When you let it go, you will feel an indescribable joy. God will not hold onto your sins nor count them against you. You will sense a release in your spirit the moment you repent. And it's not a one-time event. Each time you find yourself doing what you know you ought not do -- or not doing what you know you should -- stop and talk to God. Admit you've messed up so you can truly prosper.

Today's Reading:
Proverbs 28:13; Acts 3:19; John 8:11; Romans 8:1
Hebrews 12:1,2; James 4:17

April 24
Same God Back Then, Same God Now

God, maker of heaven and earth, is a miracle worker. He demonstrated His power through the prophet Elisha. When Naaman had leprosy, he came to the prophet to be healed. Elisha told him to go dip his body in the Jordan River seven times. He complained that he was being told to go dip his body in the river of his enemy. Yet, when he did his skin was as smooth as a baby's skin. On another occasion, God demonstrated His miracle working power when Lazarus got sick and died. Jesus was asked to come to come to Lazarus before he died, but instead Jesus waited four days and only arrived after Lazarus had been buried and his body was decaying. His sister complained about Jesus not coming earlier. Still, He called Lazarus back from the dead. This week a little girl in Ghana was in a coma, barely alive. During the Women Connecting with Christ Bible Study I teach, we prayed for that little girl. Within 48 hours God brought healing and she was walking around the medical unit. God is still working miracles. Trust Him and believe He can work in your situation. What a Mighty God we serve!

Today's Reading:
2 Kings 5:11-14; John 11:36-40

April 25
Let Go Of Control

When God allows a circumstance to come about you can trust Him, knowing He loves you. Rest assured He desires to see you blessed in the end. A situation may be challenging, but you are never alone. He will be with you and see you through it. When the children of Israel were delivered out of their bondage in Egypt, they complained all along the way. At the sign of any challenge, they questioned God, despite His just having moved a whole sea on their behalf. Naaman complained when Elisha told him to dip in the Jordan, because it wasn't the manner in which he thought the healing would come. Naaman wanted Elisha to come and speak some words of healing instead. Thankfully he decided to be obedient and was blessed with healing. Martha even complained to Jesus because he didn't show up before Lazarus died. She didn't know God had planned to glorify Himself by raising him from the dead. What situation are you trying to control in your life? Let God take the wheel. If you do, I can guarantee He will get you to your best destination: right downtown on perfect will of God boulevard!

Today's Reading:
Exodus 14:11,16:3; 2 Kings 5:11,12; Psalm 77:3-15
Luke 15:2; John 11:21

April 26
Not The End

When you are going through a trial it can be difficult to remember it is not the end. Just like enduring a bumpy plane ride does not reflect your ultimate destination, so too having a challenging time does not reflect where you are going to land in Christ. The fact that you are facing a challenge is an indication that God knows you can withstand it. He never lets you be tempted beyond your capacity to handle what you are facing. And He provides a way of escape for you to hold up under it. Though He allows rain on the righteous and the unrighteous, God has told us we will have showers of blessings. The things you are going through are building your character and will ultimately cause you to be mature in the Lord. They will not end in death. They will bring God glory as you joyfully endure them like a good soldier.

Today's Reading:
Psalm 23:4,84:6,7; Ezekiel 34:25; Matthew 5:45; John 11:4; 1 Corinthians 10:13; 2 Timothy 2:3; James 1:3-5

April 27
When They Come To You

Interestingly King David experienced what many have in relationships. When he was younger, he went to take food to King Saul and those who served alongside him in battle with their enemies. His brothers were among the soldiers. When they saw him, they immediately ridiculed him for coming to the battlefield and inquiring about Goliath, the Giant whom they all feared. They even mocked him by inquiring about the little sheep he normally watched. He eventually went on to not only face the Giant, but to slay him. Later when he came to be known for his exploits and he was being pursued by the king he would succeed, many came to him to serve under his leadership. His brothers were among those who came to him. You may have experienced a time when others disparaged your character or suggested you were not good enough, only to later seek you out for their assistance or just to be associated with you. When that happens, be like David and receive them with grace. Let God deal with those who come against your character.

Today's Reading:
1 Samuel 17:23-28, 23:1, Romans 12:19

April 28
No Worries

One of the biggest wastes of time is worrying. Not only does it consume you emotionally, but it also eats up precious moments of your life that you can never get back. Anxiety will weigh you down. But a good word will make your heart glad. Therefore, it's better to spend time meditating on God and His word than on your problems. And God promises to keep you in His perfect peace when you keep your mind on Him. God invites you to cast all your cares on Him. He wants you to bring every one of them to Him in prayer and leave them there. He has promised to never leave you nor forsake you. You are blessed when you trust in Him. When you go through waters you will not be overtaken by them. When you go through fire it will not drown you because the Lord your God is with you. He is your everlasting strength. You have no reason to worry or to be afraid.

Today's Reading:
Psalm 56:3; Proverbs 12:25
Isaiah 26:4, 28:3, 41:10, 43:2; Jeremiah 17:7
Luke 12:22-32; Join 14:27; Philippians 4:6,7; 1 Peter 5:7

April 29
For His Glory

Whatever you achieve is the result of God giving you the ability and the grace to do it. Your gifts and talents are all given by Him. Without Him you can do nothing. As you go through life always recognize your achievements are intended to bring glory to God. He works in you to achieve His purposes. He strengthens you to do whatever you do. He gives you the ability to produce wealth. He gave you good health and your mental capacity. There is no plan or insight that can be achieved unless He allows it. Whatever you do, do it with all of your might, knowing you're doing it unto Him. That's what He did for us. He gave us His best when He sent His only begotten Son. Jesus set the best example of living a life to please God. His obedience brought glory to His Father. You are wise to live in the same manner. Live a life that is surrendered and obedient to Him, so that He may be glorified.

Today's Reading:
Ezra 7:18; Proverbs 21:30; John 4:38, 11:40, 14:13, 15:5
Romans 11:36; 1 Corinthians 10:31; Philippians 2:13

April 30
Don't Let It Happen

Don't let your heart be troubled is what Jesus told the disciples who followed Him. It was just before His crucifixion. It almost seemed oxymoronic for Him to say He was about to die, but don't let your heart be troubled. Much like the tensions in your own life which can weigh you down if you allow them, the news the disciples faced was difficult and challenging. How could they not let their hearts be troubled? Jesus gave them the answer immediately. He said, trust in God and in Me. The reason you don't have to let your heart be troubled is also the method by which you can do it: Trust in God. Trust means rely upon; being confident and secure in God. When you face a problem, you can confidently believe that God will take care of you, or you can believe the problems you face are greater than God. You have a choice. Focus on your problems and be filled with anxiety or focus on trusting God and everything He has said whenever you have issues. If you choose the latter, your heart will not be troubled.

Today's Reading:
John 14:1-6

May 1

Avoid The Spirit Of Accusations

One of the oldest tricks the devil uses is accusation. Indeed, he is known as the accuser of the brethren. It's important for you not to buy into this habit. Never accuse anyone of things you can't prove. Caution yourself against trying to attribute motive to a person's actions. In the book of Job, his friends accused him of sinning even though he was a righteous man. They assumed because of the multiple calamities he experienced; he must have sinned. They were wrong. Indeed, their speculation was far from the truth. If you believe someone has done something, the best thing you can do is ask them. Otherwise, you stand in danger of being used by the devil. That's how offenses and brokenness in relationships often occur. Once a person is offended it can be very hard to win them back. Feelings are hurt and wounds can cut deep. Guard again making accusations and walk in love.

Today's Reading:
Job 1:8-22; Proverbs 18:19; Revelation 12:10-12

May 2
He Will Hide You

What do you do when your heart is heavy, and you are feeling despair? Do you get a drink, a drug or a joint? These options all work to harm your body and mind, which also serves as the temple of God. Instead of those destructive escape mechanisms, find refuge in God instead. Just like the psalmist, you can take refuge under the shadow of God's wings. You can find comfort for your soul in His presence. When your heart is overwhelmed go to the Rock of your salvation. He will hide you from the worries and frustrations of the world. He will give you the strength you need to fulfill your responsibilities. As you enter His presence begin to give Him praise. In His presence there is fullness of joy! That joy in Him is your strength. Rather than escape from your pain by using artificial and harmful substances which leave you hungover - and worse than you were before you indulged in them - you can take refuge in your God, your Rock and your Redeemer.

Today's Reading:
Nehemiah 8:10; Psalm 16:11, 36:7, 61, 91:1-2

May 3
Your Aroma

Your fragrance could be nice and yet you could have a bad aroma - to some people. When you are in Christ, God is able to diffuse the fragrance of His knowledge through you everywhere you go. For you are the aroma of Christ. To those who are perishing your aroma smells like death. Even without you making any effort to do so your presence can bring conviction of their sin. As Christ's ambassador you carry His fragrance. Consequently, they can be repelled by you because there is no fellowship between darkness and light. You are the light of the world. Darkness and light cannot coexist in the same space. The spirit in them can war against the Spirit in you without you ever saying a word. Whereas to those being saved, you have the aroma of life. You are kindred spirits, and their spirit can bear witness with your spirit that you are a child of God.

Today's Reading:
Matthew 5:14; 2 Corinthians 2:14-17, 5:21, 6:14

May 4
Favor

Favor is defined as acts which display one's fondness or compassion for another. It is grace, kindness, kindheartedness. God will bless you with His favor. His favor cannot be purchased. It is bestowed upon you as His righteous child. He will demonstrate His fondness for you in big and subtle ways. For example, I saw the favor of God when I decided to return my rental car late once I was informed my flight was delayed. I expected to pay a late fee for the late return and to be assessed for having slightly less than a full tank of gas. Instead, I was favored to not only be able to turn in the car without paying a late fee, but I was also extended grace for the gas as well. The attendant made sure I knew his name was Michael, the name of the archangel sent to war for God's people   I cannot help but be reminded God has sent guardian angels to watch over you, minister to you and keep you in all your ways because you are His child. Expect God's favor to manifest in your life today and always.

Today's Reading:
Psalm 5:12, 30:5, 91:11; Proverbs 8:35; Hebrews 1:14

May 5
Who Do You Say He Is?

On one occasion Jesus asked His disciples, "who do men say that I am?" They responded, "Some say John the Baptist, some Elijah, and others Jeremiah or one of the prophets." And then He asked them the question we all must answer for ourselves, "who do you say that I am?" I say He is the only begotten Son of the Living God. He was born of a virgin, died on the Cross, rose on the third day and is seated at the right hand of the Father. I say He is the maker of heaven and earth. All things were made by Him and for Him. Without Him nothing could exist. He is the Bright and Morning Star. He is the Rose of Sharon and the lily of the valley. He is Wonderful, Counselor, Almighty God, Everlasting Father and Prince of Peace. He is my Rock and my Redeemer. He is Jehovah Shalom, my peace. He is the Lamb of God. He is the Savior of the world. He is my strength. He is my healer. He is my way maker. He is the reason that I am and the source of my joy. Without Him I am nothing and I can do nothing. He is the Way, the truth, and the life. No one can come to the Father but by Him. Who do you say that He is?

Today's Reading:
Psalm 19:14; Isaiah 9:6; Matthew 16:13-16
Luke 1:26-32; John 3:16; 14:6

May 6
Let It Go

You cannot walk forward very long while looking back and expect to get where you're going safely. Likewise, you cannot live your life always focused on the past and experience the fullness of your life in the present. At some point you will encounter a problem. The enemy relishes keeping you occupied with thinking about what happened in the past, what you did or didn't do and how bad things were. You can choose to accept what you cannot change with the help of God. You can decide like the Apostle Paul to forget those things that are behind and press towards your destiny in Christ that is filled with blessing upon blessings. If you dwell in the past, it will rob you of your peace and distract you from embracing the present and the future God has for you. The enemy of your soul would love for you to stay trapped in the past, but that is not God's desire. Keep pressing into Him and walk confidently into all that your Heavenly Father has for you.

Today's Reading:
Isaiah 48:9,18-19; Jeremiah 29:11; Philippians 3:12-14

May 7
When You Are Speechless

Sometimes you are simply at a loss for words. You may feel overwhelmed by an emotional issue, financial stressors, health challenges, relationships, or other concerns. You could find yourself speechless. The Holy Spirit will not only guide you into all truth, but He will also give you the words to say. Seek His guidance. Jesus said if you stand before judges don't worry what you will say. The Holy Spirit will give you the words. And there may be other times when you don't know what to pray. Remember the Holy Spirit intercedes for you. When He prays, He always prays in agreement with God's will. Who else knows the thoughts of a man except his spirit. Even more important is the fact that the Holy Spirit knows God's will. So, the next time you find yourself at a loss for words, ask the Holy Spirit to give you the words to say. And when you don't know what to pray, trust the Holy Spirit to pray for you.

Today's Reading:
Mark 13:11; Luke 2:26; John 14:26; Romans 8:26,27

May 8
Praying For You

When you are overwhelmed or simply don't know what to do, be encouraged. You have a prayer covering. Jesus is living to make intercession for you. He is praying 24/7 on your behalf. Others may tell you they are praying for you. Whether they do or not you can be assured that He is always praying for you. He knows what you have need. He is able to understand what you're going through because He walked as a man and experienced what you're experiencing. He was homeless, incarcerated, attacked in His character, physically assaulted, grieved as a loved one was murdered, misunderstood by His family, lied on and disparaged. Nothing you encounter can surprise Him. Plus, since He created everything, He knows everything. Again, nothing surprises Him. Therefore, as you face various temptations and trials, you do not need to worry. Jesus has your back. He gets you. He will see you through no matter what.

Today's Reading:
John 17:16-26; Romans 8:34; Colossians 2:6
Hebrews 4:14-16, 7:25

May 9
Daddy's Love

You have a superpower working in your favor - the Heavenly Father's love. He loves you with an everlasting love. He loves you so much He sent His only begotten Son to die for you. He has drawn you closer to Himself with His loving-kindness. You love because He first loved you. He calls you His friend. He will bless those who bless you and curse those who curse you. He is the maker of heaven and earth, your light, your salvation and your strong tower. He favors you and has blessed the work of your hands. Because He is for you, who can be against you? He has put a hedge of protection around you, your household and everything you have. Therefore, you don't have to fear anyone. No weapon formed against you shall prosper. When you walk in obedience to His ways, blessings upon blessings will follow. Remember who your Daddy is and how much He loves you.

Today's Reading:
Genesis 1:1; 12:2,3; Job 1:10; Psalm 27:1; Isaiah 54:17
Jeremiah 31:3; John 3:16; Romans 8:31; James 2:23

May 10
Posture Yourself To Hear God

Knowing God's will is not reserved for a few. He wants you to know His will by getting to know Him. He is not seeking to be obscure. He makes His ways known. Like a cable box is to a satellite signal, so is God's Word to those seeking to know God and His will. The Holy Bible connects you to His voice. As you meditate on His Word daily you will tune your heart to hear Him. You will begin to understand His ways and recognize His patterns. He will speak to you deep within, guiding you as you make your life's decisions. When you pray you may sense Him speaking to you through a specific verse or biblical passage. He will become like a close friend whose response you can anticipate because you know them so well. It all starts with positioning yourself to communicate with Him. Get to know Him through knowing His Word and spend some time communing with Him in prayer. Prayer is speaking from your heart, as well as listening to His.

Today's Reading:
Colossians 3:16, Psalm 1, 119:15, 119:105

May 11
Know You Are Loved

You may feel like no one loves you, even more so in this time of social upheaval and seemingly increased polarization in society. You may not have family nearby or you may even be estranged from those who may be as close as next door. Still, you are loved whether you have family and friends near or far. Guard against going by whether you feel loved at a given moment. That's not the best approach because feelings can deceive us. Always measure your feelings against truth. The truth is God loves you with an everlasting love. Nothing you can say or do will ever change His love for you. It is forever and unconditional. It will never change because He never changes. You also don't have to earn God's love for you. He gives it to us freely. So no matter what you go through, no matter who may or may not make you feel appreciated, no matter whether you feel like a great success or a failure on a given day - remember nothing can separate you from the Love of God.

Today's Reading:
Psalm 103:11; Romans 8:38, 39; 1 John 4:10
Hebrews 13:8

May 12
Hindering God's Plan

One of the greatest hindrances to being anointed and used by God is your refusal to surrender your will. When you gave your heart to Christ you professed Him as your Savior. He also wants you to honor Him as your Lord. "Lord" means master or owner. Do you not know you are not your own? You've been bought with a price: the precious blood of Jesus. You may acknowledge He is your Lord, yet you don't choose to obey Him. He asked, "why do you call me Lord, Lord and do not do what I say?" If He is your Master, then obey Him. The only means by which you can truly manifest your love for God is your obedience to His Word. Everything short of this is lip service. He has said it this way, "these people honor me with their lips, but their hearts are far from me." As you let go of your will, God's perfect will, plan and power can manifest in your life.

Today's Reading:
Matthew 15:18, 16:21-26; Luke 6:46, 22:42; 1Corinthians 6:19; Philippians 2:9-11

May 13
God's Goal For You

Romans 8:28 is quoted more often than many other verses in the Bible. And we know that all things work together for the good of those who love God. Yet it's verse 29 that reveals why God working things together. God has predestined you to be conformed to the image of His Son. He doesn't want Jesus to be an only child. To the contrary Jesus was intended to be the firstborn among many brothers and sisters. God wants all of the qualities that reside in Christ Jesus to abide in you. He wants Christ to be formed in you. He allows hardships and difficulties, the proverbial sandpaper of life, to rub you until your edges are smoothed. He allows heartaches to push you towards communing with Him. He knows the more time you spend with Him the more you become like Him. He is using all the issues and circumstances of your life to bring you to the ultimate goal. Like a silversmith uses heat to burn away the dross. God uses everything in your life to drive out those things that hinder you from reflecting His image. All things are working to conform your character to be like Christ's.

Today's Reading:
Proverbs 25:4; Galatians 4:19; Romans 8:28,29

May 14
Choose What Is Better

When Jesus visited their home, 2 sisters responded differently. One spent time getting ready while the other spent time with Jesus. We too have this same choice to make daily. In the business of life, we can schedule our day in such a way that Jesus is not a part of it. Like Martha, we can find ourselves around others who are seeking Him, yet never seek Him for ourselves. Or we can choose the better option of communing with Him daily. Spending quality time learning about Him has to be intentional. Just as He called the disciples to be with Him before He sent them to serve Him, He wants to be with you. If you take a math class, you won't do well just knowing someone that knows math. You won't do well just having the class curriculum or the textbook. You will be tested to see if you've actually studied. Likewise in life we will have tests. They will test our faith and our knowledge of the Word. The more we know the Word the more successful we will be in passing. Everyone will take one final test. The question is: Do you know Him? Only those who know Him will pass and enter into their heavenly home. Be like the one who chose what was better.

Today's Reading:
Matthew 7:23; Mark 4:14; Luke 10:38-42; John 1:1, 17:3

May 15
Keep Your Heart Tender

Remember when you were a new Christian? You were sensitive to God's heart and wanted to do what you believed was right. You read your Bible and made every effort to obey God's word. You wanted to stop doing things that you thought were not pleasing to God while making every effort to do the things you believed would please Him. If you were like most you wanted to tell everyone you were saved. You wanted everyone to know what God had done for you. Sadly, in time you can lose your fervor and let your heart harden. You can stop reading your Bible as frequently as may find you share your testimony less and less. I want to encourage you to stay sensitive to the Lord. Always be ready to give the reason for the hope you have. To stay fresh in your relationship with God and excited about sharing your testimony stay in His Word. Stay connected to others equally desiring to stay close to God. It will keep your heart soft and obedient to His will.

Today's Reading:
2 Chronicles 34:15-28; Mark 5:20; John 4:39
1 Peter 3:15

May 16
Poster To Move The Hand Of God

One of the most powerful things you can do to see God move in your life is too fast. Turning down your plate and turning up your prayers gets God's attention. Fasting has become popular as a weight loss tool but there is a difference between these types of fasts and spiritual ones. For weight loss you merely abstain from eating. For a spiritual one, your focus is kept upon hearing and heeding God's voice. You demonstrate to God your value for Him and His word above all else. You humble yourself before Almighty God and He, in turn, exalts you. In lieu of food consumption you consume scripture, listen to the ministries of preaching and teaching, while maintaining a posture of prayer. There are several types of fasts. As you commit to a fast determine whether you will do an absolute, normal or partial fast and for how long. Pray to ask God to strengthen you as you commit your time of fasting to Him. Watch how much clearer you will be able to hear God. Experience an increase of His supernatural power operating through you, as He answers your prayers. God honors humility. Fast regularly. You will be blessed.

Today's Reading:
Exodus 34:28; Esther 4:16; Daniel 10:2-7; Jonah 3:4-10
James 4:6; 1 Peter 5:6

May 17
Travel Ready

When I received an email from an airline telling us we were travel ready, I was confident that all the things we needed to do to prepare for our trip had been done. First, we had to create an account. Then we had to identify our flights. Lastly, we had to upload our proof of vaccination. It made me stop and think about what you need to be travel ready. If you want to follow God's path, you will have to do some things to prepare. First you need a heavenly account. You can establish your account by connecting with Romans 10:9,10. Confess with your mouth the Lord Jesus, believe in your heart God has raised Him from the dead, and you shall be saved. Secondly, you need to let the Holy Spirit identify the traveling plans you will use while here on earth. You cannot lean to your own understanding. Instead, acknowledge and He will direct your path. When you are unsure, ask Him. Lastly, you will reach your ultimate destination only if you have proof you are cleared for entry. Jesus said He is the way, the truth, and the life. No one comes to the Father except by Me. He is the only way to get to God. Are you travel-ready?

Today's Reading:
Proverbs 3:5-7; Jeremiah 33:3; John 14:1-6,17:3
Romans 8:14,19:9,10

May 18
Called To Minister

I was leading the devotional time with other staff members when I asked one of them to lead us in a prayer. Later when I encountered a coworker in the hallway, he told me not to call on him to pray during those devotional times without prior warning. I shared that I often get called on the spot to pray in situations, to which he replied that was different since I am a minster. I beg to differ. Every believer in the Lord Jesus Christ is a minister. Your ministry is to let others know about God's love. He will empower you to do His work. God has called you to lay down your life just as Jesus laid down His life. Laying down your life means sharing the gospel and the practical things people need in life, including their need for food and clothing. If you have a friend who has a need, and you are able to meet it, you are called to minister to their needs. When prayer is needed, you have a responsibility to approach the Thone of God. This is a part of your ministry. Many think the only one God has called to serve Him are those who have titles. This is not so. Your podium may not be in a pulpit, but you are called, nonetheless.

Today's Reading:
Romans 8:29-30; 2 Corinthians 5:18,19
James 2:1417; 1 John 3:16,17

May 19
Called To Peace

The times we live in are filled with division. There is political division. There is racial discord. The world needs peace. You are called to a lifestyle of peace. In fact, you are called to make every effort, as much as it depends on you, to live at peace with everyone. Try to keep concord, harmony, and tranquility in the interactions you have with others. This doesn't mean everyone will be at peace with you. Some are quick to take offense. Still, you can choose to be peaceful. In fact, the word of God encourages you to maintain a peaceful demeanor even when others do not. Hence, God will not hold you accountable for the lack of peace in your relationships so long as you've made every effort you can to be at peace with others. And when you do, God will make your enemies live a peace with you. He will bless you for being a peacemaker. He calls peacemakers His sons. The Lord will guide you with His peace, if you pour out your prayers and petitions to Him with thanksgiving. Indeed, God's way is a way of peace. Keep your mind on Him and He will keep you in His peace. Live in peace.

Today's Reading:
Proverbs 16:7; Isaiah 28:3; Matthew 5:9; Romans 3:17
Colossians 3:15; 2 Thessalonians 3:16

May 20
Be Guided By The Word

You may hear people say they don't know what they should do, or they aren't sure about God's will for their lives. You may have days when you are not clear about your next step. Yet, God has given us very specific directions applicable to each of our lives. If you use them as guides, you will find yourself better positioned to be successful in all of your endeavors. The Bible provides a set of principles for you to live by. If you allow them to guide you, they will be like a light for your steps along the path of life. Remember when Dorothy was told to follow the yellow brick road in the Wizard of Oz? Or when Luke was told to stay on target in Star Wars? They were both given directions that would lead them to their desired destination. This is exactly what the Word of God does. If you continue to study, it and follow its' guidance you will find many of the questions you have about what your next steps should be are already answered. In sum, if you constantly obey the ways of God's Word, you will discover His perfect will for your life. You will be guided into the exact place He has ordained for you to be.

Today's Reading:
Psalm 119:105; Proverbs 4:20-22,29:18,30:5
John 8:31-32

May 21
Fight Right

You are called to peace, but you will still have to fight
sometimes. However, your weapons are not the weapons
of the world. Your weapons are spiritual; they are
mighty; and they can tear down strongholds. When you
fight, start with praise. In doing this you invoke the
presence of the Lord to be on your side. He camps out in
the presence of praise. The more you praise Him the
more evident His power and presence will be in your
circumstances. Instead of packing a pistol, strap on your
sword of the Spirit which is the Word of God. Prepare
your feet with the gospel of peace. You are not fighting
with people but principalities. And they know the Word.
Your job is to know it better. That way when the father of
lies tries to defeat you by deceiving you into believing
you can't be victorious in any given area of your life, you
will already know the truth. Your breastplate is your
righteousness - your right standing with God – and it
will protect your heart. Faith is your shield that will
deflect your enemy's attacks, along with your helmet of
salvation. You fight the right way when you use God's
weaponry and not the weapons of the world.

Today's Reading:
2 Chronicles 20:20-22; Psalm 8:3; 2 Corinthians 10:4
Ephesians 6:10-16

May 22
Take A Stand

As a saint of the Most High God, you are called to stand up against wickedness and sinfulness. You are the Lord's representative in the earthly realm. As His ambassador you have been strategically placed to plead His case to others who don't know Him. It may be on your job or with your family. Wherever there is a clear distinction between what is right and what is wrong, you are to take a stand and share God's way in a loving fashion. When the world's ways are pushing up against you, stand firm in Christ. Stand knowing that the Lord will fight your battles as you obey His voice. He will cause your enemies to live at peace with you; and in many instances He will move those out of your path who try to hinder His will for your life. Also there will are times when He will not remove the enemy's tactics because He wants you to be the opposition to set an example. He wants you to speak up for righteousness. It won't always make you popular, but it will make you right with God. After you've done all to stand, stand.

Today's Reading:
Exodus 14:13,14; 2 Chronicles 20:17; Psalm 94:16
Proverbs 16:7; 2 Corinthians 5:20; Ephesians 6:13

May 23
Kingdom Living

When you are living with Kingdom principles you trust in the Lord. You don't just listen; you do what the Word says. You choose to not simply live by what you can understand; instead, you acknowledge and put your trust in God and allow Him to direct your path. You meditate on His Word knowing He will give you wisdom and understanding. You know when you seek first His Kingdom then the things you need will be added to you. As a Kingdom minded believer, you sow into the things of God. And you know He shall supply all your needs according to His riches in Christ Jesus. When you are living on Kingdom principles, you connect with a church that believes we should all bring the whole tithe into the house of the Lord. And you rest knowing He said when you do so He will pour you out so much blessing you won't have room enough to receive it. You know as you give, it will come back to you pressed down, shaken together, and running over. Such is the heritage of those who do not merely give lip service to the things of God, but who choose to live according to His kingdom's principles.

Today's Reading:
Proverbs 3:5,6,4:5; Malachi 3:10; Matthew 6:33
Luke 6:38; Philippians 4:14-19; James 1:22

May 24
Find Favor

The currency of the kingdom of God is not money. It is favor – God's unearned blessings. Some people think they need luck. Luck is of the world. It is random. Favor is from God and He intentionally favors those who follow His plan. The scripture is clear. Walk in the ways of the Lord, obey His Word and He will favor you. And it will flow to 1000 generations. You will find favor with God and with man. Favor with man is an intangible, unexplainable blessing. It is amazing how God will have complete strangers bless you. The other day I was buying some breakfast. After I placed the order, I decided to add another item. The cashier told me to have it for free. God will show you favor at seemingly random times. Recently when I checked into my hotel, they told me I had a complimentary upgrade. And, because God is merciful, He will show you favor even when you don't deserve it. Favor ain't fair. It is for those who diligently seek Him, those walking in the prayers of those who went before them, and for those upon whom He will have mercy. Thanks be to God for favor!

Today's Reading:
Deuteronomy 30:1-10; Proverbs 3:4; 8:35; 22:1
Isaiah 56:1-5; Acts 7:46; Romans 9:15

May 25
Lip Service

King Saul was the first human king of Israel. The people had cried out to have a king because the other nations had one, though they already had far greater. They had the King of kings. God Almighty was their God. Nonetheless God gave them a king. Saul proved to be a disappointment to God because he didn't obey His command. He chose to please the people, instead. When God commanded him to destroy the Amalekites, he kept the best of their possessions because the people wanted them. He even sought to have it appear as though he was pleasing God by asking the prophet Samuel to share a time in worship with him, following his disobedience and God's rejection of him as king. His goal was to create an image of obedience. You can be like Saul and the people of Israel who said they would obey God's will only to disobey Him when faced with worldly influence. Obey God at all times. Be a doer of God's Word. Don't just talk about it, be about it. Then you will hear our Father say, "well done."

Today's Reading:
Exodus 19:8; 1 Samuel 15:22, 30; James 1:22

May 26
Resist Negative Reports

One of the greatest challenges to you walking by faith, is listening to things contrary to the promises of God. Negative messages produce doubt. Doubt is contrary to faith. It is a lack of confidence. When you listen to people tell you things that cause feelings of uncertainty, you are quenching your faith. This is exactly what happened when Moses sent spies to scout out the promised land. Only 2 of the 12 came back with a good report. They spoke out of fear and questioned their ability to triumph over the land's inhabitants. The people listened and wept. They complained, even saying that they should have stayed in Egypt even though God had been faithfully providing, protecting, and promising them they would be blessed. Instead of listening to God, they were listening to the negative feedback. Clearly, they ignored that God was with them. This was a mistake! Remember to reject the negative voices in your midst. Focus on the promises of God. Meditate on what God says. Build up your faith by abiding in the Word and rejecting everything that is contrary to what God says. Above all, remember the Lord your God is with you!

Today's Reading:
Numbers 13:17-33,14:1-4; Joshua 14:8
Philippians 4:8; Romans 10:17; Hebrews 11:1

May 27
Another Level

You have a choice every time someone offends you. You get to decide whether you will forgive. To withhold forgiveness is like drinking poison and expecting the other person to die. You only hurt yourself when you fail to forgive. Bitterness towards one person can infiltrate other relationships like gangrene eats away a person's whole body. Forgiving is a fundamental part of being a Christian. Still, there is another level. It is one that is beyond the basics and moves into the Divine. It is when you can forgive others for their sake and not for your own. When you read about Stephen's murder, you learn his last words were "don't hold this sin against them." God loves you this way. Can you do the same for others? You may be inclined to think they don't deserve it. Neither do you. Many won't understand how you can show kindness to those who have done evil against you. But when God infiltrates your heart with His love, you learn to display the same grace to others that you receive from Him. That's another level of Christlike living. That's when you can say, "I have been crucified with Christ and I no longer live, but Christ lives in me."

Today's Reading:
1 Kings 8:33-36; Mark 11:25; Luke 23:34; Acts 7:50
2 Corinthians 5:19: Galatians 2:20; Hebrews 12:15

May 28
Hardships Ain't Fair

When we go through difficulties it can be overwhelming. The fact that we are Christians doesn't exempt us from pain and struggles. Jesus said in this life you will have trouble. But He also said to take heart because He has overcome the world. Being in Christ means you too are an overcomer. When you encounter hardships, you may feel no one understands what you are experiencing but the Bible tells us there is nothing you're facing that is uncommon to man. That is the beauty of our communion with one another. You can share your struggles and be motivated to press on when you know someone else has done the same. You can be spurred on by the testimony of others. When you go through trials remember God is not allowing anything to occur that He hasn't equipped you to handle. Also, share your story with others. It can be a source of strength for those facing similar trials. When it feels like too much, talk to God about it. He knows exactly how much you can bear. Trust the Lord. He wouldn't have let you go through it unless He had equipped you to get through it.

Today's Reading:
Psalm 34:6,18,19,42:5-11; Matthew5:45; John 16:33
Romans 8:31,37; Revelations 12:11

May 29
You Won't Go Away Empty

When God freed His people from their bondage in Egypt, He gave them favor in the sight of the Egyptians. They left the land not only free but with gold and other things of value. Job lost all of his wealth and his children when the devil was allowed to attack him. He was struck with horrible illnesses. Yet, when it was all said and done, God gave him twice as much as he had lost. His latter days were more blessed than his beginning. Indeed, the wealth of the wicked is to be stored up for the just. God is the same today, yesterday, and forever. The same way He was in the past, He is today. You may be going through a season of struggles, and it may seem like the tide will never turn. But hold on. Your story is not finished. You haven't seen the end. You will see the blessings of the Lord in days to come. He is a rewarder of those who diligently seek Him. No good thing will He withhold from those who walk upright. I decree the blessings of the Lord over your life. I declare that your latter days will be greater than your former ones. You will not go away empty!

Today's Reading:
Genesis 9:11-16; Exodus 3:21; Job 42:10,12; Psalm45:12
Isaiah 61:6; Romans 8:32; Hebrews 11:6

May 30
Right In Front Of You

The only way you can follow God's will for your life is to know it. It is not something He keeps secret. He is not hiding Himself or His plans from you. If you are unsure, simply ask Him. When you want to know anything these days, it's common for someone to tell you to "google it." You can find information about anything. Likewise, God is not hiding His will from you. You simply need to take the time to search for it. Spend time in His Word with a laser like focus. The same way you use a search engine to pull up information on the internet, you can find out what God has said about anything related to your life simply by seeking it out. He will speak to you through His Word and in your heart. If you start to veer off course you will hear Him saying, "This *is* the way, walk in it." Once you make finding His will a priority for your life, and not merely something that is optional, you will find this to be true: His commandment is not hidden from you, nor is it far off. It is not in heaven nor is it beyond the sea. But the Word is very near to you, in your mouth, and in your heart, so you may do it. God's will is right in front of you, if you choose to know it.

Today's Reading:
Deuteronomy 30:11-14; Isaiah 30:20,21; Jeremiah 29:13,33:3; Romans 12:1,2

May 31
Draw Near

You may have experienced times where you felt like God was far away. When you lose a loved one or you feel the conviction of the Holy Spirit, you may feel like God is far away. But in fact, He is near the broken hearted. He is an ever-present help in times of trouble. Still, you may have seasons where you feel He is not with you. There is a solution to counteract these feelings. Kneel before the Lord and recall His Word in prayer. You can pray: "Father, You said if I draw near to You, You will draw near to me." Then delve into His word. Renew your mind through Holy Scripture. If you have sinned, repent. Turn away from whatever it is and turn to God. Lastly, repeat these steps. The process of restoration is like taking an antibiotic. When you initially start taking it, you may not notice a difference! But little by little you start to feel the effects of the medicine. In the Spirit, when you draw near to God and read the Word, you will gradually begin to feel His presence and the warmth of His love again. It may sneak up on you. You may not be aware of when it occurred, but you will just know.

Today's Reading:
Deuteronomy 4:7; Psalm 73:28, 91:1; John 15:1-5
Hebrews 7:19, 10:22; James 4:8

June 1
Laying It On The Line

It takes courage to serve your nation by putting your life
on the line to protect others. They put their lives on the
line to save us from any form of attack. Jesus did the
same thing. He died for the sins of the world. He laid it
all down so you could live. He didn't focus on anyone's
skin color or ethnic backgrounds. He gave no thought to
their job titles or educational accomplishments. He laid
His life down for all. Likewise, God has called you to
serve others by laying your life down for them. He wants
you to sacrifice whatever gifts and talents you have to
draw others to Him and advance His kingdom. Jesus
made the supreme sacrifice to bring you to God. Are you
willing to lay your agenda down for others, regardless of
their age, color, ethnicity, or religious background? Do
you only share the gospel with those who look like you?
If so, I challenge you to ask God to allow you to see
others as He sees them. He died once, for all. God wants
you to also put it all on the line so that He can use you to
bring all those you encounter in life to know Him as their
personal Lord and Savior.

Today's Reading:
John 15:13; Philippians 2:29,30; Hebrews 9:16
1 Peter 3:18; 1 John 3:16

June 2
Faith To Be Healed

You play a vital role in your healing. When you read scripture about the times Jesus healed people, you will find over and over how He references faith. When the woman with the issue of blood believed she could be healed by touching the hem of His garment, she was healed. She simply reached out and touched Him in faith. In another instance, a soldier asked Jesus to heal his servant. As Jesus approached the soldier's home, the soldier told Him He didn't need to enter His house. He believed Jesus could simply speak a word and his servant would be healed. Yet when Jesus went to His own hometown, He could do no miracles there due to the collective lack of faith demonstrated by those who were familiar with Him. This not only speaks to you having faith, but it also points out the importance of staying connected with people who will believe God along with you. You can choose to have faith in God to see His miraculous healing power manifest in your life or you can operate in unbelief. Believe God is able and willing to heal you. Pray the prayer of faith and watch as He works miracles in your life.

Today's Reading:
Matthew 9:21,29, 15:28, 17:16-20; Mark 6:1-6
Luke 7:1-10, 8:40-50, 18:42; Acts 14:9; James 5:14

June 3
Twice As Nice

The Word of God tells us it is not good for man to be alone. In fact, all throughout scripture this truth is espoused. He tells us it is better for two to work together than one because they will reap more from their labor. If one of them falls the other can help them up. They can keep one another warm. They can withstand attacks better and most importantly, where two or more believers are gathered, God is in their midst. Consequently, it is good to collaborate with others as much as you can. Even if you can achieve something on your own, it is not God's perfect will for you to be a loner. Instead, He ordains you to be a part of His body and function as such. The natural body has many parts. Not one of them can function fully without working in tandem with the other parts. So too, in the body of Christ, God wants you to work and minister with others. When Jesus sent the disciples out, He sent them in pairs. When Paul traveled, he was always with a companion. Learn to work with others in everything. Your life will be far more successful. It is the only way to fulfill God's perfect will for your life.

Today's Reading:
Genesis 2:18; Ecclesiastes 4:9-12; Matthew 18:29
Luke 10:1; 1 Corinthians 12:12-19

June 4
Yes, You Can!

You can do all things through Christ who strengthens you. If you have faith of a mustard seed, you can move a mountain. No matter what it is you are facing, you can achieve your goals. You are more than a conqueror. When David faced Goliath no one believed he had the capability to be triumphant. But David believed he could do it and he chose his slingshot as his weapon. He had experience using it to kill lions and bear. He realized that though the obstacle he faced were different, the skills he had developed in other circumstances were sufficient. Your skills are transferable to deal with new challenges. Your past experiences have prepared you for whatever you are facing today. Trust what God has put in you. You are enough to get the job done. David chose 5 smooth stones and prayed to God to let him be triumphant. Like David, if you believe, you will receive everything you ask for in prayer. You can accomplish anything you set your mind to achieve. Don't let naysayers discourage you. Instead, believe what God says about you! Trust the ability God has given to you and be victorious.

Today's Reading:
1 Chronicles 17:2; Proverbs 23:7; Matthew 21:21,22;
Luke 17:6; Philippians 4:13; Romans 8:37

June 5
What To Do

Freedom in Christ it is refreshing. It's like taking off a great weight. You no longer have a desire to live by rules but a heart to live in love. You no longer want to operate based upon your limited understanding or to simply please your flesh. You want to do what please God. You learn to walk by faith and not by sight because you choose to obey His Word and the unction of the Holy Spirit even when it's contrary to the world's view and the popular stance others may take. Instead of trying to figure everything out on your own you learn seek God. You begin to appreciate the fact that God will give you wisdom when you simply ask for it. His Word becomes like a flashlight. It illuminates the way you should go. As you follow Christ, He begins to unfold His plans for your life. He will show you each step of the way. Begin your day by meditating on truth and seeking God in prayer. His wisdom is far above yours. He is concerned about every facet of your life, including who you marry and where you work. If you will heed His wisdom, then the Holy Spirit will direct your path so you do exactly what God created you to do.

Today's Reading:
Psalm 119:11; Proverbs 3:5-7; John; Romans 8:13,14
2 Corinthians 5:7; James 1:5

June 6
But Should You?

While all things are permissible to you, not all things are beneficial. Even though you are free to do anything you want, it is good to make every effort not to offend others. People may be watching you to find any contradictions between what you say and what you do. Some become eager to identify any hypocrisy to discredit your testimony or even affirm their unbelief in God. Still others are watching because they are hungry for God and want to know how to live for Him. They are looking to see Christ operating through your life as an example of how they ought to live. You have liberty in Christ. And with this liberty comes great responsibility.

Consequently, when you speak, do your best to speak in agreement with God's word. Do whatever you do with the ability He has given to you so that in all things He is glorified. You are not your own, you were purchased with the precious blood of Jesus. Hence, your actions should be pleasing to Him. Walk circumspectly and not foolishly. Seek to u the Lord's will so your actions will be pleasing to Him and edifying to others.

Today's Reading:
Romans 14:16; 1 Corinthians 6:12,19, 10:23-33, 14:40;
Ephesians 5:1,15-17; Philippians 4:13; 1 Peter 4:11

June 7
Know And Be Known

Salvation is based on a relationship with God through His Son Jesus. It is to know God. It is reflected when you have a change of heart and want to please God, not merely have it your way. When you truly know Him, He knows you. You may go to worship to hear the preacher share the Word of God. Yet, you still spend time in your Bible getting to know God for yourself when you have a personal relationship with Him. You may ask others to join you in praying over a matter, but you set aside time to talk to God about it for yourself as well. When the seven sons of Sceva, a Jewish priest, encountered a man who was demon possessed they tried to cast out the evil spirit by invoking Paul's name. It didn't work. The spirit spoke back and said, "Jesus I know, Paul I know, but who are you?" The sons of Sceva knew "about" Jesus but they didn't know Him for themselves. When you know Him, your actions reflect this relationship. You not only hear the Word, but you also do what it says. The Holy Spirit bears witness that you are a child of God. These things are evidence that you know God and He knows you.

Today's Reading:
Jeremiah 15:15; Matthew 15-23; John 14:7; 15:10, 17:3
Acts 19:11-20; Romans 5:5, 8:16

June 8
You Haven't See It All

Eyes have not seen, and ears haven't heard all that God has in store for those who love Him. Whatever hardship you encounter cannot compare to the glory of God that is yet to come upon you. He will not withhold anything good from you as you continue to walk upright before Him. Remember, He gave you the most precious gift He had to offer. He gave up His only begotten Son. And if He was willing to give you such a phenomenal gift, it should not be a surprise that with Him He will freely give you all things! You haven't seen anything yet! It will get better right here on earth.

Still there is more! Like a buyer who puts down money to confirm they will buy a house, God also gave you His Holy Spirit as a deposit guaranteeing what is to come for you. Even when God allowed an angel to show the Apostle John some of wonderful things you will experience someday in the future, John wasn't allowed to share it all. Consequently, some things you simply will not see until we all get to heaven. You have many more benefits of His love that you will experience in the future.

Today's Reading:
Psalm84:11; Isaiah 64:4; 65:17; Romans 8:18,24
1 Corinthians 2:9; 2 Peter 3:13; Revelations 10:4

June 9
Know The Depth Of His Love

Like the Apostle Paul, I pray that you, being rooted and established in love, may have power, together with all the Lord's holy people, to grasp how wide and long and high and deep is the love of Christ, and to know this love that surpasses knowledge—that you may be filled to the measure of all the fullness of God. You are not expected to do this alone. Paul prayed you would reach this understanding together with all of His people. This is so crucial to understand. God wants you to operate as a part of His body. We too often try to achieve God's will for our lives as loners. This is not His will. You are a part of something far greater. You are invited to put your resources (gifts and talents) together with the rest of God's family. When you embrace togetherness, you tap into the power to grasp the depth of God's love for you. He blesses you and surrounds you with His favor. He preserves you. His love for you is greater than all of the space between here and heaven. And as strong as angels are, not even angels (or demons) are able to separate you from God's love. His love for you runs deep.

Today's Reading:
Psalm 5:11,12, 36:5-7, 103:11; Romans 8:35,37-39
Ephesians 3:14-19; 1 John 3:1, 4:8

June 10
Words Can Hurt Too

There is an old saying you may have said as a child.
Sticks and stones may break my bones and will never
hurt me. Unfortunately, it's not true. Your tongue is
powerful. You have the power of life and death in your
mouth. Your words can cut like a knife if they aren't
season with the word of the Lord. Choose your order
wisely. Be quick to listen, slow to speak and slow to
become angry. How often have you suffered from foot in
mouth disease. Perhaps, you later realized you shouldn't
have said what you said. The Lord's natural brother
James admonished us to work to tame our tongue. Like a
little spark that can end up burning down a forest so too
your tongue is small compared to the amount of trouble
it can stir up. Speak to others in love. You are speaking
life or death each time you open your mouth. Use every
opportunity to build others up with your words, not tear
them down. What you speak can harm not only the
hearer and your relationship with them, but it can also
hurt your own life as well. Seek to say things that are
edifying. Speak life.

Today's Reading:
Psalm 36:1-3; Proverbs 13:3; Matthew 12:33-37
Luke 6:45; Ephesians 4:29; James 3:2-12

June 11
Oh Give Thanks

Giving thanks to God should be easy. He breathed life into your body. He knit you together in your mother's womb. He has kept you through every trial and tribulation. From every fall to every foolish decision, He has seen you through all you have experienced. When I was a child, I was hit by a car and could have died. But God! Think of all of the times you could have died or should have experienced far worse than you did because of your own choices or the actions of others. The fact that you can read this is a reason to thank the Lord. Everything you experience, in every triumphant moment and every disappointment He is with you! Hallelujah! His presence provides the strength that you need in every situation. He is good and His mercies endure forever. Surely that alone is enough for you to give Him thanks. All riches and blessings come from Him. Most of all, when you think about the sacrifice of His Son so that you can be forgiven of all of your sins, your heart should overflow with thanksgiving every day! Oh give thanks to the Lord, for He is good. Yes, He is good.

Today's Reading:
1 Chronicles 16:30,34, 29:10-13; Psalm 75;1; 2
Corinthians 9:13-15; Philippians 1:3, Colossians 3:17
1 Thessalonians 5:18

June 12
Well Able

What you say to yourself when you face challenges is even more important than what you say to others. As a man thinks so is he. If you keep saying things to yourself to suggest you are never going to be successful, you will prophesy your future. Speak life over your life. Caleb and Joshua went into the promised land with 10 other scouts to spy. The ten spies came back with a report that the land was too much for them to conquer. But Caleb and Joshua came back and decreed they were well able to overcome every challenge and succeed in taking the land. The people believed the negative report. They were discouraged and became fearful. Consequently, they never entered the land God promised to them. Caleb and Joshua, on the other hand, did enter and received the blessings God had for them. The woman with the issue of blood talked to herself. She said, "if I can just touch the hem of His garment, I shall be made whole." And she was! Tell yourself today, "I am equipped by God to take on anything that happens in my life. I am more than a conqueror in Christ Jesus. If God be for me who can be against me." You are well able.

Today's Reading:
Numbers 13:30; Ruth 1:20,21; 1 Kings 17:8-16
Matthew 9:21

June 13
You Are What You Think

How you think - and what you think about- will help to set the trajectory of your life. When you are always thinking negatively, you will gravitate towards negative things in your life. You cannot control what pops into your thoughts, but you can determine whether a thought continues to linger in your mind. When you find yourself thinking about things that are depressing, discouraging or breed discontent, then change the channel of your mind. Choose to think about things that are lovely, positive and of a good report. In every situation there is something praiseworthy on which you can focus. Instead of a sickness you are facing encompassing all your mental focus, choose instead to meditate on God and His Word. He promises to keep you in perfect peace if you keep your mind on Him. You can fix your eyes on Jesus who is the author and finisher of your faith. He endured the cross and you too can endure anything that happens in your life. Remember, better days are coming. Once you begin to think the way God wants you to think – in agreement with His word – you will live your life the way God wants you to live. You will walk in the blessing God wants you to have. Your thinking is the key.

Today's Reading:
Isaiah 26:3, 40:28-31; Philippians 4:8; Hebrews 12:2,3

June 14
To Destroy The Works Of The Devil

Jesus came to destroy the works of the evil one who perverts our souls. He cancelled the devil's power when He was crucified, buried, and rose from the dead. He demonstrated that it is He who has all power in His hands. Consequently, for those who believe, the devil has no authority in our lives. When Jesus encountered sickness, or any form of oppression by the enemy, He rebuked it. A man with a withered hand was in the synagogue on a sabbath day. Jesus told the man to hold out his hand, and when he did it was healed. All throughout the Holy Bible there are accounts of Jesus casting out demons that were tormenting people, and healing multitudes throughout the regions in which He traveled. He wants you to be set free from the devil's grip. If you have been feeling bound or oppressed in any way, if you are battling sickness, or your family is caught up in any type of lifestyle that reflects they are being controlled by something other than the Holy Spirit, then cry out to Jesus. He came to destroy whatever the devil is doing in your life and the lives of others.

Today's Reading:
Colossians 2:13-15; James 3:16; 1 Peter 3:9; 1 John 3:8

June 15
To Preach The Kingdom

After He was led by the Spirit into the wilderness to be tempted by the devil for forty days and nights, Jesus was ministered to by angels. The first thing He did afterwards was to begin to preach the Kingdom of God. His first words were, "repent for the Kingdom of God is at hand." He let everyone know He had been sent to proclaim liberty to the captives of sin. He preached that our faith would make us whole. He wanted us to know it is not our works that saves us but rather our belief in the work He did on the cross. The Jewish nation had been seeking their righteousness by keeping the law. They had to constantly kill animals to make atonement for their sin. Jesus' message was revolutionary because He let us know that keeping the law was not sufficient to be in right standing with God. It requires repentance and belief in all that transpired during His death and resurrection. Are you in right standing with God? If you have not done so, I say to you. "Repent for the Kingdom of God is at hand." And if you have put your faith in Jesus, then rest in knowing you have eternal life.

Today's Reading:
Matthew 4:17,23, 9:35; Mark 1:14;
Luke 4:43, 8:1, 16:16, 24:46-49; Galatians 3:8

June 16
To Make Disciples

One of the key principles to the Kingdom of God is duplication. While Jesus was sharing the good news of the Kingdom of God, He also made disciples. A disciple is a person who follows the teaching of another. Jesus went to people and invited them to come and follow Him. His example was one that I had to learn to embrace. I was always hesitant to encourage others to follow me. I always thought they should just automatically volunteer to follow. But I came to realize, after looking at His pattern, Jesus was bold and forthright. He invited people to be His disciples. He went around preaching, healing the sick and declaring the kingdom of God, and He called His disciples to do the same thing. You are God's ambassador. Your role is to represent Him on earth and to advance His kingdom throughout the earth. Just as Jesus sent the disciples out, He is sending you to make other disciples and to promote His kingdom. You are called to continue the work Jesus began. He has called you to be His disciple, and to share with everyone you encounter, "repent for the kingdom of God is at hand."

Today's Reading:
Matthew 4:19, 16:24, 19:21; Mark 3:13,14; Luke 9:2,60
John 21:22; Acts 28:31

June 17
King of Kings

The way of this world tends to pull you in the opposite direction of the Kingdom of God. The world teaches that whoever wants to be the leader should be served by others. Jesus taught whoever wants to be the greatest serves others. He came to serve, not to be served. The world operates with pride and selfish ambition, but Jesus said blessed are the poor in spirit because the Kingdom of heaven will be theirs. Jesus taught us to pray for God's Kingdom to be manifested on earth. Each time we pray for God's will to be done on earth as it is in heaven, we are praying for His Kingdom to dominate the dictates of the world and everything in it. Wherever there is a kingdom there must be a king. When He was being judged by Pilate just before his crucifixion, Pilate asked Him if He was the King of the Jews. He told him His Kingdom is not of this world and that He is indeed King. Praise be to God! When Jesus returns his thigh will have written on it, "KING OF KINGS AND LORD OF LORDS." Confess Him as your King and Lord today. Don't wait. Tomorrow is not promised.

Today's Reading:
Psalm 24:10; John 18:33-37; Hebrews 7:1-3
1 Timothy 6:13-16; Revelation 17:14, 19:16

June 18
To Give Us Power To Testify

When Jesus revealed Himself to be the Messiah of the world, He immediately began preaching and teaching, "repent for the Kingdom of God is at hand". He also began to heal those who were sick and drive out demons from those who were possessed. He then sent out His disciples to do the same things. He gave them power over sickness, disease, and all other works of the devil. What may get lost is why He empowered them (and you) to do these things. His purpose is for you to be His witness to the world that He is who He said He is - the Son of the Living God. He wants you to be His witness so others can believe. The signs and wonders you have been given power to perform are tools through which you can give foolproof evidence that His Word is true, and He is God. Jesus often said things like, if you do not believe My Words then at least believe the miracles. That miracle-working power is made available to all that have made Him their Lord and Savior. He has called you to do the same things. Use it and testify.

Today's Reading:
Mark 3:14,15; Luke 9:1, 10:19, 23:8; John 14:11; Acts 1:8
Ephesians 6:10; 2 Timothy 1:7

June 19
To Guide You

One day I was trying to park in a space that required me to back in between 2 cars. My car's rear camera provided guidance with lines to show me how to do it. Yet, I ended up going back and forward unnecessarily. I kept looking at the cars around me instead of focusing on the camera monitor. I was distracted by what I thought could have been an obstruction instead of focusing on the direction I was given. Have you ever been so caught up looking at things around you that you didn't trust what God was telling you? Jesus came to provide you direction. His Word is a lamp to your feet and a light for your path. Are you following His guidance? Or are you allowing things around you to cause you to deviate? Follow the path set before you. Trust the Lord your God that He is leading you in the right direction. He loves you. He has plans for you. His plans do not include harming you. In order to walk in the blessings of God, trust His leading. Like those balloons with arms in front of stores blowing around in the wind, other things will always try to catch your attention. Fix your eyes on Jesus.

Today's Reading:
Psalm 119:11; Mark 4:24
John 13:15-17, 14:6,15-18, 16:7-14; Hebrews 12:1-3

June 20
Our High Priest

Under the Mosaic law, several men served as priest, and of them was appointed to serve as High Priest each year. They served in the temple. Once a year, the High Priest would enter the Most Holy Place on the Day of Atonement. His role as High Priest was to intercede for the believers. His assignment was to present the blood of animals to sacrifice for his sins and the sins of the people of the nation of Israel. The blood could only cover their sins. Hence, the sacrifices had to be made over and over, again. But we have a Great High Priest who entered the heavenly tabernacle once. He presented His own Blood which was spotless. He went in once, for all. Unlike the blood of animals, Jesus' blood was pure. His Blood cleanses us of all unrighteousness forever. Now we have a High Priest who sits at the right hand of the Father making intercession for us. Consequently, we are able to go boldly before the throne of Grace, to receive mercy and find grace in our time of need. Go before the Lord with the confidence today knowing Jesus has opened the way for you to receive the help that you need from God.

Today's Reading:
Leviticus 21:10-15; Matthew 26:3; Acts 9:1
Hebrews 3:1-6,19,20, 4:14-16, 5:1-11, 7:20-28, 10:19-25

June 21
Our Mediator

A mediator's role is to resolve any conflicts; to be a go-between with two entities. Jesus is our Mediator. Your sin separated you from God. In fact, the wages of sin is death. But Jesus came and died in your place, forgiving all of your sins. He is able to mediate between you and God. You now can live with the confidence of knowing that even when you miss the mark and fall short of the Lord's glory you are still forgiven in Christ Jesus. No more sacrifices are necessary or warranted. Under the old covenant, the people could not speak directly to God for themselves. They could pray in the outer court, but they could not go into the inner sanctuary. They relied on the priests and High Priest to seek God. That is why only Moses was able to go up on the mountain to receive the 10 Commandments. Jesus took away the division between us and God. Upon His death the curtain in the tabernacle dividing the people and God was torn in half to provide direct access to the Father. Go before your God in prayer today with assurance He will hear you and He will answer you directly.

Today's Reading:
Exodus 20:19; Deuteronomy 5:5; John 14:16
Ephesians 2:13; 1 Timothy 2:5; Hebrews 8:6, 12:22-24

June 22
Jesus Came To Set You Free

People were bound by the law of God before Jesus came on the scene. Their sin kept them in bondage. They sacrificed animals for their sins over and over again. Then came Jesus! Thanks be to God, Jesus paid the penalty for your sins and set you free from all things related to sin. You are no longer bound by a guilty conscience or the fear of death. You are free from the consequences of breaking the law. You have been set free by God's grace through your faith in Jesus Christ. Since Jesus died for every one of your sins, you are free to live in Christ without the fear of death. Death no longer has any power over your life. You now have the Spirit of God living on the inside of you. And where the Spirit of the Lord is, there is freedom! Yet, though you are free from the ultimate results of your sins, you are called to walk in the holiness of God. Your freedom in Christ is not a license to sin. On the contrary, since you received this freedom at a great cost, use your freedom to honor God. Do your best to please Him with all your actions. Your liberty was purchased with the precious Blood of the Lamb. It didn't come cheap.

Today's Reading:
Galatians 5:1,13; Romans 5:18,22, 6:6,7,14,18; 8:1.2
2 Corinthians 3:17

June 23
Model Of Living With Intentionality

Whenever God does something, it achieves more than one end. So too, in His death Jesus not only delivered you from the power of sin, but He also modeled how you should live. He lived and died with intentionality. As He said, "No one takes it from Me, but I lay it down of Myself. I have power to lay it down, and I have power to take it up again." He died as an exercise of His will, not because He was forced to do so. And He did it out of obedience because it was a command He had received from His Father. In doing this, He set the standard by which you should live. How often do people say things like, "I know God will change me when He gets ready?" Newsflash! God has been ready for your change for over 2,000 years. It is your willingness to die to yourself that will determine when you change. No, you will not have to die a physical death to follow Him, but you will need to die to your flesh if you want to follow Jesus completely. Be intentional with your obedience to God. Say no to your fleshly desires and yes to God your Father. It is only when you die to you – your will - that you truly live in Him.

Today's Reading:
Luke 9:23-2-25; Romans 5:8, 6:5-14
1 Corinthians 15:31; 2 Corinthians 4:10, 5:14-17

June 24
To Overcome

Some have the false belief that once you give your life to the Lord, everything should be easy. While this sounds wonderful it is not the truth until you get to heaven. The Bible says God allows it to rain on the just and the unjust. Jesus never said you would only have pleasantries. We will encounter the consequences of sin as long as we are on the earth, but you can still be of good cheer because Jesus has overcome the world. You are in Him and He is in you, so you too are an over comer! No matter what challenge you face, you have a superior force to overtake it. We don't overcome by fighting with our hands. We use the weapons of our warfare. Love is the most powerful force on the planet. You overcome evil with good. Instead of being controlled by the ways of the world, be transformed into the image of the Son of God by renewing your mind in His Word. You are well able to overcome every obstacle to your blessings, destiny, and purpose in Christ Jesus. You are more than a conqueror. You have power to overcome every evil spirit because greater is He in you than he who is in the world.

Today's Reading:
Numbers 13:30; John 16:33; Romans 12:21
1 John 4:4, 5:4-5, Revelations 2:11, 3:11, 26, 21:7

June 25
Your Avenger

There is a present and a future time of vengeance. In the present, the Lord will avenge you against all of those who oppose you. He will fight your battle. Do not try to take revenge on anyone. The Lord says we are to give place to His wrath, because vengeance is His. When you give place to God's wrath you don't take matters into your own hands. You get out of the way. Your job is to walk in love towards others and obedience to God. In fact, the Word of God tells us if our enemy is hungry, we are to feed them. If they are thirsty give them a drink. This is how we give place for God to do what only He has authority to do. If you think about it, you are not only in sin when you repay evil for evil, you are limited in your capacity to get back at those who offend you anyway. Your God has far greater power than you. He can be far more effective at dealing with those who come against, lie, and dishonor you. Let God be God. In the future, when Jesus returns, He will bring destruction to those who oppose righteousness and His people. Repay evil with good, then you won't be overcome by evil.

Today's Reading:
Psalm 58:10, 94; Luke 21:22; Romans 12:14-21; 2 Thessalonians 1:6-9; Hebrews 10:30

June 26
Forgiver In Chief

One of the most challenging facets of walking with God is being able to forgive others. You have the assurance of being completely forgiven of every sin you have ever committed when you accept Jesus in your heart. Jesus set the example by paying the ultimate price for your sins. He died and shed His blood for the remission of our sins. Yet, the Bible states numerous times if you will not forgive others their sins, then God will not forgive yours. Peter asked Jesus if 7 times was enough to forgive his brother. The number 7 means completion. In essence, Peter believed 7 times was the total amount of grace anyone should be extended. However, Jesus' reply probably shocked him. Jesus said you should forgive not 7 times but 70 times 7 times. In other words, you should forgive as many times as someone sins against you. There is no limitation to God's forgiveness towards you. That is why you are admonished to forgive others just as in Christ, God forgave you. And like with any other sin, if you are struggling to forgive, then pray. Ask God to help you and He will.

Today's Reading:
Matthew 6:14-15, 18:21-22, 26:28; Mark 11:25
Luke 22:34; Ephesians 4:32; 1 John 1:8–9

June 27
A Friend

What a friend you have in Jesus. He will never leave you nor forsake you. When God spoke to Moses, He spoke to him face to face, as a man speaks to His friend. He called Abraham His friend because Abraham believed Him. Abraham's faith was credited to Him as righteousness. We are counted as Abraham's descendants by faith. When Jesus was about to ascend back to heaven, He shared with His disciples that He would no longer call them servants, but He would call them His friends. As friends they were told God's plans. So, too, He has revealed His plans to you all throughout the Bible. Jesus also shared what makes you able to be called His friend; keeping His commandment to love others, just as He has loved you. Be like Abraham and believe God. The evidence of your faith is your actions. When you believe God, you act in accordance with your confession of faith. Lots of people claim to know Him but they live in ways opposite to what He commanded. Faith without works is dead. In essence, the true proof of your friendship with God is doing the things He has told you to do in His Word.

Today's Reading:
Exodus 33:11; Proverbs 17:17, 18:24; Luke 16:19; John 13:35, 15:10,13-17; James 2:19-24

June 28
Chief Cornerstone

A cornerstone is a brick laid to build a structure. It sets the foundation upon which everything else is erected. It sets the edges and connects the walls to make the corners of a structure. The chief cornerstone is set in place first so that everything else that is built must align with it. If it is not properly set the whole building will be out of order because the foundation is set up around it. Jesus is the Chief cornerstone of the church. He is the basis upon which everything is established. The apostles are the foundation of the church. They walked with Jesus. They, like a natural foundation, were established in alignment with the Chief cornerstone - Jesus. They led many to know Him and thereby set the foundation for the church. We are the church, the small stones which make up the building. Though we may meet inside of a structure we refer to as the church, it is not the building that makes the church. It is the church that makes the building. You are the church and Jesus is the Chief Cornerstone that has set the order. Make sure your foundation is the apostles' teachings, so you fit into the structure the Lord has created.

Today's Reading:
Psalm 118:22; Isaiah 28:16; Acts 4:11
1 Corinthians 3:9-10, 6:19; 1 Peter 2:6-7

June 29
Alpha And Omega

God had declared He is he Alpha and the Omega, The
Beginning and The End. Alpha is the first letter of the
Greek alphabet and Omega is the last. It signifies the fact
that before anything existed, God was already God.
There was never a time He didn't exist, nor will there
every be one. There is no other God. He has no
comparison or competitor. In the beginning He created
heaven and earth. Time began with Him just as your
existence did. You were created in His mind before
existence was manifested. He is your beginning and your
end. Believers have the blessed assurance spending your
eternity with Christ in heaven. However, as surely as
there is a heaven, there is also a hell for those that do not
believe. He knows when this earth will come to an end.
No one else knows the day or the hour, not even the
angels in heaven. You can rest assured He has your
beginning and your end in His hand. He knew every day
ordained for you before one of them came to be.
Therefore, there is no need to fret. You may not know
what the future may bring, but you do know the One who
will bring the future to be. He is Alpha and Omega.

Today's Reading:
Psalm 90:1-2, 139:1314; Isaiah 41:4,44:6,48:12;
John 1:13; Colossians 1:16; Revelations 1:8,11,21:6,22:13

June 30
Prince of Peace

Before you knew to do right or wrong you were already a sinner. It is in your spiritual DNA. Thus, you were in a place where you were unable to have a personal relationship with the Lord because God cannot have fellowship with the darkness of sin. Thankfully God had a plan from the foundation of the world to restore our peace. Jesus' death reconciled us back to God. He is our peace. His sacrifice serves as a bridge to connect us back to the Father. He is the only way. No one can come to the Father except they go through Him. His way is one of peace. The fruit of His Spirit is peace. His peace gives you the capacity to love others even when they don't love you. He empowers you to walk in peace. Your goal should be to live at peace with everyone, as much as it depends on you. Peacemakers are blessed. They are the ones who shall inherit the Kingdom of God. Not only did He give you peace with God, and the power to be at peace with others, He gave you access to peace from God. The peace of God surpasses all understanding. Rest in His peace today.

Today's readings:
Isaiah 9:6, 26:3; John 14:27, 16:3
Romans 5:1; 8:6, 15:13; Philippians 4:6-7
Colossians 3:15; 2 Thessalonians 3:16

July 1
You Have Everything You Need

When God made you, He made you wholly equipped to accomplish the purposes for which He created you. If you meditate upon His precepts and follow His commands, then you will be the best version of yourself that you can be. It is in learning and keeping His Word that makes you successful in God's sight. His divine promises have given you everything you need for life and godliness. Consequently, you can achieve much by the world's standards and still not live up to God's will for you. Make efforts to do the things you can in order to be successful in your endeavors, but do not confuse the world's definition of success with God's. Remember, the fear of the Lord is the beginning of wisdom. Without it you will miss out on God's best for you. As you resolve to take better care of your health, achieve professional goals, pursue educational achievements, or whatever it is you have determined to do, make sure obeying God's Word is high on the list of achievements. In doing so, you will set yourself up for the greatest accomplishment you can possibly attain. You will one day hear God say, "well done, my good and faithful servant.

Today's readings:
Exodus 4:10-12; Leviticus 26:3-9; Deuteronomy 10:12-13
Psalm 145:15-16; 1 Thessalonians 4:7; 2 Peter 1:3

July 2
It Will Do What It Do

God's Word is full of promises. He will keep His word. As you read His Word, you can rest assured what He has spoken will come to pass. His Word will not return to Him void. It will accomplish the purpose for which it was sent. Have you ever been reading your Bible and suddenly it seems like a verse is leaping off the page? It is in these types of moments which provide the basis for you to experience God in a very personal way. He uses His Word to let you know He is working on your behalf. Perhaps you have been praying about a particular thing, God can use His Word to assure you He has heard your cry and will work things out in your favor. Maybe you are in a time of uncertainty, God's Word can exhort you to know everything is going to be alright. He even uses it to reveal things that are yet to come. His Word will not return to Him without accomplishing His will in the earthly realm. These are reasons it is so important to spend time in God's Word. Set yourself up to not only hear from God, but to be assured by God. No matter what you are going through, be encouraged. For God keeps His Word. He will fulfill His promises to you.

Today's readings:
1 Kings 2:4; Jeremiah 1:11-12, 13:10, 24:7; 39:18
John 5:24, 8:12,12:48, 14:23,15:7

July 3
Steadfast

God is calling you to stand firm in your faith. God wants
you to resolve in your spirit that you shall not be moved.
Be like Jesus - the Rock - who is the same today,
yesterday, and forever. Undoubtedly you will face
challenges to your faith. Look at David when he faced
Goliath. He had to look past the massive size of his
enemy in order to be successful in his battle against him.
David could have easily responded like the army of Israel
and been afraid to fight. But David knew he was the one
with the real advantage because he served the True and
Living God. He focused on who was with him. He knew
he had nothing to fear. If God be for you, who can be
against you? Who or what are you facing that looks
insurmountable? What is your Goliath? Do not let what
you see cause you to cower in your faith. We walk by
faith and not by sight. Put your trust in God. Be like a
Doberman, known for biting into something with such a
firm grip it won't let go. You serve the Maker of heaven
and earth, who will never leave you nor forsake you. He
will not, indeed He cannot, fail. Hold on to your faith,
come what may.

Today's readings:
Psalm 18:1-2, 96:10, 112:7; Daniel 6:26; Romans 12:12
1 Corinthians 15:58a; Colossians 2:5; Hebrews 3:14,6;19

July 4
Satisfied

When you are born again God gives you spiritual gifts that equip you to accomplish His will for your life. Your natural ability, combined with your spiritual endowment, provide everything necessary to accomplish God's assignments for you. It's God's will for everyone to be diligent to work and take care of themselves to the best of their ability. In fact, the Word tells us to work to eat our own food. This is a natural example of a spiritual truth. "My food", Jesus said, "is to do the will of the Father who sent me." Being idle and waiting for someone else to do the spiritual work while you make no effort to co-labor with God will leave you hungry. Seek God's face. Follow the Spirit's leadership and you will find a contentment unparalleled by anything earth has to offer. It will far surpass the "high" of having money, sex, drugs, or alcohol. It will provide a fullness and sense of wholeness that only following God's will can allow. Follow the Holy Spirit's prompting and obey God. Once you begin to do what He shows you to do, He will direct you to do even more until your assigned work is completed.

Today's readings:
John 4:4; Ephesians 2:8-10; 2 Thessalonians 3:10
James 2:26; Revelation 22:12

July 5
Not Forsaken

The Apostle Paul was shipwrecked and beaten. He was imprisoned and lowered out of a city wall in a basket. He was left for dead after having been attacked by a mob. Despite all of this he recognized he was never forsaken. He knew his circumstances did not mean God was no longer with him. In fact, Jesus forewarned that in this life you will have trouble. But He admonishes you to take heart because He has overcome the world. You might be tempted to think that your troubles mean God is not concerned about you. That's not true. Paul endured far more than most of us ever will, yet he was keenly aware God was still with him. Let Paul's testimony encourage you any time problems seem to be breaking loose in your life. He reminded us, though we are hard pressed on every side, we are not crushed; we may be perplexed, but we are not in despair. Trouble does not mean the absence of God in your life. In fact, He promises to be an ever-present help in your time of need. Whenever there is trouble, remember God is there. Instead of doubting His presence, look for Him. He is always there. He has promised to never leave you or forsake you.

Today's readings:
Deuteronomy 31:8; Psalm 46:1,118:5; John 14:16,16:33
2 Corinthians 4:8

July 6
No Matter What

You are going to mess up. That is a given. Thank God He sent Jesus to die for all your sins. It may be hard to comprehend this truth but every time you sin, the blood of Jesus covers them. David was a king of Israel. He had several wives and a prosperous kingdom. He enjoyed God's favor. But sin still tripped him up. He became an adulterer and a murderer, yet God forgave him. Only God knows why He loved David despite his sinful behavior but perhaps Psalm 51 provides some insight. David acknowledged his sin before God. He repented, humbling himself before a holy God. I believe it was not David's choice to sin, but rather what he did following it that moved God to favor him. God honored his humility. He was an Old Testament "type of Christ" and the ancestor to the Lord Jesus. He was the fulfilment of God's promise that David would always have a son on the throne. Like David, Jesus humbled Himself in acknowledgement of sin – the sin of the whole world. Because of Jesus' sacrifice and humility, you too are favored and forgiven. You are forgiven for every sin you have, or ever will commit, no matter what.

Today's readings:
Psalm 32:1-2; John 3:17,10:27-28; Romans 8:1
1 Peter 3:18

July 7
Purposefully Led

Before Serena and Venus Williams were born, their father drafted a 72-page plan for how he could develop two of his children into being the top tennis players in the world. Part of his plan was to move to Compton, a place in the inner city of Los Angeles known for gangs and violence. As a part of his research on successful athletes, he noted how many of them had come out of similar geographical locations. He reasoned it would make his daughters tough and able to handle the pressures of professional tennis. Similarly, when the Israelites were coming of Egypt, God led the Israelites to the promise land by way of a long journey. He didn't take them the shortest route because He knew they weren't quite ready for the battles they would have likely encountered. Today God is still leading His own. He may lead you in ways you do not understand. But just as an earthly father chooses what he thinks is best for his children, how much more does your all-wise and loving heavenly Father guide you according to what is best for you. Trust God. Follow the path He sets before you to experience your best life.

Today's readings:
Exodus 13:17-18; Proverbs 3:3-5; Matthew 4:1-2, 7:11
Luke 4:1-4,11:13; Romans 8:14

July 8
Not Without Revelation

When God wanted to bring His people out of Egypt, He first told Moses. When He was about to destroy Sodom and Gomorrah, He discussed it with Abraham in advance. He does nothing without first revealing it to His servants. In the Old Testament these conversations with God were limited to as select few. Today, God has fulfilled His promise to pour out His Spirit on all flesh. Women, men, and children can hear directly from Him to know what is yet to come. He told both Elizabeth and Mary she would be with-child. Joseph had a dream when the angel told him to take baby Jesus to Egypt where He would be safe from Herod. God will also speak to you. Psychics and palm readers are a foolish waste of money. Their prophecy is not of God. They operate in the occult, darkness and the demonic. Likewise, stay away from *horror*-scopes and instead go to the One who put the stars in the sky. He will not leave you ignorant; if you seek Him for guidance and keep your mind and spirit saturated with his word, He will speak to your heart that which you need to know in advance. If He doesn't reveal it to you, then you don't need to know.

Today's readings:
Genesis 16:18-21; 1 Samuel 20:2; Joel 2:28; John 16:13

July 9
All it takes is One

You are enough! One vote can decide an election. One person can put 1,000 to flight. One person decreed it, and it did not rain for 3 yrs. Your fervent prayers alone can move the hand of God. You, plus God, are a majority. Everything God has ordained for you to accomplish He has equipped you to do. The choice is yours. You can choose to doubt your abilities, or you can move forward by faith recognizing the Lord goes before you making all crooked roads straight. Eleazer was one of David's 3 mighty men. He found himself alone on the battlefield against the Philistines because the army fighting with him fled. He battled all day until his arm was tired and came away victorious. He had won the battle alone by the power of God. I wonder how much time and energy has been wasted over the annals of time by people who spent precious moments wondering if they were capable of being successful. Doubt can keep you from ever receiving God's blessings. Choose to take your rightful place as more than a conqueror. Stop waiting for the approval of others. If God has made a way, then take that path He set before you and be victorious.

Today's readings:
Joshua 23:1-10; 2 Samuel 23:8-10; 1 Kings 17:1-7
James 1:5-8, 5:13-18

July 10
Always There

There is one thing that is unchangeable and unending and that is God's love for you. And the beautiful thing is He's always in your midst. As David said in Psalm 139, you could go down to the deepest depths and God would still be there. You can't do anything to escape or be driven from His love. Indeed, it is a banner over you at all times. He is hovering over you pronouncing to every creation on earth and in heaven, to every demon and angel, this is my child whom I love. Sometimes when a baby is upset, a parent will soothe them by singing a song to comfort and quiet them. Likewise, God will rejoice over you with singing. He is rejoicing over you. You bring Him joy. Think of how a new puppy makes you smile as he wiggles his tail. How much more does your Heavenly Father smile at the sight of you. The psalmist said it well when they penned this line, "over my head I hear music in the air, there must be a God somewhere." I would add this, there is a God; not only is He somewhere, but He's also everywhere!

Today's readings:
Song of Solomon 2:4; Jeremiah 31:3; Zephaniah 3:17
John 3:16; Romans 5:8,8:37-39; Ephesians 5:2
1 John 4:8-10,16,19

July 11
Blessings and Favor

There are key principles throughout scripture that will allow you to see blessings and favor in your life. First, when you delight in Him, it pleases God. He will grant you the desires of His heart because your heart will align with His. Second, choose to obey God. When you do things His way, you will be blessed and favored. God looks at your heart and your motives. God is not fooled. He is omniscient. He knows everything, including your thoughts. He wants your whole self, including your heart. Also, following those who are following Christ is a kingdom principle many miss. In our era of independence where society tells you to do whatever you want without concerns for any rules, you may think it's unnecessary to mimic those who walk in the Lord. Yet, the first thing Jesus said when He called His disciples is, "follow Me." As you see the men and women of God living out their faith, observe and apply what you see and hear. This list of basic truths, though not exhaustive, has been proven to bring blessings and favor to those who live by them.

Today's readings:
Numbers 31:31; 2 Chronicles 17:3-12
Psalm 37:4, 40:8, 119:2; Proverbs 3:5; 1 Corinthians 11:1

July 13
God's Goal

One of the greatest promises of God is that all things are working together for the good of those who love God and are called according to His purpose. The beautiful thing about the word "all" is it encompasses everything in your life. Your failures are working together for your good as much as your triumphs. Romans 8:28 is often quoted, but what does it really mean to be called according to His purpose? The text reveals the reason God works things together and the good He is seeking to achieve. First off, He foreknew you. He knit you together in your mother's womb. He also predestined you to be like Jesus. His wants others to see Jesus when they see you. The reason all things are working together for your good is so God can duplicate the prototype He created in His Son. Like Jesus, you have God's power because the Holy Spirit lives in you. Like Jesus, you have the Word of God, and the mind of Christ is available to you as you constantly renew your mind in His Word. What God wants is to see you abiding in Jesus and His life in you. All things are working together for your good to conform your character to be like Christ's.

Today's readings:
Romans 8:28-29; Galatians 4:19; Philippians 2:5
Hebrews 13:20-21; 1 Peter 3:15-16

July 14
Hindrances to God's plan: Self Will

There are numerous hindrances to being blessed and used by God. The first is probably the greatest. This barrier is prevalent throughout scripture, your life and mine. It caused Moses to miss entering the promised land. It caused Saul to be stripped of his crown as king of Israel. It is probably the only hindrance that is completely within your own control. It is disobedience to God. Your refusal to surrender your will to God's will. You were born with a will; your ability to act or choose. Your will is exercised when you put your faith in God. It is also reflected in your obedience or disobedience. Saul chose to spare the life of a king and he kept valuable items even though God told him to destroy everything. Obedience is better than sacrifice. Like Jonah, who chose to go in the opposite direction when the Lord told him to go to Nineveh, you may find yourself in a storm as a result of your own actions. Sometimes the circumstances created by your disobedience may be far more than you anticipated. Learn to let go of your will, and grab hold of God's so His plan and power can manifest in you.

Today's readings:
Numbers 20:7-12; 1 Samuel 15:1-3,7-22; Jonah 1:1-3
Matthew 16:21-23

July 15
Hindrances To God's Plan:
Ungodly influences

Eve's decision to eat of the fruit God forbade her to consume led to our eternal relationships with God being misaligned. Instead of focusing on what God said, she listened to the devil. She not only fell for the temptation to partake, but she also gave some to Adam, who did the same thing. Adam's decision changed the trajectory of all of mankind. Jonah's shipmates were impacted by his disobedience. They lost all their goods and all of their food because they were aboard a ship with him. Similarly, a young man was sent by God to prophecy to King Jeroboam. God told him not to stop and eat within the city's limits once he had completed his assignment. Sadly, for him, he was deceived by an old lying prophet who invited him to dinner. The deceiving prophe-*liar* told him God had said it was ok for him to share a meal with him. The younger man listened and went against God's will. When it came time for him to leave, he was attacked by a lion along the way. It was all because he listened to the counsel of the ungodly. Make no mistake about it, bad company corrupts good character.

Today's readings:
Genesis 3:1-7; Exodus 32:1-4; 1 Kings 13:1-28
Psalm 1:1-3; 1 Corinthians 15:33

July 16
Hindrances To God's Plan: Greed

Another very dangerous hindrance to God's plan for you to live your best life is the love of money and possessions. It is so easy to get caught up in wanting more and more. God is not anti-money. You can live a healthy and holy lifestyle with wealth. It is the love of money, not money itself, that is the root of all evil. When it reaches that place where the more you get, the more you want. When your desire for things exceeds your love for God and His will, it becomes a problem. Like all things in the Bible, your relationship with prosperity should be balanced with moderation. Seeking God's Kingdom first is your best choice. Otherwise, if you choose to seek more abundance as a priority you may be like Gehazi and get more than you bargained for. He was Elisha's servant, who sought to go behind his boss' back to obtain a reward the prophet had refused to accept. Only, instead, he gained more than he expected because he ended up with leprosy. Love God with all your heart, mind, soul and strength and you will not have to worry about the things you need. Your God will ensure you have them.

Today's readings:

Numbers 22:1-35; 2 Kings 5:15-27; Ecclesiastes 5:10
Matthew 6:24,33; 1 Timothy 3:2-3,6:810; Hebrews 13:5

July 17

Hindrances To God's Plan:
Other Sources

When you put anything ahead of God in your heart, you are practicing idolatry. Allowing yourself to be swayed by another voice, including your own, is putting something before God. Reading horoscopes and seeking revelation from another spirit are also repulsive to God. Rebellion is like witchcraft to Him. Stubbornness is the same as iniquity and idolatry. He rejected Saul from being king because of his refusal to obey. Notice how these behaviors all flow from your heart. If you dissect them, the root of them all is what caused Satan's fall from grace: wanting to be in control. You seek out palm readings so you can know what's going to happen. You get angry and jealous because you can't have what you want. You try to be like other people so that you can feel comfortable. You can unwittingly sacrifice your own blessings by refusing to allow biblical truth to be your guide and accepting God's will for your life. Don't miss out on your blessings. Embrace His ways and reap the benefits and experiences He has planned for you. He is your source for blessings and victory in your daily walk.

Today's readings:
Leviticus 20:6; 1 Samuel 15:23; 2 Chronicles 13:6
Proverbs 18:27; Jonah 2:8; Galatians 5:19-21

July 18
Hindrances to God's plan: Fear

Healthy fear warns you to avoid being harmed in
circumstances, whereas unhealthy fear can cause you to
freeze and fail to accomplish God's will. Sometimes fear
is a spirit that controls you. It is demonic spirit, but God
is greater, and He can deliver you. Consider how Moses
was very fearful. When God came to him in a burning
bush to tell him to go back to Egypt and lead His people
out of captivity, Moses began to make excuses about why
he couldn't do it. He had a speech impediment, he told
God. The people wouldn't believe God had sent him, he
complained. He did not think he was qualified. God
addressed each of his complaints by reminding him of
who He was. He said, "I Am that I Am". He told Moses it
was He who made his tongue to equip him to speak. He
showed him the power he had by instructing him how to
use his staff. And, most important, He told Moses He
would be with Him. Likewise, when you face your
Pharaoh - whatever name it goes by – remember you are
surrounded by angels, protected by God, and filled with
His Spirit.

Today's readings:

Deuteronomy 31:6; Joshua 1:9
Isaiah 41:10; Matthew 6:34 Romans 8:29
2 Timothy 1:7; 1 John 4:8

July 19
Successful failure

Many a failure has turned out to be a blessing in disguise. Bubble wrap was a dismal failure as its' intended purpose of being wallpaper. But when IBM decided to use it to ship its' computers, a worldwide success was born. WD-40 got its' name because the first 39 attempts to make an aeronautical lubricant were unsuccessful. Wheaties were in a sense a failure. Someone who worked for a company that sold bran gruel – a less flavorful product - created it accidentally when he spilled it on a stovetop, and it crackled into flakes. With a little doctoring, the Breakfast of Champions evolved. Billions of dollars later they are still being consumed. The point is you should never give up your dreams. When you make a mistake, do not beat yourself up. God is on your side working all things together for your good. God can use your failures to bless many. Apostle Paul started out as a persecutor of Christians but turned out to be the greatest conveyor of the faith who ever lived, having written the majority of the New Testament. Do not be afraid to fail.

Today's readings:
Psalm 73:26; Proverbs 24:16,28:13; Acts 9:1-16
Romans 5:3-5,8:28; 1 Corinthians 12:9-10

July 20
Keep God's Attention

One of the most powerful things you can do to see God move in your life is turn down your plate. Fasting and praying gets God's attention. He honors humility. Incorporate it into your life routine. Meditate on scripture. Look for ways in which your sacrifice can be someone else's blessing. Denying yourself and seeking God will keep your heart sensitive to the things of God. You will be more attuned to His movement and will for your life. You will see outcomes manifesting in ways you had never thought or imagined as God does exceedingly more than you ask Him to do. Look at Nineveh. Jonah was sent there to forewarn them of God's coming judgment. The king's response to the prophet's pronouncement was to order everyone and everything to humble themselves. He put on sackcloth and ashes as a symbol of his humility. When God saw the response of this gentile nation, He relented from bringing the calamity. If fasting changed the outcome of an entire nation, then imagine how much your life and those of your loved ones can be impacted.

Today's readings:
Exodus 34:28; Esther 4:16; Isaiah 58:1-14; Daniel 10:3
Jonah 3:4-10; Luke 4:1-4; Acts 13:12,14:23;
1 Corinthians 7:5

July 21

Speechless

"Shucks folks, I'm speechless," said the Cowardly Lion. For some this is never the case. You may be one of those people who is always talking. Yet, you may feel like you don't know what to say when it comes time to pray. I have encountered people who say they don't know how to talk to God. Perhaps you see Him as unapproachable. Or you may feel your prayers are not good enough, especially when you've heard others pray who seemingly do so with ease. You may feel like you do not know how to pray adequately. However, your capacity to converse with God is within you. Imagine talking to someone who is not only interested in hearing from you but is eager to listen. God's ears are attentive to the prayers of the righteous. Sometimes your heart may feel so burdened with a problem you simply don't know what to pray. In those times you can allow Holy Spirit to pray through you. When you pray this way, in unknown tongues, your spirit is speaking to God. You can be assured you will have what you are asking for because it will always be in line with God's will. God honors prayer that agrees with His will. Praying in the Spirit is powerful and effective.

Today's readings:
Psalm 34:15; Matthew 6:8-13; Romans 8:26-27
1 Corinthians 14:13-18; 2 Corinthians 3:17

July 22
Corroborating Witness

When Jesus walked the earth, He was seen by many both before and after His resurrection who could later testify to what they had seen. The facts they shared are what we read in our Bible today. When He was about to ascend to heaven, Jesus gave the disciples instructions to go to Jerusalem to wait for the promised Spirit of Truth to be poured out. The Holy Spirit was poured out on all believers on the Day of Pentecost. As Jesus promised, He gave you power to boldly share your faith. Through your testimony others can come to know Him and the blessings you have experienced from having a relationship with Him. Nobody can tell your story like you. Just like word of mouth is the best advertisement for a business, your testimony is the best way to help others to know the Lord for themselves. You are walking evidence of the fact that Jesus is real. Be a corroborating witness to the goodness of God. Share with others what He has done for you. Allow His power that resides in you to give you courage. Boldly tell the world of the great things He has done. Let everyone know that Christ Jesus is real and loves them.

Today's readings:
2 Samuel 1:16; Proverbs 28:1; Mark 16:14-18
John 1:34,3:11,5:39,10:38; Acts 1:8,2:1-4,14:3

July 23
Yokes

A yoke is a type of harness. It restricts movement. It can be used to control direction. Jesus said His yoke is easy and His burden is light. He invites you to take on His yoke and find rest for your soul. His yoke stands in contrast to the world's yokes. You've probably experienced some of those yokes that aim to conform you to their patterns. Have a drink, take a hit, drive a luxurious car, etc., to fit in with them. Those yokes can be burdensome and heavy. You can feel as though you just don't measure up. But thanks be to the Lord our God, you don't need to wear any of those yokes to please God. You are accepted into the Beloved of God without making extra efforts. There is only one qualification to walk under His yoke. It is your faith. When you put your faith in Jesus, He invites you to cast your cares on Him. He will give you peace that is so light it can make you feel as though you are walking on clouds. Jesus never requires us to do anything to wear His yoke other than putting your faith in Him; once you do, then you can receive the unsurpassable peace only He can give.

Today's readings:
Leviticus 26:3; Isaiah 10:27; Matthew 11:29-30
Acts 15:1-21; Romans 12:1-2; 2 Corinthians 3:17, 6:14

July 24
What You Say To You

Your tongue has the power of life and death in it. It can not only kill relationships with others, but it can also kill you! What you say to yourself is crucial. If you say things that suggest you cannot accomplish something, then the likelihood is you won't because you've convinced your mind you cannot. As you speak to yourself you are creating thoughts. Those thoughts begin to manifest in your life. When Jesus encountered the woman with the issue of blood, He did not know she was there initially. Unlike the countless others who He healed, she was healed based upon what she said to herself and her faith in Him, not because He spoke to her or touched her. She demonstrated how powerful your self-talk can be. She told herself she could be healed if she could just touch the hem of His garment. And that is exactly what occurred. Negative thoughts may creep into your mind but instead of feasting on the negative, take every thought captive that would lead you to say negative things about yourself. Replace those toxic thoughts with what God says about you. Only speak to yourself truths that agree with God's Word.

Today's readings:
2 Samuel 23:2; Psalm 139:14; Proverbs 18:20-21
Deuteronomy 28:2; 2 Corinthians 5:21; James 3:1-12

July 25
Cast Your Cares

The w|Word of God tells you to cast all your cares on the Lord. He is inviting you to release your frustration, pain, and anxiety upon Him. If you are like most, you think you have released your burdens only to find yourself bothered again by the very thing you were praying about earlier. Casting means to "to throw upon or place upon". When you truly cast your cares, they are no longer on you. You are giving them to Him. The weight of your burdens will be on the Lord. He will carry them. How heart breaking it must be for the Father to see you struggling and bearing the weight He wants to carry for you. You lose sleep and walk around anxiously trying to figure out the solutions to your problems, while the Lord is beckoning you to hand over your concerns to Him. Put all of the heaviness of your circumstances on Him then watch and see how He chooses to work it out. He will speak to your heart and let you know what you must do, but the problem will be His, not yours. If you want to live the life God wants you to have, give God everything that concerns your heart – give Him the weight that keeps you loaded down.

Today's readings:
Deuteronomy 28:1; Joshua 23:14; Psalm 55:2
Matthew 11:28; Romans 14:17; James 1:22; 1 Peter 5:7

July 26
God Sees You

When Sarah could not become pregnant, she made a plan to have her Egyptian maidservant Hagar sleep with her husband Abraham, so that she could produce an offspring through her. However once Hagar became pregnant, they began to have conflict. Sarah began treating Hagar harshly. Hagar ran away and found herself alone. She likely felt dejected, unappreciated, and lonely. She stopped at a spring and an angel of the Lord spoke to her. He assured her that God had seen how she was being treated. He told her God already had a name for the child within her womb. His name was Ishmael, and he would be a great nation. We know his offspring today as Arabs. God saw her, and He already had a plan in place concerning her and her unborn child. He sees you and knows what is causing you concern. Nothing is hidden from His sight. Others may not see what you're enduring, and it can feel like no one cares. You can feel isolated and alone. But be encouraged, because God sees all that concerns you and He has plans to get you through it all. Never give up. God's plan for you is still unfolding.

Today's readings:
Genesis 16:1-13; Psalm 139:13; Jeremiah 29:11
Hebrews 4:13

July 27

God's Prescription For A Blessed Life

God has set forth numerous ways for you to be blessed, in the Holy Bible. When you serve God, He will bless your food, making sure you have provision. He promised to also take sickness away from you and all connected to you who serve Him. Some turn their noses up at those who are less fortunate and shun those who seek help. But God says when you give to the poor with a good attitude, He will bless you in everything you do. He always gives back far more. God cares about those who are downtrodden. He will bless you when you bless them. Serving Him wholeheartedly is a sure-fire way for you to be blessed whether you are in the city or out in the wilderness. It will even bless your unborn offspring and your property. You will posture yourself to see blessings over your household and the money you produce. On the contrary, doing the opposite will reap the opposite. Many make lots of money and yet find themselves bankrupt when they don't follow God's principles. It is God who gives you the capability to produce wealth. Trusting God leads to God's favor over your life.

Today's readings:
Exodus 23:25; Deuteronomy 15:10,28:2-8
Psalm 84:11-12; Proverb 8:34,19:17; Luke 6:35

July 28
Keep Swinging

Hank Aaron said, "My motto was always to keep swinging. Whether I was in a slump or feeling badly or having trouble off the field, the only thing to do was keep swinging." Jesus' actions reflect this concept. He was clear and focused on finishing His course. He went through criticisms and rejection. They belittled Him so badly in His hometown He could not do any miracles there. He endured whippings with a cattail and being spat upon. Yet, Jesus endured it. He could have chosen to quit at any moment. He could have called down legions of angels to destroy everyone who muttered a word against Him, but He chose to persevere through every trial and tribulation to reach the goal the Father had sent Him to accomplish. He focused His eyes on the future and for the joy set before Him, He endured. Have you ever been discouraged and considered quitting? Keep pushing. Keep persevering. You won't know what the future holds until you allow yourself to move forward to see what will be. Rather than quit when those times occur just keep swinging.

Today's readings:
Isaiah 26:3; 40:31; Matthew 24:13; Romans 5:3-5
1 Corinthians 10:13; Hebrews 12:1-2; James 1:12,25

July 29
Forget about It

When my son was young, we would watch the movie *Lion King*. When one of the lead characters was trying to encourage Semba not to dwell on his past, he told him, "you have to leave your behind in the past." Well, though his wording wasn't quite correct, his intention was spot on. You are blessed with a brand-new opportunity with each new day. Why waste it on something that happened previously? What is done is done. Forget about it and move forward. Great athletes keep very short memories. If they sit and ponder the mistakes, they will never win the game. Likewise, you are not going to be perfect until you reach heaven. Do not waste time condemning yourself because of a mistake. God does not condemn you. He forgives you. This is the day the Lord has made, use it wisely to move forward. You were given brand new mercies today. Mercy is the gift of God that causes you to not be treated as your sins deserve. He casts your sins into the sea of forgetfulness. Don't go fishing for them. Leave what is behind you in the past and press on to see what the end is going to be!

Today's readings:
Lamentations 3:22-23; Micah 7:19; Psalm 25:7, 118:24
Philippians 1:6,2:13, 3:13-14; Romans 8:1

July 30
Always With Love

The true nature of God is love. What that looks like as it is manifested through human beings is what is often referred to as the golden rule. You demonstrate this when you love your neighbor as yourself. Love is clearly defined in scripture as much by what it is, as it is described by what it is not. It is patient. This means when you love you will suffer with a person for a long time without ceasing to care for them. It causes you to be benevolent towards others and look out for their needs. You are not envious when you walk in a lifestyle of love. Instead, you rejoice with those who rejoice. When you are being prideful, rude, quick to anger or selfish you are not demonstrating love. Rather, your willingness to bear with others, believe what is true, remain hopeful, and endure - while maintaining a loving attitude - is a true reflection of God's love operating in and through you. But, even if you give to the poor, pay your tithes, speak in tongues, and have great faith, it will be unpleasing to God if not rooted in love. He said none of these things matter if you are not loving. Walk in love.

Today's readings:
Matthew 19:19; 1 Corinthians 13; Galatians 5:6
Philippians 2:1-4; 1 John 4:7-8

July 31
Not Optional

Within 24 hours I learned of two people who suddenly transitioned into eternity. Neither was expected to pass away. Literally, they were here one minute and gone the next. It seems cliché when it is said that no one knows the day, nor the hour, God will call you to give an account for your life. Cliché or not, tomorrow is not promised to anyone. Just like we will have to deal with the consequences if we cause someone to be hurt – even though we didn't know we would do harm - we will be held responsible for our sin even if we don't know the Bible. Tell everyone you know God commands us to repent. You may think you will have time to get right with God just before you die. But that is not necessarily true. Sometimes death comes suddenly. And as Solomon said in Ecclesiastes, you will not win the war to retain your spirit when that war comes. You have a destination with death. You will not be able to postpone or ignore it. Will you be ready? Today is the day of salvation. If you have not done so, repent and turn to God. Ask Him to save your soul. Share this truth with others, before it's too late.

Today's readings:
Proverbs 27:1; Ecclesiastes 8:8; Matthew 6:34, 24:36-39
Acts 17:22-31; Hebrews 9:27; James 4:13-15

August 1
Stay Hungry

Never become totally satisfied. Your hunger will spur you on to be filled even more. This is true both in the natural and in the spiritual realm. Jesus said those who are hungry are blessed and they shall be filled. When you read the Lord's description of His chosen people, He talks about how He found them in the wilderness. They were destitute so He fed them. But once they became fat, they no longer worshipped Him. They became obese consuming His blessings. Their hearts strayed and they began to sacrifice to foreign gods. This is what happens when you become complacent in God. You start approaching your relationship with the Father as mundane and routine. It leads to you being lazy about pursuing Him and staying in His Word. Crave His word like a baby needing pure milk. Your constant pursuit of God will give you peace that surpasses understanding. You will find it easier to obey His Word and hear His voice. As long as you stay hungry, let Him be central in your life, and search His Word for direction, He will satisfy your soul and keep your from pursuing the artificial "gods" of this world that can lead to destruction.

Today's readings:
Deuteronomy 32: 9-15; Psalm 42:2; Proverbs 16:26
Matthew 5:6; Luke 6:21; 1 Timothy 2:22; 1 Peter 2:2

August 2
Teach The Children

Children are the next leaders of the church. They are an important part of the body of Christ. You are Christ's ambassador who is called to teach them. You have the capacity to prepare the children in your life to be lifelong lovers of Christ. Some think it is the Sunday school teachers' job to teach them about the Lord. However, the job to teach children belongs to parents and those who know them. It takes a village to raise a child. As you walk along, go for a ride, visit a park, share a meal or engage with children in some way, help them to see and understand God. They can catch on easily because their hearts are still tender. When you train them early, you set them on a course for success. Taking them to church is important. Talking to them and modeling how to apply what the Bible says is even more significant. Daily application of the Word of God will leave an indelible mark upon their lives. If you don't have children in your life, volunteer in the children's church or befriend the children in your neighborhood so that you can help prepare the next generation to be disciples of the Lord Jesus Christ.

Today's readings:
Proverbs 3:16,13:24,22:6,29:7; Psalm 8:2; Ezekiel 20:18
Matthew 19:14; 1 Corinthians 13:11; Ephesians 6:4

August 3
Division Destroys

Maybe you say you are a Christian and speak up for the things of God in one instance, but in another you quietly blend into the way of the world. Perhaps you feel confident you can trust God when it comes to some things, but in others you walk in fear and anxiety. Doubt quenches faith. Scripture says your duplicity will destroy you. Similarly, a house divided cannot stand. Jesus was accused of casting out demons by the power of the devil. He made it clear that if He was casting out devils by the power of the devil, then the devil's kingdom would be destroyed. Fighting against the thing you say you are for will lead to destruction, in other words. When you are engaged in things contrary to your confession of faith or goals, sooner or later you begin to chip away at your own efforts. Likewise, two people cannot walk together unless they agree on the direction and path to take. Unity makes things possible. In fact, when the body of Christ is unified, God commands a blessing. When you are joined to a cause, get rid of any attitudes or behaviors inconsistent with your aim. Walk in unity and reap the blessings from God that come forth from it.

Today's readings:
Genesis 11:1-9; Psalm 133; Proverbs 11:3; Amos 3:3
Matthew 12:22-30; Philippians 2:1-2; James 1:6-8

August 4
Become Like Children

Children are very trusting and likely to believe anyone.
They are resilient. No matter how often they may
experience disappointment they will keep trusting. They
easily forgive when they are wounded by someone. If a
child hurts another child's feelings, they may cry or
become disturbed, but it is not unusual to see that same
child playing with the one who caused them to feel badly
a short time before. When a parent disappoints a child,
the child will quickly forget all about it. They will
lovingly seek their parent out if they are separated.
Children love unconditionally. Rather than judge a
person, they will extend love to those who society deems
to be less than desirable. You too can have the same
trusting, forgiving and loving heart of a child. It requires
you to surrender your will to the Father's will. Through
His Spirit within, you have the power to love anyone no
matter how many times they have sinned against you.
You have been given a measure of faith enabling you to
believe God even when things seem hopeless and there is
no rational reason to believe otherwise. Become like a
little child in your faith.

Today's readings:
Exodus 25:2; Psalm 14:2, 34:11; Matthew 11:14,18:1-5
Romans 5:5,8:21; Hebrews 11:1; 1 John 5:2

August 5
New Testament Sacrifices

The Old Testament was based upon the law. Each sin
was to be atoned for by the sacrifice of the blood of
animals on the altar of God. The Old Testament practice
of sacrificing animals was not enough to take away the
sin, though. Rather, they were more like temporary
appeasements. Without the shedding of blood there is no
remission of sin. In the New Testament Jesus came to
satisfy the sin-debt for all of mankind. After His perfect
Blood was shed, there was no longer a need for
additional blood sacrifices. But Paul does identify one
additional sacrifice you can offer to God: yourself! He
said you should offer yourself to God as a living sacrifice.
This means to lay down your own life for God's life to be
lived in you. He wants a living sacrifice. The problem
with the New Testament sacrifices is they keep getting
up from the altar. Living sacrifices that are not totally
surrendered to God, keep wanting to have their say and
do things their way. God wants better of you. Offer
yourself as a living sacrifice, holy and pleasing to God.
This is your minimum service to the God who paid the
ultimate price for your freedom from the bondage of sin.

Today's readings:
Malachi 1;8; Mark 12:7; Romans 6:23,12:1
Ephesians 5:2; Hebrews 10:1-18

August 6
Thorns Included

As the Frankie Beverly song that has stood the test of time states, joy and pain are like sunshine and rain. You cannot have one without the other. When you encounter trouble in this life you should not think it is strange or that God is angry with you. All too often people view their challenges through the lens of retribution for their iniquity. They think God is paying them back. Contrary to the sinners who do not know God, you are not treated as your sins deserve. You are blessed by the fact that Jesus bore your sins upon Himself. By doing so, He took away the punishment. Still, everyone will encounter sorrows in this life. No one is immune. Just as everyone has sunny days, rain pours out on the just and the unjust. However, you have the blessing of knowing that Jesus will carry you and your burdens. Like a rose which comes with thorns, life comes with challenges. As the beauty of the rose is worth the thorns that accompany them, the blessings of life are worth the difficulties you may encounter. The lows make the highs all the sweeter. Don't get so caught up in the negative that you overlook and undervalue all the positives in your life.

Today's readings:
2 Chronicles 15:4; Job 5:7,14:1; Psalms 46:1; Nahum 1:7
Matthew 5:45,6:25-34; John 16:33

August 7
Birthing Pains

Some things are foretold in scripture which will come to pass to bear witness to Jesus' return. He told us to expect to hear of wars and rumors of wars, nations rising against nations, and kingdoms against kingdoms. There will be famines, pestilences, and earthquakes in various places. But note, these are not the signs of the end. Instead, just as when a woman is about to give birth, she must go through labor pains, so too these are merely signs of the beginning of the preparation for His return. Time is drawing closer, but it is not the end. It is critical to remember He said do not be troubled. These things must come to pass, and you will do well to obey His voice. If you ignore Him, you will allow yourself to be stressed over what He told you to expect. Would a mother be stressed over her labor pains? Let not your heart be troubled. There are other things which also must come to pass before His return, much as a mother's labor is part of a baby's birth. May you rejoice and find peace in Jesus' parting words, "I'm with you always even to the end of the age." He is with you now and will be with you forever.

Today's readings:
Psalm 122:6; Matthew 24:3-14; Mark 13:5-13
Romans 8:22; 1 Thessalonians 5:25; 2 Thessalonians 3:1

August 8
In A Time Like This

What you can and should be doing in a time like this is set forth in scripture. Jesus said, "men always ought to pray and not lose heart," and we should both "watch and pray." Being watchful allows us to see what is happening so we can pray and take action. Use wisdom. Be prudent to posture yourself as best you can for what is yet to come. While you should do what you can, you should not place your trust in your own capability. No matter what you can or cannot do, God is the real source of your security. Find your strength in Him. Pray for those who are in authority. Pray for the peace of Jerusalem and the city where you live. Like Solomon prayed, if our country and our allies go out to battle, you can pray asking the Lord to hear in heaven and maintain their cause. Ask God to go out before our army. Pray for those who preach the gospel, that the Word of the Lord will quickly reach the ends of the earth. Pray with the Spirit in order to pray God's perfect will. Pray for the lost, that they may come to know Christ before it is too late.

Today's readings:
1 Kings 8:44-45; Psalm 122:6; Jeremiah 29:7
Matthew 24:20; Mark 13:33; Luke 18:1,21:36
Colossians 1:9; 2 Thessalonians 1:11, 3:1

August 9
Little By Little

Many seek success overnight, but doing things God's way requires you to be patient. When a farmer plants a seed in the ground, it would be ludicrous for them to expect a crop the following day. Instead, they patiently water and fertilize it. Then after some time, they expect to receive a harvest from their seed. Interestingly, when the Jews were delivered by the Lord out of the bondage of Egypt, He did not allow them to possess the promised land all at once. He let them gain control of it little by little. His reasoning was that if they got it all at once it would be too much for them. They would be overtaken by the wild animals. They had to learn to master the smaller portions of the land first and then they would receive more. Likewise, Jesus espoused this concept as whoever shows themselves faithful over a little can then be trusted to be faithful over much. Rather than think you are somehow behind schedule for accomplishments you think you should have completed, trust the process. Know that God knows exactly how and when you should progress so that you can have success without success overtaking you.

Today's readings:
Exodus 23:29-30; Deuteronomy 7:22
Proverbs 20:21, 28:20; Luke 16:10-12; James 5:7,10-11

August 10
Saying Ain't Doing

One of the verses in the Bible that always makes me laugh was spoken by one of my favorite Biblical characters, the prophet Samuel. God had commanded Saul to annihilate all the people, property and animals associated with the Amalekites. But instead of obeying, Saul bought back the king of the Amalekites along with the choice animals and items. Samuel questioned his obedience by asking, "what then is this bleating of sheep in my ears and the lowing of the oxen which I hear?" Or, in modern day terms, "Why did you bring back the Gucci bags?" The king tried to justify his actions by suggesting he had bought the items back in order to make sacrifices to the Lord. But like God, the prophet was not impressed. And he followed up with one of the key verses in scripture on honoring the voice of the Lord. "To obey is better than sacrifice." It is not enough to merely know what God has said. Like Korah and those who banded with him in rebellion to God's chosen leadership, you could be swallowed up by your own disobedience. You cannot walk in the blessings God has promised you by merely hearing His word, but you will be blessed if you obey what it says.

Today's readings:
1 Samuel 13:13-14,15:13-23; John 8:31; James 1:21-25

221

August 11
Rejoice

This is the day the Lord has made. Rejoice and be glad in it. Rejoice means to be in a state of gladness, happiness and well-being. It is more than a feeling. It is a verb requiring action. Paul declares you should rejoice in the Lord, always. The choice to rejoice is based upon your focus. When you are struggling to find joy do what Paul told Timothy to do; fan into flame the gift that is within you. Stir up the gift! Feed your spirit the Word of God. Meditate on the goodness of God. Focus in on the blessings of God. Let the Son shine in your soul! It's harder for you to rejoice when all of your focus is on gloom and doom. When I think about Jesus and all He has done for me, as the psalmist said, I can dance, dance, dance all night. Rejoice with those who rejoice. You can even rejoice when you are persecuted for your faith, knowing the promise of God to bless you. The key to rejoicing is gratitude for all the Lord has done. There is also another form of joy, a noun, which is joy given by God. If you are struggling with making the choice to rejoice, ask God to pour out His oil of gladness in your heart. Choose to rejoice today!

Today's readings:
Psalm 118:24; Luke 5:23; Acts 14:17; Romans 12:15
1 Corinthians 12:6; Philippians 3:1, 4:4

August 12
A Battle Cry!

Call on the Lord when you are in distress. He will answer you. It is better to trust in the Lord than to put confidence in man. Nations may surround you, but in the name of the Lord, you will destroy them. You shall be lifted above your enemies all around you. Though He has chastened you severely, the Lord has not given you over to death. Blessed are you because you come in the name of the Lord! Like David against Goliath, your enemy thought you would be too small to withstand them, but you are standing in the name of the Lord. He is your light and your salvation. Do not fear. What can man do to you? God is your strength. Do not be afraid. Though an army encamps against you, do not let your heart fear. Though war rises against you be confident in this: you shall see the goodness of the Lord in the land of the living. Wait on the LORD, be of good courage, and He shall strengthen your heart. Wait I say, upon the Lord! And remember when all is said and done, you shall dwell in the house of the Lord, forever.

Today's readings:
Psalm 27, 118

August 13
Burning Within!

I said I wasn't going to tell nobody, but I couldn't keep it to myself. It is like fire shut up in my bones! These are the types of things you may find yourself saying when you sense God calling you to share the good news of the gospel of Jesus Christ. Every believer is called to share their faith. And when you are called to preach and teach, it is a desire you cannot easily ignore. Paul said, "woe unto me if I don't preach the gospel." You may find your family and friends roll their eyes when you start telling what you believe to be a timely word from the Lord. After all, a prophet is not without honor except for in his or her own household. But others who God has drawn may find your words life-giving as they hear you expound upon the truth. Don't be like Jonah and run from the calling. Whether He has called you to be an evangelist to share your faith wherever you go, a prophet, an apostle, a pastor, a teacher, an administrator, an assistant, or some other area of gifting, know that He has a purpose for you to fulfill. Like the preacher who cannot help but preach, do whatever He has called you to do.

Today's readings:
Proverbs 15:23; Isaiah 50:4; Jeremiah 20:9; Acts 20:27
1 Corinthians 9:16; 2 Timothy 4:2

August 14
The Anecdote For Anxiety

It is so easy to be anxious. Just turning on the news can rob you of your contentment if you allow it. Thankfully the Lord has given us several ways to avoid feeling anxious. He told us, "Anxiety in the heart of a man weighs him down, but a good word makes him glad." Fill your heart with the Word of God. Read verses about being able to do all things through Christ who strengthens you, and how you are more than a conqueror. When you are reminded, the Lord is your Shepherd and you shall not want, it makes it harder for you to be concerned about what lies ahead. And then you can boost your serenity by praying about everything that is bothering you, casting all your cares upon Him. He promises to take your burdens and in exchange give you His supernatural peace. While you may be trying to figure things out, He is working them out and granting you the privilege of resting your soul in Him. Lastly, rather than worry, seek first the kingdom of God and He will add all that you need for your life. Meditate, pray, and seek God's kingdom. In doing so you will find yourself walking in joy, peace, and provision.

Today's readings:
Psalm 94:19; Proverbs 12:25; Matthew 6:25-33
John 14:27; Philippians 4:6-7; 1 Peter 5:7; 1 John 4:18

August 15
God's Shifts

When the Israelites came out of bondage in Egypt they were accompanied by the Lord's presence in a cloud. It hovered over the Tabernacle they erected every time they stopped. So long as the cloud lingered, they knew to stay where they were. But as soon as it lifted, they packed up and moved with it. Learn to sense God's shifts in your life. Knowing how to discern His guidance will help you to avoid pitfalls. Notice how the cloud never stayed in one place at the same amount of time when it stopped. When you learn His ways and understand His shifts, you too will see He cannot be boxed into a script. The key is to learn His voice and obey it. Many have made bad decisions based on their own desires or their own timing instead of heeding God's voice. When He leads you, He always leads you with an underlying peace. When you override His peace to proceed to do what you want, you are no longer in flow with the Lord's leading. That will not lead to God's best for you. Learn to shift with Him. When He moves you move, just like Him.

Today's readings:
Numbers 9:15-21; Psalm 34:14; Proverbs 3:17
Philippians 4:6-9; Colossians 3:15

August 16
Closing The Gap

There is a gap between your spiritual status and your daily life. When you were born again, you were spiritually transformed immediately. God's nature is now inside of you. Still, if you are honest, you can identify areas of your life that have not changed completely. The things you do or say, and the way you behave or display attitudes, do not always reflect the spiritual transformation that has taken place within your spirit. Your soul – your mind, will and emotion – have to catch up to your new spiritual condition. This process of sanctification is being carried out in you by the Holy Spirit. You are being transformed into God's image so that you will look like Him both inside and out. The gap between the new spiritual you on the inside, and your old behaviors can be frustrating. You may feel like Paul. The things you don't want to do, you do. And the things you want to do, you don't do. Yet, you can be encouraged to know God does not condemn you for the gap. Instead, He is working in you to accomplish His will. He who has begun a good work in you will see it through to completion until the day of Jesus Christ.

Today's readings:
2 Corinthians 3:18; Galatians 4:19; Romans 8:29
Philippians 1:6, 2:13; 2 Peter 1:5

August 17
Living In The Gap

There is often a period between the time God gives you a vision and when it comes to pass. When Joseph's brothers sold him into slavery, he kept a positive attitude and served his master well. He was young and handsome. His master's wife was enamored with him and sought to expand his services! But Joseph was a man of God with great integrity. He resisted her advances, but she lied and said he tried to rape her. His master had him placed in prison. Once again, he excelled. As a model prisoner he ended up in charge of the prisoners' duties. He was treated with respect by the officials. After he interpreted his cellmates' dreams, God opened a door for him to stand before the Pharaoh, who was the equivalent of their king, to interpret his dreams. From there he became Egypt's prime minister before whom his whole family would eventually come to bow just as he had dreamed beforehand. You may find that many years may pass before you see the fulfilment of a promise from God. Though the vision tarries wait for it to come to pass. He will bless you far beyond your expectations.

Today's readings:
Genesis 18:1-12,37:5 -10; 37:23; 41:41; Psalm 107:17-19
Habakkuk 2:3; 1 Peter 1:6-7

August 18
The Woman With The Issue

She was sick for 12 long years. Her body hemorrhaged every day. She was shunned and called unclean. She had gone to every doctor. They took her money but couldn't fix her problem. Finally, she heard Jesus would be passing through the area. She told herself if she could just touch the hem of his garment she would be healed. Despite her shame, her rejection, her uncleanness she made her way through the crowd that had gathered to see Him. She was broken financially and in spirit. She knew He was her only answer. She persevered and pressed until she touched His hem. Immediately the bleeding stopped. This woman taught a valuable lesson. She overlooked the insults and rejection of others to step out in faith. When they told her she was unclean she did not accept it as her final estate. She told herself if she did what she could, God would do the rest. She convinced herself not to let their view of her define her destiny. What you tell yourself is more important than anything others have to say to you or about you. Despite whether others think you belong, always listen to what God's Word says instead.

Today's readings:
Leviticus 15;19; 20:18; Ezekiel 36:17
Matthew 9:20, 11:28, 14:36; Mark 6:56

August 19
Naaman's Slave Girl

She was just a girl. She had no say in her circumstances. Having been captured in war, she was a slave serving the wife of Naaman. He had garnered the respect of his master as a great and honorable man because by him the Lord had given victory to Syria. He was a man of power and influence. Yet, she was just the opposite. She was a Jewish girl living under his roof. She had no power; but she had something he didn't have. She had a relationship with God. She knew if Naaman could make his way to the prophet Elisha, he could be healed. She approached this powerful man to tell him about her Great and Mighty God. She spoke the truth to power. Her boldness was based on her relationship with God and her confidence in Him. She demonstrated what you can do as well. When you have truth, and God impresses upon your heart to make it known to those in authority in your life, you can respectfully approach them with the information you have. After praying for guidance from God, you can humbly appeal to them to hear you and consider the wisdom you have to offer. Your faith is your calling card.

Today's readings:
2 Kings 5:1-14; Nehemiah 1:11, 2:1-3

August 20
Hannah

Hannah wanted a child, but she was barren. Barrenness can leave you feeling inadequate and empty. Is there an area in your life that feels like you cannot meet the standard that others seem to be able to accomplish? What God has for you shall come to pass. What do you do in the meantime? Hannah gives the example: she went to the house of God and prayed. She was praying so intensely in the temple that the prophet Eli saw her lips moving and assumed she was drunk. She assured him she was not. Rather, she was beseeching God. She felt so bad about her circumstances she wouldn't eat. Like Hannah, you could reach a point where you do not have an appetite but let me encourage you to eat anyway. Your body is God's temple. It needs the fuel of food to be able to carry out God's will for your life. Eli prophesied God would answer Hannah, and He did. Her first son was born, and she named him Samuel. His name means "heard by God". Samuel came to be because of his mother's intercession. When you are facing a problem take it to the Lord in prayer. He will hear you and answer your prayers.

Today's readings:
1 Samuel 1:1-18; Matthew 21:22; 2 Corinthians 10:12
1 Thessalonians 5:17; James 4:2,5:16b

August 21
The Woman Caught In Adultery

They used her as a pawn to try to trap Jesus. They
figured He would say something that would not align
with God's Word. Surely, He would not pass the test
when the Pharisees brought Him a woman who had been
caught in the act of adultery. According to the law she
should have been stoned to death. Jesus did not
respond, initially. He bent down and wrote something on
the ground. Then He stood and said, "Let anyone among
you who is without sin be the first to throw a stone."
Then He bent down and resumed writing. When He
looked up again, they were all gone. She stood there
ashamed and embarrassed by her sin. She knew she
deserved to be punished. She did not make excuses. She
humbly stood there knowing her guilt. Jesus asked her if
anyone was there to condemn her. She recognized there
was not, and He told her He did not condemn her either.
She gratefully walked away when He said, "Go and sin no
more." When you are dead wrong, rather than pridefully
excuse your behavior, humble yourself. He is faithful to
forgive and cleanse you without any condemnation.

Today's readings:
Psalm 66:18; Proverbs 28:9; Isaiah 59:2; John 8:1-11
Romans 8:1; 1 John 1:8-10

August 22
The Syrophoenician woman

Someone who was told "you don't take the children's bread and throw it to the dogs" could have chosen to take offense and missed their blessings. People pull away from the things of God for things which seem relatively small while others have wounds that cut deep. They leave with church hurt. Fortunately, this sister didn't allow her feelings to get in the way of God's favor. Her faith catapulted her into the annals of biblical history. She approached Jesus to ask Him to deliver her daughter who was demon-possessed. He had come to minister to the Jews. The long-term plan of God was for the gospel to expand into the gentile communities once the gospel had been preached to His chosen people. Yet, her faith was so bold she moved Jesus to answer her prayer. Because she didn't allow an offense to take root, her daughter was delivered. You can miss out on a lot of opportunities and blessings by allowing an offense to get in the way of God's move in your life. Choose to overlook an offense as she did. Press past your emotions to follow God, no matter what anyone else says or does.

Today's readings:
Proverbs 17:9, 19:11; Matthew 6:15; Mark 7:24-30
Romans 16:17; 1 Peter 4:8

August 23
The Woman At The Well

At that time, Jews did not associate with Samaritans. But Jesus went out of His way to reach her. He told His disciples He needed to go to Samaria, though it was miles outside of His route. By the time the woman showed up the day was half spent. Yet, Jesus waited for her. He will go out of His way and wait for you too, even when you have strayed outside of His will. She was astonished that He was speaking to her. She told Him about how her ancestors worshipped on the mountain even though the Jews said they needed to worship in Israel for it to be acceptable. Jesus made it plain that it wasn't about the "where" but the "how" of our worship that counts. He told the woman all her business including her sin, and yet He still offered her the eternal, life-quenching water of the Holy Spirit. She ran to tell everyone and didn't hesitate to acknowledge that He knew about her indiscreet lifestyle. It was her testimony. It was the bait she used to hook the fish. She didn't allow her past to make her ashamed. She won many to Christ. Whoever wins souls is wise.

Today's readings:
Psalm 139:1-4; Proverbs 11:30; John 4:4-26
Hebrews 4:13

August 24
Widow With Two Mites

Jesus sat by the door watching the deposits being placed
in the offering. He noted how the rich people who gave
large sums at the temple did not give as much as the
widow who gave only two copper coins. The rich were
able to give without it being a problem, whereas the
widow gave out of her own need. Her gift was sacrificial,
and it got God's attention. The story of this widow
woman challenges you to examine your own heart. See if
in fact you have demonstrated a willingness to support
the work of the Kingdom of God. Thanks be to God we
are not condemned for not giving. But like her we can
experience God's admiration as we prayerfully share out
of our resources to advance His Kingdom. God has
promised when you give it will be given back to you:
good measure, pressed down, shaken together, and
running over as He causes others to pour into your life.
It reflects the precept that you experience the promises
of God with the same measure that you apply the
principles of God. Whoever sows sparingly reaps
sparingly and whoever sows generously also reaps
generously. She is a testament to this truth.

Today's readings:
Mark 12:41-44; Luke 6:38, 21:1-4
2 Corinthians 8:12-14 9:6-11; James 2:5

August 25
The Widow Of Nain

In the time of Jesus' ministry, it was not easy for a widow to survive without aid. This widow faced the double challenge of surviving without her husband and her son. As she was preparing to bury him, the pain of her loss was palpable. Jesus was in Capernaum. He encountered a group of Jewish elders who came on behalf of a Roman centurion soldier. They pleaded with Him to come and heal the man's son. He began to walk towards the officer's house but before he could get there the officer sent another group to tell Him he didn't need to come. He knew all He needed was a word from the Lord for his son to be healed. Meanwhile, the widow was preparing to bury her son. As the funeral procession was making its way through the streets of Nain, Jesus showed up, touched the coffin, and raised her son from the dead. The fact that He timed His arrival to perfectly coincide with the exact place where this weeping widow would be passing by, lets you know God has His eye on you. Like this hopeless woman, He knows your despair and your needs. He will always show up at just the right time.

Today's readings:
Lamentations 3:32; Luke 7:11-17; Romans 5:6
Philippians 4;19; Hebrews 4:14-16

August 26
The Sinful Woman

The truth is that we do not know who this woman was for sure. What we do know for certain is that a sinful woman wiped the feet of Jesus with not only her hair but her tears. She wept as she poured expensive oil on His feet. His host watched, thinking if Jesus had known who she was He wouldn't have allowed her to touch Him. Yet, He did know. Jesus told a story of how when you have a substantial impact on someone's life, they usually have a much greater appreciation and devotion to you for all you have done for them. On the other hand, if someone has only experienced your sacrifices and grace on a smaller scale, they wouldn't typically be as devoted. Those who were familiar with this woman were obviously aware of her sinful behavior. She is a model of all who come to know Jesus as their Savior. He accepts all sinners. Maybe like her, you are so grateful for His redeeming love and grace it has brought you to tears. As Jesus noted, when a person who has been forgiven of much, they love Him much. How about you?

Today's readings:
Matthew 26:6-13; Mark 14:1-9; Luke 7:38-50
John 11:2, 12:1-11; 1 Corinthians 15:9-10

August 27
Pilate's Wife

Claudia came from a highly connected family. She learned of the late-night trial of Jesus that lasted into the wee hours of the morning. She did not rest well that night. When the Lord was brought to her husband to be incarcerated, she was uneasy. She sent Pilate a note while he was interrogating Jesus that morning. She told of her dream that bothered her so much. She risked being out of order by interrupting her husband's official duties. Yet, she was compelled to speak. She let him know the dream she'd had was so disturbing she did not have any peace. She told him to let The Lord go. Pilate tried to encourage the crowd by letting one prisoner go, but instead of Jesus they demanded Barabbas be released. Claudia was obviously very sensitive to the things of God. When you have a relationship with God He will speak to your spirit, sometimes in the wee hours while you sleep. What grieves His spirit will grieve yours, as well. He will show you what is to come. Like Pilate's wife, keep your ears and heart focused on the Lord. As He leads you, speak what the Lord has spoken to you.

Today's readings:
Deuteronomy 13:1—3; Job 33:14-15; Jeremiah 23:28
Joel 2:28; Matthew 27:15-23; John 16:12-15

August 28
Elizabeth

She was of the line of the patriarch Aaron. She had
grown old and had always desired a son. But with each
passing decade her hopes for conceiving were looking
more and more unlikely. She could have grown bitter
and no longer worshipped God. Yet, scripture described
her as righteous. When the angel visited her husband
Zacharias to foretell their son's birth, he told him his
prayers had been heard. Though she was elderly, she
conceived and gave birth to John the Baptist. She did not
abort her mission, as some are in the habit of doing.
Instead, she carried him and nurtured him. Beyond
merely giving birth to the person Jesus proclaimed as the
greatest man who had ever lived up to the His coming to
earth, she honored the directions of the angel Gabriel
that she would be pregnant with a child whose hair
would never be cut and who would never drink wine. He
lived to baptize the Savior and to tell the world of His
coming. Her steadfastness in her faith, her sacrifice and
endurance, her obedience to the word of the Lord to
train up her son in the way he was called to go are
exemplary attributes you would do well to emulate.

Today's readings:
Isaiah 40:3; Malachi 3:1; Matthew 3:1,11:11,14:1-11,17:13
John 1:19-26

August 29
God's But

One of the most fascinating truths about the Word of God is the power of God's but. He allows you to see how His but can and will make a difference in the lives of those who know Him. There are numerous examples throughout the Bible. A man's heart plans his way, but the Lord directs his steps. You do not have to be overtaken by evil when people come against you, but you can overcome evil with good. Joseph was hated by his brothers and even sold him into slavery, but God was with him. So too, you may have many weapons formed against you, but none of them will prosper. When you heard the words of truth you were dead in your sins, but God has made you alive in Christ because of His great love for you. We were all still sinners, but God demonstrated His love for us by sending His only begotten Son to die for our transgressions. Though they found no cause for his treatment, they crucified Him, but God raised Him from the dead. Your flesh and your heart may fail; *But God* is the strength of your heart and your portion forever. You may have many afflictions, but the Lord will deliver you out of them all.

Today's readings:
Genesis 50:20; Psalm 34:19; Acts 7:9, 13:28-30
Romans 5:8, 12:21; 1 Corinthians 3:6

August 30
Grumbling

If hallelujah is the highest praise for God, then grumbling must be the lowest form of expression of displeasure with God. When you grumble you are throwing shade on God. You are indirectly saying His provision is not good enough. You are expressing your displeasure with the state of your life. When you are pleased with God's provision, you shout out hallelujah. You tell others of how good He is. But when you aren't happy with the state of your affairs, and you grumble, you are indirectly telling God of your displeasure. It is like somebody saying a snide remark alluding to something concerning you, but they are not bold enough to say it directly to your face. Even when you complain about the way you are treated by others, you are ultimately complaining about God. Observing the way He responded to the Israelites when they grumbled in the desert will help you see how God feels about your complaints. Instead of murmuring, choose to maintain a grateful attitude. Nothing can happen in your life unless He allows it; and one way or another whatever you are going through is working for your good.

Today's readings:
Exodus 16:8; Numbers 11:1-3; John 6;42-43
1 Corinthians 10:9-10; Philippians 2:14-16

August 31
For This Reason

Ephesians is one of the epistles Paul penned from prison. Chapter three is an extremely important treatise on the status of every non-Jewish believer. His explanation of our inclusion into the family of those redeemed by the blood of the Lamb is a truth every believer needs to understand. This profound truth upended the prior revelation of how God related to mankind. He started by revealing Himself to the Jewish nation. His covenant with them was not directed to gentiles. We learn gentiles are no longer alienated but are a part of His family. He now reveals his manifold wisdom to the principalities to demonstrate His profound love and mercy towards us. We now have access to God. We have boldness with confidence in Him. We now belong to God. Because of these truths, like Paul, I can now bow my knees to God and pray with the assurance God hears my cries. For this reason, I not only believe He hears me, but I also believe as I pray in alignment with His will, I can be confident I have what I have asked of Him. For this reason, I can expect to receive exceedingly abundantly above all I ask or think, according to the power that works in me.

Today's readings:
Ephesians 3

September 1
One Thought Can Change Your Life

One thought can change your fortunes and the world.
What you think about is the seed to your actions. There
is nothing you've ever done without first thinking about
it, even if the thought was only momentary. God thought
about the creation of heaven and earth. Samson thought
about reaching the pillars in the coliseum, where the
Philistines had taken him after gouging out his eyes, and
he killed more in his death than he had in his lifetime.
The woman with the issue of blood thought if she could
just touch the hem of Jesus' garment, she would be made
whole. Bill Gates and Steve Jobs both thought they could
build personal computers. I thought I could write a daily
devotional. Whatever you think about, you can achieve.
Set your mind on Biblical truth and live to please God.
Do not set your mind on satisfying your flesh unless you
want an ungodly lifestyle. Keep your mind refreshed in
the Word. Choose wisely what you think about because
your life depends on it.

Today's Reading:
Proverbs 16:3, 23:7; Matthew 9:2; Romans 5:5-8
Ephesians 4:23; Philippians 4:8

September 2
An Issue Of The Heart

Your heart tells everything about you. People tend to look at your outward being. But God looks at your heart. From your heart your mouth speaks. Good things come from your mouth when you have a pure heart. On the other hand, if you allow your heart to be steeped in bitterness your words will destroy. Oft times pain is the source of the things you speak when your heart is filled with bitterness. Ask God to heal your heart when this is so because you will give an account to Him for every word that comes from your mouth. Since your heart is the wellspring that you draw from to speak, it is imperative to guard your heart. The Lord will help you, when you pour out your prayers and petitions with thanksgiving, He will guard your heart. Pay attention to what you allow in your ear-gates and eye-gates. Trust the Lord with all your heart and He will direct your path.

Today's Reading:
1 Samuel 16:7; Proverbs 3:5, 4:23; Matthew 6:21, 12:36
Luke 6:46; Romans 5:5

September 3
You Don't Have Many Fathers

God allows us to have spiritual relationships through which we are bought into or developed as members of His Kingdom. He uses those connections to speak to us. Paul's admonition tells us that while you may encounter many instructors, few are those who are called to father (or mother) you in the things of God. They are not only used by God for you to be born but they also help you to identify your purpose and to mature in your walk as a Christian. You are to imitate them. Their words should carry great weight in your life. Paul not only instructed his spiritual son Timothy in the ways of ministry, but he also guided him in his choices for where he served and utilized his gifts. As you make life choices seek the wisdom of those God has created to serve you as spiritual guides. These Divine connections in your life are created by God and should be treated accordingly.

Today's Reading:
1 Corinthians 4:14-16

September 4
Stand In Your Authority

One of the greatest challenges to your walk in Christ is temptation to sin. Sin will kill your witness and stifle your ability to fulfill your purpose. You may be inclined to blame the devil for the inclination you have to do what is contrary to God's will. But it's not the devil. It is you exercising your will. As a child of God you have power over all the works of the enemy. The Holy Spirit lives in you. He empowers you to resist the devil. When you submit to God and resist the devil, he will flee. What then causes you to falter? Your desires are the culprit. If you are yearning for a thing, person or whatever it may be that draws you away from living holy, you choose to give in to that yearning. You can also choose not to do so. Temptation is rooted in your own desires. What tempts you may not tempt someone else unless they share the same desire. You don't have to give into that desire. You have power over your flesh because the fruit of the Spirit is self-control. Walk in your authority to live righteously.

Today's Reading:
Matthew 26:41; 1 Corinthians 10:13; Galatians 5:22
James 1:12-15,4:7; 1 Timothy 6:9

246

September 5
The Invisible Reality

Some don't believe God exists because they cannot see Him. But as surely as the wind blows and you cannot see it, trust me, there is a God who is Sovereign over all. There are some things you simply cannot comprehend or see with your natural mind. You must be born again. Unless you are born of the Spirit of God you cannot see things from His standpoint. You could be surrounded by a move of God and not know it even if you tripped over it. You have no natural capacity to fully grasp spiritual truth. It must be interpreted through a mind renewed by the Spirit of the Living God. And even when you are born again, much like a car that needs a tune up or a steering column that needs a realignment, your mind needs to constantly be renewed by His Word. Otherwise, the world can draw your course. Keeping your mind saturated with the things of God is the only way to ensure your vision can stay aligned with His.

Today's Reading:
Colossians 1:15; John 3:1-3; Romans 12:1,2
1 Corinthians 2:14-15

September 6
Be Encouraged

Your life may be full of challenges. You may be facing difficult situations. Your family may be in turmoil. Your loved one may be sick. Your money may be funny - it's low while your bills are high. Your demands may feel as though they outweigh your energy level. Whatever the case nevertheless tell yourself, "Better days are coming". Remind yourself you can make it. This too will pass. Be like my spiritual daughter laying in a hospital feeling too weak to lift herself, who got up and walked anyway after telling herself, "I can do all things through Christ who strengthens me." God has promised even when you pass through the waters, He will be with you and they will not overtake you. Even when you walk through the fire, you will not be burned. Be encouraged knowing that the Lord your God is with you no matter what.

Today's Reading:
Deuteronomy 31:6-8; Joshua 1:9; Jeremiah 29:11
Isaiah 40:31, 43:2; Psalm 42:11
2 Corinthians 13:11

September 7
Not A Hint

The oldest trick of the enemy is to lure you away from your purpose through your own desires. We all have desires. You can allow them to lead you astray if you're not careful. On any given day you may hear of someone who got caught in a compromising situation because they started longing for something that wasn't of God. Lots of great leaders have lost their positions of power because they allowed themselves to be led by their desires instead heeding God's wisdom. Make sure you guard your heart. Set up parameters to protect yourself. Keep some accountability partners in your life. Avoid circumstances that give off even a hint of sexual immorality, or any other thing that takes you outside of the will of God in any area of your life.

Today's Reading:
Genesis 3:1-6; Judges 16:1,6; 1 Corinthians 6:18-20

September 8
Agape Love Isn't An Emotion

If you fall in love, you are euphoric and giddy. Everything is lovely. Your love for the other person blinds you to their faults. Eventually the euphoria wears off and you start to notice everything they do that you don't like. You can no longer go by your feelings of love to love them. If you encounter someone who is unkind to you or others, you may see them as unworthy of your love. Or, if there is someone in your circle who does something that hurts you, you may not feel like being loving towards them. In each of these instances you have to choose to love the other person in spite of how you feel. God is love. His command is that we love each other. Feelings don't have anything to do with it. Love is a choice. When you choose to love regardless of the feelings you have, the feelings you have will usually change. They will follow your will to imitate God and love unconditionally.

Today's Reading:
John 13:34-35; Romans 5:5; 1 Corinthians 13:1
Ephesians 4:32; 1 John 3:16, 4:7-8,11

September 9
Rejoice In The Lord Always!

This is the day the Lord has made. Let's rejoice and be glad in it! Joy (a feeling of great pleasure and happiness) is medicinal. It's like penicillin for your soul. The palmist is telling us to choose to be joyful. Think of yourself in a store shopping for a dress or some pants. You could pick black, brown, yellow, red or any other color. Likewise, you can choose to rejoice. You can intentionally focus on what brings you joy. Being attentive to the beauty of God's creation like the breathtaking sunsets, moonlight, birds, or the ocean can soothe your soul and cause you to feel joyful. Or you can take the time to think on how much God has blessed you. The most obvious source of joy is God's Word. Flooding your soul with scripture saturates you in the Word and stirs up your spirit. The fruit of the Spirit is joy! The joy of the Lord is your strength - grace sufficient for any trials you may endure. It will give you the fortitude to get through anything. Rejoice in the Lord always! Again, I say rejoice!

Today's Reading:
Nehemiah 8:10; Psalm 16:11, 118:24; Romans 14:7
2 Corinthians 12:9; Philippians 4:4; 1 Thessalonians 5:16

September 10
By And By

There is an old saying that says, hindsight is 20-20. I can imagine how Jesus' parents must have felt when He was twelve years old. They had gone up to Jerusalem for the annual Passover feast. When it was over and time for them to return home, He was nowhere to be found. They were looking among their relatives, but no one had seen Him. It was like an ancient version of the movie "Home Alone." They had traveled for a whole day before realizing He wasn't with them. They went back to Jerusalem where it took them three more days to find Him. He was in the temple sitting among the Biblical scholars. They were astonished at His wisdom as He conversed with them and asked them questions. When His parents approached Him, Jesus asked them why they were seeking Him. He expected them to know He had to be about His Father's business. But they did not understand. In your life you may have experiences you simply do not understand. You may be confounded by the things the Lord allows to occur or seemingly leads you to but in the fullness of time, as He told Peter, you will understand it better by and by.

Today's readings:
Proverbs 3:5-6; Matthew 15:16-20; Luke 2:42-50
John 13:4-7, 14:5

September 11
No Looking Back

No matter what has happened in your past, you can choose to move on and not be bogged down with guilt or condemnation. If you repented of your shortcomings, then God has forgiven you. If your heart is aching, God will heal you. He is close to those whose hearts are broken. If you have suffered financial loss, rest in knowing that God can restore just like He did for Job when he lost everything. God can bring favor into your life and bless you with even more than you lost. However, if you stay focused on the past instead of what is before you, it will hinder those blessings. Leave the past in the past and embrace what God is doing in your life today. Decide to forget about what is behind you and press forward in the Lord. When we hold on to the past, we aren't postured to receive what God has for us right now. Lot's wife learned this the hard way when she looked back, perhaps longing for her past, only to be turned into a pillar of salt. Looking back can cause you to get stuck. Make up your mind to focus on the gift of today, the present. Decide there is no more looking back. Walk forward into the blessings God has for you.

Today's readings:
Genesis 19:17-28; Job 32:12; Psalm 34:18; Romans 8:1
Philippians 3:12-14

September 12
Worshippers Wanted!

What if you saw a sign posted that said, "worshippers wanted?" In a sense this is what is posted in the spiritual realm. God is seeking worshippers who will worship Him in spirit and in truth. He wants you to be born of His Spirit. He is longing for people who walk in truth to worship Him. In its ultimate expression, worship is to give worth to Him. When you give the highest worth you demonstrate it by loving Him. God is not the only one seeking worshippers. The devil is too. That is why when Jesus was weak from 40 days of fasting, the devil came to Him and offered Him the entire world if He would just bow down and worship him. As Jesus replied, only the Father should be worshipped. The battle for mankind's devotion has been going on since the beginning in the garden of Eden and continues to this day. What God desires of you is a commitment to truth. And the truth is there is no one greater than Him. You should have nothing more esteemed in your life than God, maker of heaven and earth. Worship Him and Him only.

Today's readings:
Genesis 3:1-5; Daniel 3:5-10; Psalm 95:6
Matthew 4:1-10; John 4:23-24,17:17; Romans 12:1

September 13
The Name

People have sung about it, talked about it and prayed with it. It has been used in expletives, banned from usage, and even yelled out in crisis. It has been disparaged and revered. It has been the basis of debates and dissention. It has served as a unifying force. Many have come to know there is something about the name Jesus. Demons tremble at the sound of it. Wars have been fought over it. Salvation can be found in no other name but it. If you ask God, the Father, anything in the name of Jesus your petitions will be granted. Why is this name so important? Jesus is the name of the Son of God. His name embodies all that is God. All the fullness of the Godhead is represented by it. What exactly does it mean? Jesus means, Jehovah is salvation. So, every time you call His name you declare the true and living God is the Savior of the world. It is no wonder the devil has done everything to keep the Name from being spoken. You declare the devil's defeat every time you say His Name. You remind the devil, and everyone in the world, His Name is above every name.

Today's readings:
Isaiah 9:6; Matthew 28:19; Luke 1:31; John 14:13
Acts 4:12,19:5; Romans 10:9; Philippians 2:9
Colossians 2:9, 3:17

September 14
Silence

Is what Shrek told Donkey, "You have the right to remain silent, what you lack is the capacity," also true of you? There are times when the best answer is no answer at all. According to scripture, you should be quick to listen and slow to speak. The mere fact that you have 2 ears and 1 mouth suggests God prefers you to do more listening than speaking. When you are quiet, you can soak in all that transpires or is said around you. You can hear the whisper of the Lord. When you go to God in prayer, it should not be merely dropping off your desires. It should be a time to both share your heart *and hear* His. Sometimes the Lord will wake you up early in the morning to talk to you. When the prophet Habakkuk spoke of the Lord being in His holy temple, he exhorted the entire earth to be silent. Slowdown from your busyness. Be still and know that He is God. Sometimes the best answer you can give is no answer at all, but simply to be quiet, listen and let God speak to your heart directly, through His word, or through the dreams and visions He gives. Be still before the Lord and listen.

Today's readings:
1 Kings 19:9-18; Psalm 46:1; Isaiah 18:4
Habakkuk 2:20; Mark 1:35; James 1:19

September 15
He Gets You

Jesus wept is only 2 words, yet the implication is profound. Jesus, the Son of God, was crying. What could possibly move God to cry? We might have expected it in the garden of Gethsemane where He was sweating drops of blood because of the weight of His impending crucifixion. It wasn't then. Perhaps it would have been understandable for Him to weep when His cousin, John the Baptist, was beheaded by Herod. But that is not when scripture states He cried, either. His tears came when He saw Mary mourning for her brother Lazarus. Even though He knew He was about to raise him from the dead, He took time to empathize with Mary. He felt her hurting heart. It's such a blessing to serve a Savior God who can not only intervene in your circumstances but also cares about you and what you're going through. He walked the earth. He was tempted in every way. Yet was without sin. Consequently, He can sympathize with your weaknesses and understand your struggles. Jesus sees. He understands. He feels. He cares. Jesus hurts when you hurt. Jesus gets you!

Today's readings:
Isaiah 53:5, 63:9; John 11:35, 15:13
Hebrews 4:14-16; 1 Peter 5:7

September 16
A Word In Season

Saying something is one thing. Saying the right thing is still another thing. Saying the right thing at the right time is the best thing. A word in season comes from sharing what the Lord would have you to say in that moment. Listen for His guidance and don't speak out of turn. Isaiah said, "The Lord God has given me the tongue of the learned, that I should know how to speak a word in season." A word in season will edify and speak life to someone, or it may also be used to speak a word of correction or rebuke to someone. It is what Paul alluded to when he told Timothy to be ready in season and out of season to convince, rebuke, or exhort with patience. When it is "in season", it is the right time. Whenever you speak, your words should be flavored with the Word of God. Rather than being hasty to speak, you would do better to listen for Holy Spirit to guide you. The Lord will put the words in your mouth. He will also hinder you from speaking if that is His will. Whenever you are unsure, ask Him. He will give you the right words to say and the right time to say them.

Today's readings:
2 Samuel 23:2; Job 32:18; Psalm 12:6
Proverbs 12:25, 15:23, 25:11, 29:11,20; Isaiah 50:4
Acts 16:6; James 3:2 2 Timothy 4:2

September 17
Knowing What To Do

Just as it is important to know what to say, it is equally important to know what to do and when to do it. Timing is everything. Imagine a person having a heart attack, and someone calls 911. What if the first responders only showed up hours later? The person who suffered the attack could be dead. And the one who placed the call would probably be irate and feel undervalued. Doing the right thing but doing it too late is unhelpful. Scripture makes it plain: If you know the right thing to do and don't do it, you sin. Delayed obedience is really disobedience. But what about the times you don't know what to do? What do you do during those times when you don't know which direction is best? Seek counsel from those who have a relationship with God. Never seek direction from the ungodly. That is like the blind leading the blind. Both of you could fall into a ditch. You can also ask God for yourself. He said He will give wisdom to anyone who asks. Then you can be like "the sons of Issachar who had understanding of the times, to know what Israel ought to do."

Today's readings:
1 Chronicles 12:32; 2 Chronicles 20:12; Psalm 1:1
Proverbs 1:5, 4:19; Matthew 15:14; John 15:15
Romans 7:15-16, 8:26-27; James 1:5, 4:17

September 18
Purposeful Pain

There will be times when you create hardships for yourself. Like the saying, "a hard head makes a soft bottom", the truth is you can make your life more difficult by doing things contrary to the Word of God. Still, there are other times when God will allow challenges in your life to glorify Himself and show you who He really is. When Jesus encountered a man born blind, His disciples asked whether he or his parents had sinned. Jesus informed them neither the man nor his parents had sinned. He had been born blind so that God could demonstrate His great power and be glorified. Jesus spat, took some dirt, made some paste, and put it on the man's eyes. Then He told the man to go wash in the pool of Siloam. Immediately his blindness was gone. Once he was able to see, people took him to the synagogue where he was questioned by the religious leaders. They did not approve of the healing taking place on the Sabbath and were trying to discount Jesus. The man told them he did not know whether Jesus was a sinner but this one thing he knew: he once was blind and now he could see. He gave glory to God.

Today's readings:
Genesis 50:15-20; John 9:1-33, 11:4; Romans 5:3, 12:12
Ephesians 3:13; Acts 14:21-22; James 1:2-4

September 19
What Pleases God

My friend, Evangelist Mayhan has a powerful testimony. He tells how he went to Vietnam and came back to the USA strung out on drugs. He lost his family and everything he had. He was struggling when he decided to enter the program at Teen Challenge (an international ministry) where he learned about the things of God. While he was out in the streets living in the fast lane, he would call his wife Phyllis and she would hang up. She did not want to hear what he had to say. But one day he called and told her he had given his life to Christ. Instead of hanging up, she perked up and listened to him. She heard what was pleasing to her. Likewise, we can be confident God will listen to our prayers any time we ask for anything according to His will. Ask for what pleases Him, and He will hear you. If you obey His commands, then you will be pleasing to God. If you pray in agreement with His word, then you will be pleasing Him. If you pray for anything that He has said He wants, you are praying in agreement with His will. As scripture tells us, meditate on Him to understand what pleases God. Then, pray accordingly.

Today's readings:
Deuteronomy 10:12, 13;18; 2 Chronicles 14:2-5
Proverbs 21:3; Isaiah 38:3; 1 John 5:14-15 NLT

September 20
God's Medicine - A Merry Heart

I love it when science confirms what scripture tells us. Numerous scientific studies have proven a merry heart does good, like medicine. Dr. Don Colbert shared some insight from the research. Laughter, he points out, lowers stress hormones and it balances your neurotransmitters. We are a generation that depends on medications in extremely high numbers, so what a blessing to know laughter can help treat depression. In addition, laughter can help control pain. He identified a study showing 10 minutes of laughter was able to control pain up to 2 hours! Dr. Colbert also noted how laughter can boost one's immune system by increasing natural killer cells that fight against cancer and increasing healthy "good" cells. He equates laughter with internal jogging. 10 seconds of laughter is the equivalent of 3 minutes on a rowing machine, according to a study he cited. Consequently, it is also good for your heart and your blood vessels. Remember the comedians Bob Heart, George Burns and Red Skeleton all lived to be 100. So don't worry, be happy. The deeper the laugh, the better. Check out this website: DrDonColbert.com.

Today's readings:
Psalm 51:12; Proverbs 15:13, 15:15, 17:22
Romans 14:17; 15:13; Galatians 5:22

September 21
Party Canceled

I decided to give myself a party of 2; me and God were the only invitees. I set the table with my sorrows. I decorated with the blues and tuned up my violin to play my favorite song for such occasions, "nobody knows the trouble I've seen." Then I was reminded of how little I was really dealing with in the grand scheme of things. By comparison to what I know others are facing, my issues seemed minuscule. I was challenged to remember that Jesus paid the ultimate sacrifice when He suffered for our sins. I realized God was telling me the party was canceled. Perhaps you have been tempted to hold similar events on occasion. Let me share with you why these events are forever banned in the Kingdom of God. Say it out loud: I am accepted, adopted, beloved, blessed, called, chosen, filled with the Holy Spirit, forgiven, graced beyond measure, grounded in love, heaven bound, heir of God, justified, known by God, more than a conqueror, qualified, predestined, purposed, reconciled, redeemed, sealed, the temple of God, and victorious. Record it on your phone. Put it on repeat should you ever forget these truths. Cancel all pity parties.

Today's readings:
Psalm 139:14; Ephesians 1:3-14,17; Colossians 1:12-14
1 Corinthians 6:19-20; Hebrews 13:12

September 22
It's Only A Test

Some people hate taking tests. Yet, it is fair to say if you want to pass a class or receive a certification, the likelihood of you not being tested is very low. God also takes you through tests. His tests are to see how much you apply His word. He tests your heart. Your heart is reflected in the heat of the moments of life. It shows who you really are and what you really believe. When things get difficult, the true you will surface. If you are one who depends on alternatives for coping - like drinking, drugs, complaining - you will turn to those things in your times of trouble. Your integrity or the lack thereof will shine through in the furnaces of life. Like a silversmith who heats up silver to such a high degree that the dross (the impurities) began to fall away, so God allows life circumstances to turn up to burn away the fleshly ways in your life. The silversmith knows how high the flame can be without ruining the silver. Likewise, God knows exactly how much you can bear. A silversmith was asked how he knows the silver is ready. He responded, "That is easy. I know it is ready when I can see myself." Likewise, God desires you to look just like Him.

Today's readings:
Psalm 7:9,11:5; 66:10: Proverbs 17:3; Jeremiah 17:10
Romans 5:3; 1 Thessalonians 2:4; James 1:2-4

September 23
Stay Full

One of the ways you continue to walk the talk you profess in Christ Jesus is to stay filled with the Holy Spirit. When you are filled with the Spirit of God, you are full of the fruit of righteousness. Just like being in a swimming pool will automatically cause you to be wet, you don't have to try to produce the fruit, it is the spiritual consequence of being filled with the Spirit. Likewise, when you are in a pool, your focus is on swimming. You do not focus on the fact that your skin is in water. You intuitively know that is normal. As you learn to walk in the Spirit, you begin to see the fruit as a regular part of how you live. You see goodness, for example, as a part of who you are. On the contrary, when you are filled with self you aren't concerned about pleasing God. Being full of yourself comes naturally. Being filled with the Spirit comes as you intentionally keep your heart focused on God and being engaged in activities that glorify Him, such as praying, attending church services and Bible study, and meditating on scripture. Let Him use you to tell others about Him. Yield to the leading of His Spirit as you live your life.

Today's readings:
Exodus 31:3 ,25:31; Proverbs 14:14; Luke 1:67, 4:1
Acts 1:4,13; Ephesians 3:14-21, 5:18

September 24
A Mother's Heart

Giving birth is a unique calling God has given only to
women. Along with this calling, He gave mothers an
innate desire to see their children grow and prosper. We
see this demonstrated in scripture when 2 women gave
birth to sons on the same day. One of them
unintentionally killed her child then switched her son
with another mother's living son, while his mother slept.
But the mother was not fooled. She realized the dead
child was not hers. She went to King Solomon seeking
justice. The king proposed to cut the child in half and
share him between the 2 women. The real mother had
compassion on her son and told the King to give the baby
to the other woman rather than see him harmed. The
imposter, on the other hand, declared the arrangement
to split him in half was acceptable to her. The King
immediately ordered the baby be given to the first
woman because he knew a healthy mother's heart would
never choose to see harm done to her child. Honor your
mother it is the first commandment with a promise. God
has promised to give you long life and blessings for
honoring the vessel He chose to bring you into the world.

Today's readings:
Exodus 20:12; 1 Kings 3:16-26; Psalm 27:10
Proverbs 1:8; John 16:21, 19:26; 1 Thessalonians 2:7

September 25
After The First Steps Of Faith

When Joshua succeeded Moses as the leader of God's people, He heard from the Lord to lead the people across the Jordan. Like Moses when he reached the Red Sea, he had to trust God for the waters to recede. The difference was he had to take the first steps while the water was still standing. They had to walk by faith and not by sight. They followed the priests who carried the Ark of the Covenant, representing God's presence. As the priest went forward, God caused the waters to be cut off. This enabled the priests who bore the Ark of the Covenant of the Lord to stand firm on dry ground until all of Israel were able to completely cross over the Jordan. Notice how the water did not dry up until they moved forward. Sometimes, you are waiting for God to move in your situation while God is waiting on you to demonstrate your faith in Him and His word. When God gives you an assignment or leads you in making a decision, you will not necessarily see all of His provision for every step of the journey when you begin. You must trust in God to make a way where you see no way.

Today's readings:
Joshua 3:13-17; Psalm 26:1; Isaiah 40:32, 50:10
2 Corinthians 5:7; Hebrews 11:29

September 26
Tell The Truth

I love this commercial where the couple is disputing about who forgot to bring the life jackets. The woman says the man agreed to bring them. He says she did. He pulls out his challenge flag and throws it on the ground. The replay shows him say he would "never forget" to bring the life jackets. I laughed as I thought about how it would be great to have this ability to get an instant replay on the things people have said. Disputes often have 3 versions: your version, their version, and the truth. Sadly, as you age your memory can fade and you can easily forget things. But all too often, the truth is purposely ignored. People lie. When you lie you call into question your ability to be trusted. If you lie, you discount your witness as a believer. Why would someone believe what you say about faith in God, if they know you are lying about things of lesser importance? In the prophet Isaiah's day, the land was filled with people telling lies. It sounds much like James' description of the last and evil days. Lies displease God so much so that He included this in the 10 commandments. In falsehoods there is darkness. And in Him there is no darkness at all. Tell the truth.

Today's readings:
Isaiah 59:2-4,8-15; Ephesians 4:25; 1 Timothy 4:1-2

September 27
An Apt Reply

When Jesus taught His disciples about the things which would occur after His ascension, He told them they would have to testify before people in authority. He also told them not to worry about what they should say. The Holy Spirit would tell them what to say when they needed to say it. When you stay sensitive to the Holy Spirit's leading, He will also tell you what to say. Keeping your mind renewed in His Word, spending time with Him in prayer, and meditating on how He has spoken in the past helps to keep your heart sensitive to His guidance. Isaiah declared God had equipped him to know how to speak a word in season to those who are weary. Consequently, you can also have an apt word for those you encounter as you spend time with God. Sometimes you may find yourself at a loss for words. There is a time to simply be quiet and there is a time to speak. Avoid saying things that are just meaningless, idle words. The best approach is to only say what you sense God would want you to say.

Today's readings:
Proverbs 18:21; Ecclesiastes 3:1,7
Isaiah 50:4; Matthew 12:34-36

September 28
What You Look For

Your capacity to frame your experiences is greater perhaps, than you think. You may be thinking you deal with things as best you can. But scripture suggests it is not that black and white. A critical part of what you experience is based on what you are looking for. What you expect can greatly impact what you get. The Bible says, seek in order to find. When you seek God with all of your heart, for example, you will find Him. When you earnestly seek God's divine intervention, you will obtain His presence in a palpable way. Similarly, you can predispose yourself to negativity. If you are looking for evil, seeking the negative, you will find it. Your mind will expect it. Once you have begun to always think the worst is going to happen, you will begin to see the worst in every situation. Of course, in life things will happen that aren't pleasant. But you can still choose to focus on whatever is good in every circumstance. Speak life. Look for and expect to see the goodness of the Lord in all circumstances.

Today's readings:
Psalm 24:14, 119:45, 122:9; Proverbs 11:27, 17:9
Isaiah 8:19; Jeremiah 29:13; Matthew 6:31, 7:7
2 Corinthians 3:18; Ephesians 3:20; Philippians 4:8

September 29
Jars Of Clay

You are not the main attraction, God is. He is the one empowering you to be able to achieve anything you do. Consequently, wisdom suggests all the glory belongs to Him for everything good you accomplish in your life. You aren't perfect, but you are perfectly suited for what God wants to accomplish through your life. Even with flaws, He can use your shortcomings to be a blessing to someone else. Sometimes, when others can see your flaws, they may tend to try to highlight those weaknesses. It is tool of the enemy to try to make you feel inadequate or, even worse, to feel shame and condemnation. Instead, choose to let the naysayers know you are aware of your imperfections. It gives you even more reason to celebrate God. His capacity to use you with all your flaws is evidence that He is Mighty. He is unlimited. He pours forth His all-surpassing power through jars of clay proving that the power you demonstrate comes from God, not you. And He alone is, therefore, worthy of all the honor, glory and praise!

Today's readings:
Deuteronomy 10:14; Psalm 62:11,150:1-6
Romans 15:15-17; 2 Corinthians 4:7; James 1:17

September 30
The Potter's House

God is the Potter. You are the clay. You are His
workmanship. When you consider how you are shaped,
you may focus on what you deem to be your
imperfections. A potter working with clay, has the
capacity to reshape the work of his hands to form a
better vessel out of something it makes. So too, when you
are born again, the Lord can reshape your character to
conform to the image of His Son. Imagine a piece of clay
being dissatisfied with its shape or purpose and
complaining to the potter. You would think things were
out of order. Likewise, to those who refuse to accept the
way they were made, God said, "Surely you have things
turned around! Shall the potter be esteemed as the clay;
For shall the thing made say of him who made it, 'He did
not make me'? Or shall the thing formed say of him who
formed it, 'He has no understanding'?" You are His
creation. He knew exactly what He was doing when He
shaped you in your mother's womb, and He knows
exactly what to do with you – your purpose in life - as
you yield to His Spirit.

Today's readings:
Isaiah 29:16,52:11,64:8; Jeremiah 18:1-11
Lamentations 4:2; Romans 9:21-23; 2 Corinthians 4:7
1 Thessalonians 4:3-7; 2 Timothy 2:20-21

October 1
Always Be Ready God's Way

You have what the world needs when you know the Word of God. People are hungering for truth. They are seeking to have an authentic relationship with God. That is why you are called of God to be prepared to explain the reason you place your trust in God. The Lord wants you to have your sword of the Spirit, which is the word of God, sharpened and read to be wielded, always. You should be equipped with the gospel of peace - the good news that Jesus is Lord, died for everyone's sin and is offering forgiveness to all. You must not overlook the fact that it is the gospel of peace. God offers peace to all, and as His follower you too should operate in peace. Essentially, it is God's desire for Christians to be able to give an account and defend the gospel, peacefully, with gentleness and respect. As you yield to the Holy Spirit within you, He will emanate His fruit of gentleness. in and through you. Like Paul, you have not been made perfect, so press on towards being who God has called you to be in this season. Study the Word, live up to what you understand, and walk in peace towards all.

Today's readings:
Micah6:8; Matthew5:43-48; 19;19
Romans 1:16,10:14-21,12:18; Philippians 3:13-21
2 Timothy 2:15; 1 Hebrews 12:14; Peter 3:13-16

October 2
Holy Hinderances

God's goal is to see you walking in His will. Consequently, He guides your steps. Sometimes you will encounter delays. When Paul wanted to go to the Romans he was delayed, because God had an assignment for him to preach the gospel in other places. Your delays may be because God desires to use you for His glory. He may have a different assignment that you may not immediately recognize. I recall being scheduled to attend a mini retreat with some girlfriends. I was to arrive on Friday, but I felt a little tug to stay home instead. I found out a friend had undergone a surgical procedure. I picked up her young daughter so that she could come to our house for the night. My girlfriends were disappointed when I arrived a day late, but I explained to them I believed the Lord had given me the assignment to support my other friend. In another instance, Paul told the Thessalonians he had planned to visit, but the devil had hindered him. We may not always understand why the Lord allows interruptions in our plans, but we can rest in knowing that when He does, it will work together, along with everything else in our lives, for our good.

Today's readings:
Psalm 37:23, 119:60; Romans 1:13, 15:15-22
1 Thessalonians 2:18; 1 Timothy 3:14-15; James 4:13-15

October 3
Ambassadors Wanted

God needs you to serve as His ambassador. He wants you to serve as His mouthpiece representing the Kingdom of God. Your assignment is not complicated. You are called to tell the world He knows all about their sins. Though the wages of sin is death, He has made the way so they will not have to pay the penalty for their sins. He died in their place. While sin separates us from God, He is seeking to be reconciled to everyone. He sent His Son to serve as the peace offering between us and Him. Consequently, once you accept Jesus as your Savior God no longer counts your sin against you. Your task is to let all know, everywhere you go, that they too can be forgiven of all their sins forever by acknowledging Jesus as their Lord and Savior. When they admit they have messed up, believe He has risen up from the grave, and surrender themselves to Him, they too will be saved from death. They will spend their eternity with Him in heaven, and they will be blessed to know Him as they journey through life on earth. Share this good news with everyone. Be the ambassador God has called you to be.

Today's readings:
Joshua 1:16; Jeremiah 1:7, 24:4-5
Matthew 10:16, 28:18-20; Romans 3:23,6:23

October 4
No Shame

You are not to be ashamed of the gospel of Jesus Christ. Yet, there are times when others will try to make you feel as though you should be. They may act as though you are undesirable because of your belief in the Lord. You must stand firm in your faith. You have no reason to take on the reproach. To the contrary, you have every reason to rejoice when you are dishonored for your faith. God has promised to bless you. You can avoid the impact of these things as you develop a long-term viewpoint. It is like the stock market, in a sense. Sometimes the Dow will swing so extremely low, people with investments will start selling off their stock. Those who see with an eye on the future will ride the wave. Over time the person who endures through the downward swing will prosper. So too in Christ, in the short run people who reject the Lord may mock you, reject you and even disassociate with you. But rest assured, in the long run you will be rejoicing while they will be put to shame. Blessings on blessings will unfold in your life. In the end, they will only be able to look up and see the glory they have forfeited, while you enjoy eternal paradise.

Today's readings:
Isaiah 54:4-5; 1 Corinthians 1:27; 1 Peter2:6

October 5
Way Maker

When I think of my mom's mantra, I'm reminded the Lord will make a way somehow. When your back is against the wall, you can rest assured God will provide all you need in that situation. For example, when Rachel was unable to conceive a child, she prayed, and God opened her womb. When Solomon was made king at a very young age, he prayed to ask God for wisdom. God was so pleased with Solomon's request, He not only gave him enough wisdom to be known as the wisest man to live. He also gave him enough wealth to make him the richest. I recall many times when God has been a way-maker in my life. One example was when I was practicing law. I was facing a much larger firm and one of the motions came across our fax machine a mere hour before I was due in court. As I was led of the Lord, I reviewed a summary of a new decision a court had just issued which made the perfect defense. I grabbed it and ran to court just in time to prevail. It doesn't matter the situation. God will provide a way when you seek Him and put Him first in your life.

Today's readings:
Genesis 21:1-2, 30:6,22; 2 Chronicles 1:7-12
2 Kings 2:14; Matthew 17:20; Luke 1:37
John 14:6; 1 Corinthians 2:13

October 6
With The Same Measure

One of the questions I was often asked during my 22 years as a chaplain in a woman's prison was about how I could deal with "those people". It was eye-opening to see the response of those who had determined they were better than the people I served. Most of those in the prison came to acknowledge what they did was wrong. It wasn't my place to judge them. I was there to love them. Because of God's grace, He never treats me the way my sins deserve. Therefore, I could treat them in the same manner, with love and respect. I had to overlook the faults I saw in them; the same way God overlooks mine. When I responded to those who couldn't understand why I would work with prisoners, it was clear they could identify faults in others but not themselves. Jesus taught us to deal with our own shortcomings before judging others. He said we have the equivalent of tree branches in our own eyes, trying to pick out the small splinters from others' eyes. It is better to focus on the fault you find when taking a close look in the mirror, than to look across to find it in someone else.

Today's readings:
Matthew 5:46-47; 7:1-5; Mark 4:24; Luke 6:27-42
1 Corinthians 4:7; Galatians 6:1-8; Ephesians 4:32

October 7
Choices

When you go through life you will face choices all the time. God has given you free will and your decisions result in the way you live. People make choices yet blame God. You cannot blame God when someone's ungodly actions result in terrible results. When the people of God were yielding to the influence of those who followed idols, Elijah challenged his listeners to follow the ways of the Lord; to no longer waiver between two opinions. He said they should choose to live one way or the other. And like many today who hear the plea from God to choose His ways, they answered not a word. You can sit quietly by and watch the impact of ungodly choices or speak up for what is right, while also doing what is right. You must choose. Personally, like Joshua, I decree "And if it seems evil to you to serve the Lord, choose for yourselves this day whom you will serve, whether the gods which your fathers served that were on the other side of the River, or the gods of the Amorites, in whose land you dwell. But as for me and my house, we will serve the Lord."

Today's readings:
1 Kings 18:20-21; 1 Chronicles 21:11; Proverbs 1:29-31
Ezekiel 33:1-5; Luke 12:40

October 8
God Or Men

Even though King Saul was directed by God to kill all the Amalekites and to destroy all their property, he came back with choice animals and things that were of value. When the prophet Samuel confronted him, he tried to justify his disobedience by blaming it on the people he was leading. In essence, he wanted to please the people. You are called to please God, not people, even if what you are doing makes you look foolish in the eyes of men. And sometimes this will cause conflicts with others. In the case of the Apostles, after Jesus ascended, they obeyed Him by preaching the gospel. The religious leaders locked them up, but an angel came and set them free. Undeterred they continued to spread the gospel, only to be arrested again. The Apostles explained their disobedience to the command saying, "we ought to obey God rather than man." You may have times when people you are in relationships with, or those who are in authority, will want you to do things that go against the will of God. You must decide if you will please God or men. It is better to please God.

Today's readings:
1 Samuel 15:30; Acts 5:17-29; Romans 8:5-8
1 Corinthians 7:32-34; Galatians 1:10; Colossians 1:10
1 Thessalonians 2:4,4:1-8; Hebrews 11:6,23-27

October 9
When God Heeds A Man's Voice

When Joshua was called of God to lead the Israelites out of the wilderness, he had to lead them to fight for the land they were being given. In one instance, five kings came together to oppose them. In the heat of the battle Joshua spoke to God and God heeded his request by causing the sun and moon to stand still. On another occasion, Elijah confronted the wicked king Ahab and told him it would not rain for 3 years, by his word. And not one of the words of Samuel dropped to the ground. It accomplished what he said it would. What do these all have in common? God heeded their words. God was moved to heed theirs because they heeded His. When God told Joshua to go forward, he went. When He told Elijah to leave town for 3 years, he went. Whatever God told Samuel to do, he did it. You have the power of life and death in your tongue. The power you have to cause God to respond is expounded in proportion to the faith and obedience you exercise. You will see the phenomenal power of God manifested more and more as you apply His Word to your life, accordingly.

Today's readings:
Numbers 22:20; Joshua 10:1-14; 1 Kings 17:1
Proverbs 18:21; Matthew 17:20; Luke 11:2; John 14:10
James 2:18; 1 Thessalonians 2:2

October 10
Living In Peace

Scripture admonishes us repeatedly to be about peace. God will keep you in peace when you keep your mind stayed on Him. It might seem impossible to always be thinking about God, but as you train your mind to be aware of His presence in your life, you become mindful of Him all the time. You recognize whatever you do, He is not only aware, but He is also in the midst. The more aware you become, the more you choose to yield to the leading of His Spirit. The fruit of righteousness is peace because peace is the fruit of His Spirit. Peace is what Jesus promised to give you as He was preparing to ascend. When you live at peace you cease striving with others. Rather than pursue discord, you look for opportunities to be on one accord. The Word of God says, as much as it depends on you, live peacefully with everyone. You cannot control the actions of others, so you cannot guarantee there will always be peace with others. But if being peaceful is your goal, yours is the kingdom of heaven and you will always be at peace with God.

Today's readings:
Psalm 119:65; Isaiah 26:3,32:17; Matthew 5:9
Romans 8:6,12:18; Galatians 5:22; Philippians 4:9
Colossians 3:1; Hebrews 12:14; James 3:18

October 11
How To Obtain Mercy

Mercy is pity, compassion for the ills of others, feelings of kindness, and goodwill. Though you may deserve an ill effect of your actions, God shows you mercy by not giving you what you deserve. How do you obtain mercy? The Bible speaks of three core reasons we can expect to receive mercy. The first basis upon which you obtain mercy every single day of your life is because of God's nature. He is merciful towards all. He pours out brand new mercies every day. But for that, we would all be consumed. Nothing can stop Him from being merciful because it is in His heart to be so. You may also obtain mercy in a particular situation because you ask. Cry out to God and ask for mercy. Sometimes you have not because you ask not. Lastly, you receive mercy by being merciful. To those who are merciful, He shows Himself merciful. Like anything else, you reap what you sow. Indeed, though you may deserve judgement, God will withhold it and show you mercy when you show mercy to others. Mercy triumphs over judgment. Be merciful, as your heavenly Father is merciful.

Today's readings:
2 Samuel 22:26; Psalm 18:25; Jeremiah 3:12;
Lamentations 3:21-23; Matthew 5:7,25:31-41; Luke 6:36
Colossians 3:12-14; Hebrews 4:16; James 2:13

October 12
Another Level

There is a God-like level of grace and mercy which flow
from the lives of those who walk closely with the Lord. It
was demonstrated by Moses when he led the people of
God out of Egypt. The Israelites grew restless as they
waited for him to come down from the mountain with
the 10 commandments. Instead of being patient, they
took the gold which God blessed them with and had
Aaron build a golden calf to worship. Like many, you
may grow weary waiting on God to show your next move
or answer your prayer, but do not turn away from God or
seek direction from witchcraft, horoscopes, palm
readers, tea leaves, Ouija boards and the like. God is a
jealous God. And His wrath was aroused against those
who worshipped the idol. He was justified in His anger,
but what happened next reflects the highest level of
righteousness. Moses told God if He didn't forgive the
people, He could blot his name out of the book of life. He
stood in the gap and pleaded for God to forgive them.
When you go to that next level you stop holding offenses
and you pray for those who hurt you. You esteem others
better than yourself.

Today's readings:
Exodus 32:11-14,30-32; 2 Chronicles 6:12-21
John 15:13; Romans 9:1-3; Philippians 2:1-3

October 13
Maintenance Is Required

When I purchased my vehicle, it was pristine but over time dirt and pollen started accumulating. Even birds blessed me with their "gifts." I realized I needed to wash it regularly. Likewise, I had to change the oil annually, refill the gas regularly, have the tires realigned when needed and so on. Maintenance was required. So, too, Jesus fills you with His Spirit when you make Him your Lord. To operate the way He wants, you must maintain your body by keeping it washed in the Word. You must realign yourself by repenting when you get out of sync with His direction. Drink the pure spiritual milk, the Word of God, to flow like a well- oiled machine. Doing deeper maintenance is sometimes required. When you fast and pray you empty out any built-up impurities to be renewed in your mind. The world can sometimes drain you. God's power in you can become diminished as you go about interacting, listening, serving and living in a fallen world. To be all that God has created you to be remember that spiritual maintenance is required.

Today's readings:
Psalm 1,19:9,12; Luke 8:43-48; Romans 12:1-2
2 Corinthians 5:17-18; Ephesians 5:26; James 4:8

October 14
The Weight Of Your Word

I marveled at the story of my uncle whose word is said to carry great weight. I was told his name is so honored in the small city in which he lives, everyone respects him. He could send someone to the store with no money. If the person tells the store owner my uncle sent them, the owner will give whatever is needed without hesitation. My uncle's word is his bond. A bond is a surety, guaranteeing a promise will be fulfilled. If he says it, people believe it, because he is known for keeping his word. This is just like the Lord's Word. Jesus is the Living Word. The Word is God. God cannot die or pass away. He cannot lie. He cannot speak and then not act. Likewise, this is the way scripture describes the word of a righteous man, who, it says, will keep his word even when it hurts. A righteous person will do whatever it takes to keep their word. Your word reflects your character. Your word should carry great weight. Others should know when you make a commitment to do something, you will do everything in your power to honor it.

Today's readings:
Numbers 30:2; 2 Samuel 7:28; Psalm 15:4c
Proverbs 30:5; Isaiah 40:8; Matthew 5:37
John 1:1; 2 Corinthians 1:17-18; James 5:12

October 15
What Are You Wearing?

Are you wearing the full armor of God? It will keep you
prepared to stand against the wiles of the enemy. You
can also add to it virtue, knowledge, self-control,
perseverance, godliness, and kindness. Foremost, put on
love, as it is the glue that holds the body of Christ, with
all our imperfections, together. As with all things in the
kingdom of God, the devil has a counterfeit version of
believers wearing righteousness. Therefore, beware false
prophets. Be watchful and don't be fooled. They come to
you in sheep's clothing – seeming like they are
Christians - but their true selves will shine through to
reveal they are really wolves who seek to steal, kill, or
destroy what God is doing. By contrast, Jesus died for
you to have abundant life beyond your earthly
habitation. Once your natural body, which is corruptible,
has put on incorruption in Christ Jesus, then you will
experience what Jesus died to give us all: Victory over
death! Hallelujah! When you are clothed in Him, just as
He was resurrected you too shall rise from the dead.
Remember, it all begins with being clothed in Him.

Today's readings:
Job 29:14; Matthew 7:15; Romans 13:12-14
1 Corinthians 15:53-55; Galatians 3:27
Ephesians 4:22-24; 6:10-18; Colossians 3:10-14

October 16
Embrace Your Detours

I was driving back from a weekend stay at the beach. The
route normally takes me west then north. But as I began,
my GPS told me to get off the road and make a U-turn to
go east. I pulled over to see why it was guiding me that
way. As I tried to figure it out my GPS said, "your route is
avoiding a closed road." Somewhere ahead traffic was
backed up because the road was closed. I thought about
how many times God has rearranged my plans for me to
avoid some kind of unseen dangers or to guide me back
to His will. And how often have I questioned the
disruption and leaned to my own understanding only to
get caught in a snare? Saul had an interruption along the
Damascus Road. He was headed to further his efforts to
destroy the church. But the Lord had other plans for
him. Instead of doing what he wanted he found himself
on Straight Street. God sent him straight in another
direction! Instead of destroying the church he became its
biggest advocate. You may find yourself detoured from
the place you thought you were headed. But trust the
process. If God intervenes, He has a better path for you
to take and a better plan for you to follow.

Today's readings:
Psalm 23:3,33:11,119:35; Proverbs 16:9, 19:21
Acts 8:54-9:21

October 17
Attract God's Attention

The best way to garner God's attention is to walk in humility. When you are humble, He pours His grace upon you. When you are prideful, He opposes you. Sometimes you may think you are under spiritual attack or people are against you. Stop and examine your behavior. Are you operating in humility? If your focus is strictly on pleasing yourself, the likelihood of you walking in humility is not high. Look at the example of Jesus. He lowered Himself to take on the likeness of men. He esteemed others as higher than Himself. Humility looks out for the well-being of others. You don't have to prove you know everything. Humility is not pressing to be the greatest at the expense of others. It is considering the impact of your actions on others. The beautiful thing is when you humble yourself, rather than pushing yourself up, God will exalt you. He will make you shine without you trying to do so. Your humility makes Him look good, so He makes you look good. It is wise to be humble. When you are humble, you get God's attention. He will hear your cries, save you, preserve your life, care for you and teach you His ways.

Today's readings:
Psalm 9:12,18:27l25:9; Matthew 18:4; Luke 14:11
Philippians 2:8-10; James 4:10; 1 Peter 5:6

October 18
Time To Come Home

One of the most fascinating experiences recorded in the Bible is that of the prophet Hosea. God directed him to take a prostitute for a wife. He did and they had several children, but she returned to her wayward lifestyle. God told Hosea to go back to get her from the street life to which she had returned. Hosea loved her with an unconditional love. God loves you the same way. Perhaps you have started living in a way that does not honor Him. God is awaiting you with open arms, much like the love we see in the story of the prodigal son. Like Hosea's wife, the son left the place where he was loved by his family to seek more. Maybe you have felt there is more excitement out there, or somehow felt like there is something greater you are missing. Perhaps have gone seeking different experiences outside of the house of the Lord where you are loved. If so, it is time to come home. God loves you and is willing to forgive all your sins. Perhaps you are waiting for Him to come to you, but the reality is He never left. He's been right there, waiting patiently for you to return home.

Today's readings:
Genesis 31:3; Nehemiah 1:9; Hosea 2:7; Isaiah 44:2
Jeremiah 4:1,24:7; Zechariah 1:3; Luke 15:18-24

October 19
What He Said

When I was a child, it was common to for me to get the same response when I asked my mother why I had to do something she had told me to do. Her response was commonly, "because I said so." In other words, she was not inclined to explain herself. I simply had to do what she said because she said it. In a sense that is the way God's Word can be viewed. You don't need to ask why He will fulfill what the Bible says. He will do it because He said so. His Word will not return to Him void. It will accomplish the purpose He intends as the scripture reveals. It will come to pass. In fact, heaven and earth will one day pass away, according to scripture, but His Word will stand forever. Consequently, you can stand on the promises you read in scripture. You can put your confidence in them. Consequently, when you speak the Word and agree with God in prayer you can expect it to come to pass. You know your prayers will be heard by the Lord, because any time you pray according to His will, He promises to hear you and to honor your prayer. Put your confidence in this: He will do just what He said.

Today's readings:
Numbers 23:19; Psalm 119:160,130:5
Isaiah 40:8,55:10-13; Matthew 24:35; 1 Peter 1:25
1 John 5:14-15

October 20
You Said It

There is a common belief that most people speak at a rate of 150-200 words per minute. In addition, you also speak to yourself. There is not a clear agreement about whether you speak to yourself at the same rate or, as some believe, at a rate as high as 1300 words per minute. Though the rate of self-talk is not agreed upon, there is no dispute about the fact that you do talk to yourself regularly. Your internal dialogue is crucial to your life. Negative self-talk can have an astounding impact on the quality of your life. A professor at Yale School of Medicine studied the impact of emotions on the brain. According to this study, if you persistently have a negative internal dialogue, it will weaken multiple neural structures in your brain. In turn, this change in your neural structures will make you more vulnerable to stress. Your negative self-talk can lead to anxiety, and depression. So, rather than speaking negativity, speak life to yourself. Remind yourself you are victorious. No matter what you've faced in the past, you have always survived. You can do all things through Christ Who strengthens you.

Today's readings:
Deuteronomy 28:3-14; 1 Samuel 30:6; Psalm 43:5
Proverbs 18:21; Matthew 6:30,5:21; Philippians 4:19

October 21
Just Like You Thought It Would Be

There is a theory called the Law of Attraction which is based on the premise you get back what you put out. The energy you put into the atmosphere will come back to you. What you feed yourself is what you will attract. The Biblical equivalent of this principle is you will reap what you sow. Scripture also says when you are expecting negativity you will find it. As a man thinks, so is he. It is scientifically proven that when you feed your mind negative thoughts, your mind will believe you. And it will respond, accordingly. You have the capacity to think positively and produce positive results, and vice versa. This suggests you should mind your mind. Pay attention to what you are thinking. Meditate more on what you do well, and less on how you make mistakes. Think about God's Word, His promises, His affirmations about you, and less about those things that are contrary to what God has said. When doubt creeps in about your capacity to succeed, think about the fact that you were created in God's image. Remember you are more than a conqueror in Christ Jesus. You have been accepted, chosen, and blessed with all spiritual blessings in Christ Jesus.

Today's readings:
Genesis 1:26; Psalm 130:13-14; Proverbs 4:23,11:27,23:7
Romans 8:5,28-39; Galatians 6:1-5; Ephesians 1:14-21

October 22
Proper Preparation

Rehoboam was a king in Israel. He was a descendent of King David, the man after God's own heart. But unlike David, he did not honor God. In fact, he rejected God and His commandment. Consequently, God allowed the Egyptians to come in to attack Israel and take away the gold items that had been created and dedicated by King Solomon. Instead of doing good, Rehoboam did evil in God's sight. The difference between Rehoboam and his predecessor came down to one distinction. The condition of their hearts. While David cried out to God in Psalm 51 asking Him to create in him a clean heart, Jeroboam did not. Instead, he did the opposite. He led a lifestyle in contradiction to God's Word. His ungodly actions were the result of his failure to prepare his heart to serve God. When you obey what God has told us in His Word, then you get the benefit and blessings of your obedience. You begin with preparing your heart. Hide the Word in your heart, as you meditate on it and memorize it. Trust Him with all your heart, in lieu of your own understanding, and He will direct your path. In sum, it all comes down to the preparation and condition of your heart.

Today's readings:
1 Kings 11:4; 2 Chronicles 12:1-2,14; Psalm 119:11
Proverbs 3:5-6,23:11; Romans 10:10; James 4:8

October 23
My Way

I chuckled as I thought about a situation because it reminded me so much of us all. When given the directions for how to put information in an online system my friend chose none of the options being offered. Instead, she made one up of her own, ignoring the required alternatives. Have you been guilty of the same? Rather than following the options God sets before you, you choose your own. You'd be foolish to reject the wisdom and knowledge you need to accomplish a goal. And yet, if you are like me, there have times you have done just that. God has given you the keys to success. When He directed Joshua to lead the Israelites into the promised land, He told him 3 things. First, be strong and courageous. Second, observe to do according to all the law. Lastly, do not turn from it to the right hand or to the left, that you may prosper wherever you go. He also told Joshua - and you - how to be strong and of good courage, and to not be afraid nor be dismayed: remember the Lord your God is with you wherever you go. The choice is yours: follow His directions for success, or be like Frank Sinatra and say, "I did it my way!"

Today's readings:
Joshua 1; Ecclesiastes 1:9; John 8:31-32, 15:1-8

October 24
Your Solitary Place

When you are seeking God's guidance, remember those of faith that have sought His direction and follow their examples. Take a look at Gideon. The enemy had been attacking and destroying the crops relentlessly, which resorted to Gideon harvesting his wheat in a wine vat in hopes he wouldn't be seen. The Angel of the Lord appeared, and told Gideon that God wanted him to lead a fight against their oppressors. Gideon didn't think he was qualified. So, he prayed for a sign to assure him his efforts would be successful. He rose early in the morning to seek God's answer in a place where he was alone with God. Similarly, when Moses was called to receive the commandments, he too arose early to go to the mountain of God. And David found a place to build an altar away from the crowds. Of course, your greatest example is Jesus who rose while it was still dark to find a solitary place to pray. If you want to have God's guidance, find a place to be alone with Him. Seek Him early before you start your day. It is a common thread in the lives of those who God blessed with success.

Today's readings:
Genesis 21:14,28:18; Exodus 24:4,34:4; Judges 6:36-40
1 Chronicles 21:1-21; Mark 1:35

October 25
The Sin Question

When you are confronted with other faiths, you may find
there are several elements that sound like Biblical texts.
When you hear things that sound pseudo-spiritual but
aren't rooted in scripture you must evaluate the key
underlying distinctions between faith in God's Word and
other beliefs. One of the fundamental foundations of
Christianity is what you are going to do about your sins.
According to the Bible all of us have sinned. The Bible
also tells you the consequence of your sins. You earn
death every time you sin. You cannot meditate this truth
away. You cannot merely ignore its truth or think you are
somehow exempt from it. Jesus was sent from heaven to
serve as the mediator between you and God. He took on
the sins of the whole world, including yours, so that you
can have eternal life. Some belief systems teach that you
can create your own better status. Some even deny there
is such a place as hell. Wouldn't it be sad to find out you
were wrong after you die? The bottom line is this: What
will you do about your sin? In Christ Jesus, you are
forgiven of all your sin. In other belief systems, you are
on your own.

Today's readings:
Exodus 20:20; Numbers 15; Leviticus 14:20
John 1:12-13,29,3:16; Romans 3:23,6:23; 1 John 5:17

October 26
Something Out Of Nothing

There is a theory of how the world was created; it suggests the cosmos was created out of chaos. It was just a big ball of confusion that evolved into an orderly universe. Some say there was a Big Bang and, poof, the earth was created. The suggestion is that something came out of nothing. There was no Creator. It just happened. Setting aside what you may or may not believe about God and His involvement, use your mental capacity to envision how an entire solar system came to be all on its own. Look at how your fingers and toes, arms and legs, heart, and lungs all function perfectly together. Following this reasoning, imagine, a Bulova watch with all its tiny parts being separated, tossed into the air, and landing perfectly into place to function as it ought. If you are challenged to believe this is possible, then how could you accept there was not a Creator who conceived all that is. The fool says in his heart, "there is no God," while heaven and earth declare His glory. Everything was created by Him and for Him. And unlike a Big Bang, He intentionally, fearfully, and wonderfully made you, and all you see. And He said it was all good.

Today's readings:
Genesis 1:1-31; Psalm 14:1,19:1,46:10,139:13-14
Isaiah 46:9; Colossians 1:16; Revelations 10:6

October 27
Don't Go Back

When God delivered the Hebrews out of Egypt, they encountered some tough times. They were flustered when they reached an area that didn't have fresh water. They were irritable when they wanted to eat meat and didn't have any. They railed against Moses and suggested it would have been better for them to go back to slavery than to endure the challenges of their freedom. You may encounter difficulties along the journey as you find your way in the Lord. But always remember your worst day walking in Christ is better than your best day living as a slave to sin. You are freed from the law of sin and death. You have been delivered from the bondage. Jesus shed Walk in your freedom. Never return to what the Lord has freed you from. It is like the person who works hard to get physically fit and eat healthy. When they go back to unhealthy eating and slothful habits, it is usually much harder to regain the momentum they had once built up to live better. Same is true when the Lord sets you free, and you allow yourself to go back to the old way of thinking and living, you make it harder on yourself. The better way is to stay the course. Do not go back.

Today's readings:
Proverbs 28:11; Isaiah 44:22,66:3; Matthew 12:43-47
Luke 9:62; Romans 8:13; Galatians 3:1-4; Hebrews 6:4-6

October 28
Remember The Equation

Paul prayed for the church in Rome to be filled with overflowing hope. The church was made up of a mixture of both gentiles and Jews. There were some disputes among them. Paul wanted to make sure they understood the fact that they gentiles were just as called to follow Christ as were the Jews. Though Christ came first to His own people by lineage, the Jewish nation, it was never God's intention to only save them. He had always planned to give salvation to the gentile nations, as well. Paul told the church at Rome they should accept one another. Then Paul gave them the equation to overflowing hope. He prayed they would be filled with joy and peace, and then by faith and by the power of the Holy Spirit, they would have overflowing hope. God will fill you with joy. It is the fruit of His Spirit. You can fan into flame your joy by praising Him and meditating on His Word. You can cultivate peace through prayer and by focusing on the goodness of God. In fact, He will give you peace that is beyond your comprehension. Add being full of joy to being full of peace and you will get overflowing hope. Remember the equation.

Today's readings:
2 Samuel 22:50; Romans 5:1-5,8:24-25,15:1-13
1 Corinthians 13:7; Philippians 4:4-8

October 29
Rejoice Always

You want me to do what? That might be what you are inclined to say in response to the exhortation to rejoice always. What exactly does it mean? And how can I do it considering all I am going through? Those are legit questions to which the Holy Bible has an answer. To rejoice means to be glad. Be in a state of gladness, happiness, or well-being. The root word does not merely mean you should feel glad or joyful. It also implies you have the choice to rejoice. For example, Paul exhorts those in Rome to "rejoice with those who rejoice." It is an action word. The point is to delight over what God has done. You don't have to wait until God moves in your circumstances. You can choose to rejoice in advance, as an act of your faith. In addition, God rejoices over his people, including with singing. Imagine the Lord singing over you, and let it bring joy to your soul. Joy is the fruit of God's Spirit. As He exhibits joy, you will too as you fill up on His word because your spirit will produce His fruit. Your choice to be joyful will also strengthen you spiritually. Choose to rejoice.

Today's readings:
Nehemiah 8:10; Psalm 34:19,24 Proverbs 24:17
Zechariah 9:9; Zephaniah 3:17,4:17-18; Romans 12:15
Philippians 4:1-4

October 30
Fear Not

Fear not! You are redeemed! God knows you by your name. When the waters of life arise, you will not be overtaken. When the fires of life come up, you shall not be burned. "You are Mine", says the Lord your God! You are made in His image. He is with you. He is your shepherd. He will guide you. He will make provision for you. You do not have to fear when others rise up against you. God is with you. Demons tremble at the sound of His name. He causes mountains to be moved, including powerful men and women in your life, without them even knowing it. Instead of fretting, pray. He will fight for you. Trust Him. He has given His angels charge over you to keep you in all your ways. When trouble comes, you never need to be afraid. God has not given you a spirit of fear. You have power, love, and a sound mind. You are filled with the greatest power on the planet. The Holy Spirit who raised Jesus from the dead, and granted Him power to walk on water, lives on the inside of you. If God be for you - which He is - then what can man do to you? Be strong. Be of good courage. You are more than a conqueror!

Today's readings:
Deuteronomy 3:22; 2 Kings 8:1-16; Psalm 23,118:6
Lamentations 3:57; Joel 2:21; Luke 18:2; 1 John 4:4,18

October 31

Trust

You are right where you need to be in this season. You will not necessarily stay where you are, but it is where God has allowed you to be for now. Trust God to help you. He will show you the way to go. Ask Him to guide you. When you choose to second guess His plan you may make a decision that makes more sense to you. However, bear in mind, your capacities intellectually, spiritually, and relationally are far less than His. He has a plan to help you reach the goals He has for you. It is up to you to follow His plans. When you trust God, it is like what Peter did when he walked on water. He put complete confidence in the One who called Him. He understood if God leads you to do something, then He will equip you to accomplish it. Peter took steps on water, defying every natural inclination and all scientific understanding because his focus was on the Lord bidding him to come. Once you know you're following His guidance, you too can defy the odds and even your own understanding. He is not limited to our natural capacity. It all comes down to trusting Him.

Today's readings:
Psalm 37:3-5, 40:4, 56:3-4,6; Proverbs 3:5-6, 29:6
Isaiah 12:2, 26:3, 28:4; Jeremiah 17:7

November 1
The Call Of Duty

You may be familiar with the late Queen Elizabeth II, the longest reigning monarch of England. You may or may not agree with the monarchy. Still, it is hard to not admire her commitment to her duty as the Queen. She was anointed during her coronation and believed her duty was not only to her country but to God. Her father was the King before her because his elder brother had served briefly as the King but then abdicated the role to marry a twice divorced American woman. He did it for love, he said. Certainly, one can understand his desire to be with the woman he loved. Yet, there is something to be said for someone who is willing to deny themself for the sake of fulfilling their duty. Paul chose to obey God's directives knowing it would cause him to suffer many times. He was shipwrecked, beaten, left for dead, bitten by a snake, imprisoned, and eventually martyred for the sake of finishing the work God had assigned to him. Likewise, Jesus only did what His Father sent Him to do, even to the point of death. He spoke only what the Father directed Him to say. You too must decide whether it is more important to satisfy your own wants, or to fulfill God's purpose for your life.

Today's readings:
Leviticus 9:6; Ezra 7:18; John 4:34,5:19,30-36,6:38
Acts 9:6,22:10; Hebrews 10:7

November 2
What He Does

When you engage to serve God with your life, do it His way. Even if you are zealous to please Him, it is of no avail without knowing what to do. When Queen Elizabeth II reached a crisis early in her reign, according to the depiction in The Crown, she called in her chief assistant who had also served her father. She sought advice about what she should do concerning Winston Churchill's inaction when London was hit with a fog that reportedly lasted numerous days and killed roughly 12,000 people. She trusted that her assistant could help her based upon his knowledge of both the monarch's role and how her father handled such matters. Once she learned what her father had done in another difficult circumstance, she had her answer. Even the devil's children mimic their father. If you want to know what to do to live out your life in a way that pleases God, do as Jesus did. He repeatedly said He only did what He had seen His Father do. Whenever you become unsure, go back to the standard set in God's Word. Mimic His actions, His attitude, and His ways. He is full of mercy and grace, kind, and gentle. He is love.

Today's readings:
Joshua 1:8; Psalm 86:15,145:8; John 8:41-44,15:26
1 Corinthians 13; Galatians 5:22; 1 John 1:5,4:15

305

November 3
He Will Let You Know

God will not leave you ignorant. Whatever is going on He will reveal. He sent us the Holy Spirit. One of His roles is to guide you into all truth. He is a revealer of things yet to come. Rather than seek out your horoscope, you can seek the Lord Who can tell you what lies ahead. This principle was reflected in the conversation Jonathan, the son of King Saul, had with David before he was king. Saul had become so jealous of David he began seeking to kill David. But when David told Jonathan, He didn't believe him initially. He made a pact with him to find out, knowing his father would do nothing either great or small without first telling him. Likewise, when Paul was about to journey to Jerusalem, he was forewarned by a prophet who took his belt and wrapped it around his wrists to let Paul see what would happen. Though people begged him not to go, Paul went because he was called to do so. The point is if you need to be aware of something, including the enemy's schemes, the Lord will not leave you ignorant. He may speak to you in a dream, like He did with Joseph. He may whisper it in the Spirit. He may speak through others. Pay attention.

Today's readings:
1 Samuel 20:2; Daniel 10:1-14; Amos 3:7; Acts 21:4-14
Romans 1:13; Ephesians 5:13

November 4
Never Forsaken

You are never alone, no matter where you go or what you do. When God heard the cries of the Israelites who were held in bondage in Egypt, He demonstrated His power towards Pharoah until Pharoah relented to let His people go. God took them through the wilderness, sustained them for 40 years and made sure their clothes never wore out. Even when they turned to worthless idols, He was still faithful to them. Even when they rebelled, He still provided manna for them to eat in the desert. He fought for them. He provided for them. Eventually, He put them in "time out". He allowed them to be taken into captivity for 70 years so that they would rededicate themselves to Him. You may feel like your failures or mistakes will cause God to turn away from you, but this is not so. He has promised to never leave you nor forsake you. And He does not lie. You can rest assured He will keep His Word for His name's sake.

Today's readings:
1 Samuel 12:22;1 Kings 6:13; Nehemiah 9:1-31
Psalm 27:10, 38:21; Hebrews 13:5

November 5
Uncover

Those who want to walk in the Kingdom of God must
come to grips with admitting they have sinned. The
worst approach is to try to cover up your error. If you try
to hide your sin, rather than confess it to God, you may
not prosper. This means you can create a hindrance to
the blessings you would otherwise receive from the Lord.
On the other hand, when you are willing to both confess
your faults to the Lord and forsake them, you will not
only be forgiven of those sins God will show you mercy.
The wages of sin is death. Sin earns you the right to die,
but God offers you mercy. He withholds the punishment
you deserve. God's desire is for you to walk in the Light,
as He is the Light. Unconfessed sins are like pouring
water on the Holy Spirit's fire within you. They quench
the Spirit and grieve Him. Sins are like spiritual poison,
bringing you agony, guilt, and shame. They are like a ball
and chain around your ankles keeping you from being
able to run your race in Christ Jesus. It is always best to
admit when you have fallen short. God already knows.
He is merely waiting for you to agree with Him.

Today's readings:
Psalm 32:3-5; Proverbs 28:13; John 3:19,12:35
Acts 3:19; Ephesians 5:8,11; Hebrews 12:1; 1 John 1:18-9

November 6
Learn From Them

All too often we ignore the lessons to be learned from others' mistakes. A friend told me how she had earned a full scholarship to college but in her zeal to join a sorority she didn't focus on her studies, lost her scholarship, and had to drop out of college. Though she had shared her story with her oldest daughter, unbelievably, her daughter did the exact same thing. Thankfully her other daughter learned through her mother's choices and graduated from college with honors. Jeremiah lamented and wept because his people rebelled against God; they did not follow His admonition to avoid other nations' gods. They ended up in captivity and eating their own children. God had warned them over and over. When He speaks to you about anything, even a positive thing to do, obey His voice. Heed Jeremiah's testimony: "The Lord is righteous, yet I rebelled against his command. Listen, all you peoples; look on my suffering. My young men and young women have gone into exile." (Lamentations 1:18 NIV) Honor God and obey His Word so that you will enjoy the many blessings of His favor.

Today's readings:
Lamentations 1-2

November 7
Good Grief

The day you accept Jesus as Lord of your life, the Holy Spirit comes to abide in you. He will lead and guide you. You may say or do something you realize is completely wrong, then feel badly about it. This is because Holy Spirit will also convict you when you sin. The grief you cause Him will make you have godly sorrow. The good news is godly sorrow is good grief because it leads you to repentance. It is different from worldly sorrow, which can even lead to death. Repentance involves changing your mind about what you've done, changing your feelings about what you've done, changing your actions to make a turn from what you've done. It involves telling God you are sorry for what you've done. And because He is merciful, He will forgive you over and over again. The punishment for your sins was already borne by Jesus on the cross. Thanks be to God! Therefore, you are not condemned by God. Instead, He lovingly takes you into His arms and consoles you. As Jesus told the woman caught in adultery, make it your aim to go and sin no more.

Today's readings:
Isaiah 53:4; Lamentations 3:32; Matthew 3:11; Acts 1:8
Romans 8:1; 2 Corinthians 7:10; Ephesians 4:30

November 8
Your Tongue

You have a phenomenal tool at your disposal. Your tongue is powerful. If you are truthful, you will be able to stand forever. On the contrary, the Bible suggests a lying tongue will be cut off because God hates lies. When you are wise, you use knowledge to speak words that are like choice silver. Your words can literally be a source of nourishment and comfort. The tongue of the wise has been called a tree of life, able to bring hope and encouragement to a weary soul. You can also speak words that break a person's spirit. A person who has a crushed spirit can more easily give up hope and wallow in despair. Use your tongue to speak wisely. Your tongue can speak life and death. Your words can cut like a sword or be healing like a balm. Amid a heated discussion it is best to settle down, reel in your emotions and think before you speak. Too often things are said in the heat of the moment that the speaker later regrets. James says the tongue as an untamable entity. Learn to master your communications to bring delight to your hearers by speaking the truth in love.

Today's readings:
Psalms 34:13; Proverbs 6:17,10:20,12:18-19
Ephesians 4:15; James 3:6-8

November 9
Covered

Noah was a righteous man who lived in a time when the Lord was so grieved by mankind's wickedness, He decided to destroy everyone and start all over again with Noah and his sons. He told Noah to build an ark large enough to take each kind of living creature onto the ark with them. After building for a few years, Noah was able to load up 2 of each kind of animal, reptile, and bird along with his family. As soon as they entered the Ark it began to rain. It did not stop for forty days. The entire earth was covered with water. The flood destroyed every living creature outside of the ark of safety. Once the waters receded and they were able to leave the ark, Noah produced wine from the vineyard he planted. He got drunk and fell asleep laying naked in his tent. His youngest son saw him and told his brothers. But the older brothers did not look at their father. Instead, they took a blanket and backed up to cover him. It was an example of what God did and does for you. Rather than expose your sin, He covers you. He hides your transgressions. You are called to do likewise. Do not repeat the shortcomings of others. Pray for them. Encourage them. Model the love of God.

Today's readings:
Genesis 9:18-23; Psalm 32:1,85:2,139:13,140:7
Proverbs 17:9; Luke 15:11-23; Romans 4:7

312

November 10
The Greatest Proof

One of the things we traditionally associate with being a Christian is attending church. Some see this as antiquated and unnecessary to follow Christ Jesus. Yet, we should gather as the body of Christ in accordance with what the Bible says about it. Jesus established the church based on the truth that He is the Son of the Living God. Scripture tells us to not forsake assembling. In other words, as children of God, we should participate in a local church. But attending church is not what Jesus identified as the defining mark of a true disciple. Yes, He established the church. And yes, He attended church. He was often in a synagogue during his earthly visitation. Yet, if we look at the scripture, we will discover what he held up as higher than even attending church. Jesus said, "Your love for one another will prove to the world that you are my disciples." Notice He did not say it is based on how much scripture you know. We can attend church, speak in tongues, pray like an angel or even prophesy, but if we do not operate in love then we fall short of demonstrating we are children of God.

Today's readings:
Matthew 6:14-15,16:13-18; John 13:34-35
1 Corinthians 13:1-3; Ephesians 4:32; Hebrews 10:24-25

November 11
Disconnected

Sometimes while I am in the middle of having a phone conversation the line goes blank. It is disconcerting when I realize I have been talking for a while before I am aware the call was disconnected. Sometimes we can experience this same thing in our relationship with the Lord. We are going along thinking all is well only to at some point realize our actions, attitude and communication no longer are reflective of our relationship with God. But in fact they are. Every time we stop spending time in His Word, it shows up. His words are no longer abiding in us. We sound more like the world than like Jesus. Our demeanor no longer reflects His character. Our words are no longer seasoned with the truth. We start going through the motions of being in Christ without the power of His anointing. Jesus told us this would happen if we do not stay connected to Him. He compared us to branches on a vine. If you cut off a branch it will no longer receive the nutrients from the vine. Soon it will wither away and die. Contrarily, if the branch stays connected it can flourish and bear fruit. Stay connected to His Word.

Today's readings:
Hosea 4:1; psalm 119:9; John 8:3132,15:1-8
Romans 12:1-2; Colossians 3:16; 1 Thessalonians 2:13

November 12
Let Go, Let God

We know the Lord gave us a new commandment to love one another, as He has loved us. He said, it was by *this* men would know you are His disciple. Since love is the greatest mark of a disciple, walk in love towards others. What is the greatest hindrance to your obedience to God's new command? Too often, you can allow your lack of forgiveness to keep you from loving. In the love chapter, 1 Corinthians 13, God says love keeps no records of wrong. Yet, I am convinced, our capacity to love is diminished because we are holding on to the hurts of the past. If you are going to obey God's command to love others, you must release them from any prior offenses to love the way Jesus loves you. He loves unconditionally. If you are a parent, your child will disappoint you. They will disobey what you tell them to do. They will even lie to avoid punishment. No matter how sweet they are, they will mess up. You have messed up many, many times. But just as the prodigal's father ran to him and covered him with his robe, you are loved and forgiven by God. The only way you can truly fulfill the commandment to love the way He does is to let go of past hurts.

Today's readings:
Matthew 6:14-15 ,18:21-22,18:35; Mark 11:25
Luke 23:24; Ephesians 4:32; Colossians 3:13; 1 John 1:9

November 13
God Causes Other To Bless You

When you are a child of God walking in your purpose, God will use others to bless you. You won't have to seek this to happen. Look at the children of Israel who were enslaved in Egypt. When God unleashed the 10 plagues against Egypt, Pharaoh finally stopped resisting God's command to let His people go. God not only caused him to set them free, He also moved the Egyptians to freely give gold and silver to the Israelites. The people of God did not ask for this to happen, but God caused them to find favor with the Egyptians. It is a principle that is a part of the Kingdom of God. He causes you to be blessed by others, when you are doing what He directs you to do. Sometimes the favor is manifested in people giving you things. I can recall when I served as a chaplain, having left my law proactive, and my salary had gone south! I was desiring to have some new black shoes. And without me asking God caused someone to show up at my house with both brand-new shows and a beautiful dress to match them. Another person asked me what size shoe I wore and gave me an entire bag filled with shoes. God can cause blessings to abound.

Today's readings:
Matthew 6:14-15 ,18:21-22,18:35; Mark 11:25
Luke 23:24; Colossians 3:13; 1 John 1:9

November 14
Your Problem Would Bless Others

My good friend is in Dallas. She was literally standing outside praising God for rain. They had been in a drought. Everything was dried up and withered. The plants, grass and trees were all dead or dying. It put my complaints about having so many thunderstorms in perspective. What you may consider annoying, someone else is praying for and would gladly receive. Having a house, even if I wish it was bigger or in a more upscale neighborhood, easily trumps the experience of the person who has no place to live. Poor sight is better than having no vision at all. God has been good to you. No matter what you have endured, He has always been there to see you through it. Experiencing the vicissitudes of life while having Christ on your side is a blessing beyond compare. Be thankful to God you don't have to face anything in life without Him. You may have a challenging assignment, boss, coworkers, or a long commute. Be grateful. It means you have a job. Remember, there is always someone else who would be blessed to get the opportunity to experience those things. In all things give God thanks.

Today's readings:
Psalm 63:5,95:2,100:4,103:2; 1 Corinthians 15:57;
Philippians 4:6,11; 1 Thessalonians 5:17-18; James 1:17

November 15
Cast Your Seed

As you invest in various places, you increase your opportunity to receive a return on your investments. You may not know which will produce the most return, so you should diversify your investment portfolio. While this is true about monetary gain, it is also true about other things in life. When you are seeking a job, you apply to various positions in hopes of landing a good one. Likewise, it is true about sowing the seed of the Word of God. As you tell your testimony to some people, share scripture with others, pray with still others you are planting seeds in various places. You can expect to reap returns. There will be those who come to know Christ as Savior and others who draw closer to Him. You may not know who will seek to have a relationship with the Lord. But that is not your worry. Your assignment is to cast the seed of the Word in various places, without focusing on the outcome of your efforts. And as you do, God will give the increase. The Word of God will not return to Him void. He will cause it to accomplish whatever His purpose is. You may not get to see it, but God will cause your seed to grow. Keep sowing.

Today's readings:
Ecclesiastes 11:1-2; Hosea 10:12
Matthew 13:24-30,31-32,37-43; Luke 8:5-15

November 16
Sow Your Seed

The principle of sowing a seed and reaping a crop is as old as time. You may have had one of those teachers who taught you about the growth process of a plant by having you take a seed, cover it with dirt and make observations about the progress of the plant's growth. This is also a biblical principal when it comes to investing in the kingdom of God. You are a part of the body of Christ. You are the church. And as such, there is a responsibility to help with the funding necessary for the church edifice to operate. The gospel is free, but the electricity, chairs, carpet, water, and maintenance are not. Pastors love God and sacrifice time and effort to keep you fed the Word of God. They forego other opportunities. It is only right they should be able to receive financial support. We know God loves a cheerful giver, who gives freely. And He has promised to bless you in return. Those who sow sparingly, reap sparingly. Those who sow bountifully, reap bountifully. You give to advance God's Kingdom, and to be a blessing to others. You reap a blessing because God honors His Word. He gives seed to the sower, so that in all things, at all times, you will have abundance for all you do.

Today's readings:
Genesis 8:22a; 2 Kings 19:29; Psalm 126:5; Hosea 10:12
Luke 6:38; 2 Corinthians 9:6-14; Galatians 6:7-9

November 17
Fulfill Your Duty

Perhaps it's an old-fashioned concept to some but honoring your responsibility to fulfill the assignments you have been given is a timeless principle. We saw an example that will likely be talked about in history classes and civics for years to come. When a group of citizens conspired to stop the certification of the election of the 46th President of the United States, the sitting Vice President refused to acquiesce to their demand for him to abandon his duty, even at the threat of being hung. Vice President Pence refused their demand keeping our country from experiencing a disarray like never before in modern history. You, too, have a duty to obey God. This is an ongoing assignment, not a one-time conviction. It is the duty of all mankind to fear God and keep His commandments. And like the Vice President, you must choose. Decide whether you will give in to the social norms or whether you will honor God's Word. Even if, like the Vice President, you face opposition, persecution or even death, your responsibility will not change. But unlike that fateful day, it is not a one-time decision. You will be required to make this choice every single day. Choose this day whom you will serve.

Today's readings:
Genesis 17:9; Ecclesiastes 12:13; Acts 23:1
2 Timothy 4:5; Hebrews 10:11-14

November 18
Remember Peter

Peter insisted that he would never turn his back on the Lord, but Jesus told him before the rooster crowed that night, he would deny him 3 times. Peter was insistent he would never do that. Yet, a few hours later when Jesus was dragged before the High Priest to be judged for claiming to be the Son of God, Peter told the hostile mob he never even knew Jesus. There is an old adage, never say never. Though you may have the greatest intention, sometimes you will miss the mark and disappointment God. It is far easier to proclaim your allegiance to the Lord from the comfort of your home than if you felt your life was endangered. Thank God, He will forgive you either way. The key is to not think of yourself more highly than you ought. There will be times you will be tempted to compromise your stance for Christ. Pray you won't fall into temptation. If someone who has placed their faith in Christ does falter, be gentle with them. You may someday need the same from others. Remember even Peter made a decision to do what he thought was never a possibility. Jesus restored Him. Praise God for the blessed assurance He will do the same for you.

Today's readings:
Psalm 32:1-2; Luke 22:31-34,54-62
Romans 7:15-23,12:3; Galatians 6:1; 1 John 1:8-10

November 19
The Best Made Plans

You are encouraged to make plans for your life. Some say you should have a 1 year, 5 year and 10-year plan. Having a plan is a good thing. However, just like American Express suggests you shouldn't leave home without it, you shouldn't make plans without seeking God. Many make plans but it is His will that will ultimately succeed. You are assured that God has a plan to prosper you. Given this truth, wouldn't it behoove you to seek Him and ask for His guidance? And any time you make plans bear in mind you can never override His ultimate will. You may plan for godly things in your life, even still leave room for God. What seems like a good idea, may not be God's plan for your life. Pay attention to hindrances. The Holy Spirit may be trying to steer you away from a plan that will not succeed. Don't say tomorrow I will do such and such. You don't know what tomorrow will bring. Instead, say if it is the Lord's will, I will do this or that. Always commit your plans to Him. He will make them successful. The way He brings them to pass may be different than the way you had expected. Nevertheless, His way is always best because He always intends to bless you.

Today's readings:
Job 5:12; Psalm 33:10-11; Proverbs 16:3,18:9,19:21,21:5
Jeremiah 29:11; 2 Corinthians 1:17; James 4:13-15

November 20
Seek Wise Counsel

King David's son rose to oppose him as king. He was shrewd. He turned the people's hearts against the king, little by little. Eventually, the king fled from the city to escape his son's attack. One man who spoke was said to speak as though God himself were speaking. He was angry with David, so he stayed behind to counsel David's son. David prayed that this great man's counsel would be foolish so he would ultimately succeed against his son. And God honored David's prayers. Whenever you are making plans always seek wise counsel. The fool has himself for a counselor, while the righteous listen to wisdom. Whether the decision you are making seems significant enough to change the course of your life, like whether to get married, or is one that seems miniscule by comparison, always seek someone who is knowledgeable about the decision you are making. At a minimum, find someone who knows God well enough to help you apply godly principles to your situation. Never seek out guidance from an ungodly person. God is the greatest counselor of all. He will guide you into all truth if you seek His face before you make any decision.

Today's readings:
Joshua 9:14; 2 Samuel 15:31,16:23,17:1-15; Job 15:8
Psalm 1,33:11,73:24,81:11-13; Acts 20:27

November 21
Forget About It

God made a covenant with you to put His laws in your heart and write them on your mind. He promised to no longer remember your lawless acts. You are not required to do what they did in the Old Testament when they sacrificed animals to cover their sins. This is no longer necessary because of Jesus. He is not counting your sins against you. He forgot about them. You can too. I can recall a time when I felt so ashamed of my actions, I condemned myself. I just couldn't believe I had messed up so badly. Then one day, Holy Spirit spoke to me. He challenged me to see the reason for my struggle. It was not merely that I had disappointed God. I had disappointed myself. I struggled to forgive myself because I thought I was better than that. My pride was keeping me from accepting the fact that I was a sinner saved by grace. By implication, I was saying my sins weren't covered by Jesus' sacrifice and my standards were higher than God's because I would not forgive myself. I had to humbly accept being forgiven by God and then forgive myself. Now, I can forget about it and leave it in the past.

Today's readings:
Psalm 25:7; Luke 7:36-50; Hebrews 10:16-18; 1 John 1:9

November 22
Your Blessings Are Assured

Balaam was approached by Balak to curse the children of
Israel when they were heading in to possess the land God
promised to them. He offered the prophet money, and
the prophet told him he could only say what God allowed
him to say. Still, Balaam went with Balak trying to curse
Israel. He could not curse what God had blessed. In
another instance, Saul was chosen to be the first king of
Israel. His father sent him to look for lost donkeys. After
a few days, he encountered Samuel the prophet who
anointed him and told the cook to bring out the choice
piece of meat he had set aside. God directed Samuel to
prepare in advance to bless Saul. Unfortunately, Saul
was not a good king because he did not fully obey the
Lord. Consequently, the Lord chose David to replace
him. Though Saul did all he could to kill David, even to
the point of driving him out of the country, David still
emerged as the king. No one can hinder God's plans for
you. You may have to go through hell, and it often will
get worse before God blesses you, but He will make sure
you have the blessings ordained for you.

Today's readings:
Numbers 22:10-12,19; 1 Samuel 9:1-24
Proverbs 19:21 Jeremiah 1:19

November 23
Delayed Obedience

You have been given a free will by God, and when you know there is something good you should do, but don't do it, you sin against God. Still, God will show you grace. Sometimes you allow your ignorance, or even plain old disobedience keep you from doing the right thing initially. Before Saul became Paul, he was looking for Christians like a bounty hunter. He had a letter from the high priest allowing him to arrest anyone who was of "the Way". Though he was initially opposed to the church, once Paul was saved, God used him mightily. He wrote the majority of the New Testament. His delay in obedience didn't disqualify him. Likewise, no matter what your background may have been it won't hinder you from being used by God. However, when you know better, God holds you accountable to do better. Your delayed obedience can also be life changing in a negative way. Failing to obey in a timely way when you know better could cost you everything, even your life. Ask King Manasseh.

Today's readings:
2 Chronicles 32:33-33:20; Micah 6:8
Matthew 21:28-32; Acts 9; James 4:17

November 24
Knowing Not Enough

When you consider the vast amount of knowledge you have about many things and compare this to the things you do, you may be inclined to shake your head. For example, you know eating sugary treats may cause you to have bad teeth and poorer health. Those who have suffered with nicotine-induced lung cancer, COPD or emphysema have acknowledged how smoking is hazardous for their health. Yet, many continue to smoke even after being diagnosed. You know that adultery, fornication, lying, stealing, maligning others, gossiping, murmuring, complaining, backbiting, entering an intimate relationship with others who do not know God, being drunk, and so on are things opposite of God's will for our lives, yet it is likely you still do some of these things. Many know there is a God. Still, they ignore His sovereignty. Instead of honoring Him, they do what seems right in their own eyes. They become fools, while thinking they are wise. It is not enough to know God exists. God's Word declares you should glorify Him. Do what He says to experience the fulfilment of His many promises and have a life that honors Him.

Today's readings:
Psalm 93:1,19:1; Matthew 7:21-23; Luke 6:46-49
John 8:31-32; Romans 1:19-22; James 1:22-25

November 25
Imitation Is Best

They say imitation is the highest form of flattery. Most would likely say they are not inclined to imitate anyone because they want to be an original. God created each of us uniquely, so this is understandable. Yet, God encourages you to imitate Him. He is love and He wants you to be a man or woman after His own heart. He wants you to love others just as He loves you. He is God of righteousness and truth. He is just in His dealings. You should strive to be the same. Paul challenged his readers to imitate him, as he imitated Christ. Would anyone identify you as an imitator of Christ? Or would be you be described more as an impostor? God wants better for you. Though you may fall short, be encouraged. You will be changed into His glory daily, as you yield yourself to Him. Meditating on His Word will transform you into His image as you continue to apply it to your life. Jesus shared how anyone who had seen Him has seen the Father. May it be so that others see Christ in you as you seek to imitate Him.

Today's readings:
Psalm 45:7,99:4; Romans 12:2a; 1 Corinthians 11:1
Ephesians 5:1-2,8; 1 John 3:16

November 26
Diligence Pays

There's an old saying. "The early bird gets the worm." Implied is the concept that being diligent pays off. Even Solomon compared the lazy to the those who are industrious. Those who work hard will be prosperous while those who are lazy will be impoverished. Likewise, the person who excels will be promoted to serve before those who do not. Those who are dedicated, industrious and who concentrate on their goals rise to the top. Being intentionally focused is what it means to be diligent. For example, a student who works to earn the highest grade in class works hard, does their homework, studies, and prepares. They pay close attention to what their instructor shares and reads all the assigned materials. They may even seek out other resources to master their subject. They make every effort to master the material and it pays off in their grade. Likewise, when you diligently seek God, He will reward you. He will bless you to experience the many blessings in His kingdom. Seek Him earnestly and with great care.

Today's readings:
Deuteronomy 6:17,28:1-2; Psalm 119:4
Proverbs 13:4,22:29; Isaiah 26:9; 2 Timothy 2:15
Hebrews 6:11-12,11:6

November 27
God Will Favor You

Favor ain't fair! God blesses you with loving kindness and grace, even though you don't deserve it. That's how much He loves you. Even Job, during his despair, recognized it was God who had blessed him with life and favor. The Bible provides insight for how you can obtain favor from both God and men. Keep God's commands and be merciful to others. God promises to be merciful to those who show mercy to others. There is a trend where people are going around randomly blessing others. In one instance, a person was approached in a store and asked whether they would prefer to receive a thousand dollars in cash or be able to bless someone else with ten thousand dollars. One person said they would choose to give away the ten thousand. He ran around the store and found someone to bless. She wept because she had children and had lost her job. And because the person had looked out for someone else, he was given ten thousand for himself unexpectedly. This is how God is towards you. Do good to others, and He will bless you.

Today's readings:
Job 10:12; Proverbs 3:1-4, 8:1,35, 11:25

November 28
All In

When God rejected Saul as king of Israel, He sent the prophet Samuel to Jesse's home to select the next king. Jesse paraded all 7 of his older sons before the prophet but none were selected. Finally, Jesse called for David, a shepherd boy. God told Samuel to anoint David as king. Meanwhile, Saul was being tormented by an unclean spirit. Some of his men told him about a shepherd boy who could soothe his soul by playing his harp. He sent for the boy, David. Because Saul was pleased with him, David became Saul's armor bearer. When Israel's army was fighting the Philistines, David's father sent him to the front line with food. While there, he heard the mocking voice of Goliath. David's experience included being a shepherd, a minstrel, an armor bearer, a courier, a great warrior and eventually a king. God use him in a multiplicity of ways. Later, another "Shepherd" began His career as a carpenter. He went on to feed multitudes, heal many sick and even raise the dead before manifesting as the Savior of the world. He, too, was used in multiple ways. You may not recognize your various strengths, but others may see them. Let go of doubt and let God use you.

Today's readings:
Job 10:12; Proverbs 3:1-4, 8:1,35, 11:25

November 29
Only He Can And He Did

The artist Prince sang a song that says, "I would die for you." It caused me to think about all that Jesus has done for us. You would like to think someone loves you enough to die for you, but as the Holy Bible says, scarcely would someone die for a righteous man. Yet, at just the right time Christ died for the sins of all of mankind. He died for you and me, even though we did not deserve it. The Stylistics sang about "you make me feel brand new". Jesus is the one who can make you brand new. If you put your trust in Him and accept His death as payment for your sins, He will make you a new creation. Your spirit will be born again. Life will have newness. The Temptations belted out, "I can make a ship sail on dry land." It made me think of the Red Sea. When God's people were up against the sea and they saw the Egyptian army chasing them from behind, they must have felt doomed. Yet, it was God who turned a sea into dry land. No matter what your situation or circumstance, remember God is able to deliver you.

Today's readings:
Genesis 6:13-14; Exodus 14:5-21; Job 9:5; Isaiah 45:7
Luke 1:37; John 1:29; Romans 5:6-8; 2 Corinthians 5:17

November 30
God Will Deliver You

In the Old Testament every time the people of God
would disobey His commands, He would allow their
enemies to triumph over them. When they would cry out
to God, He would rescue them. I recall reading and
seeing this cycle repeated over and over. I was tempted
to judge them for their disobedience when the Holy
Spirit reminded me, they were just like us. If you are
honest, you too go astray, and the Lord delivers you from
your distresses. You too may find yourself in a difficult
set of circumstances because you refuse to obey God's
will for your life. Jonah is the poster child for this truth.
He was directed by the Lord to go to Nineveh to share
His message to let them know if they did not repent of
their wickedness, God was going to destroy their city.
But Jonah deemed the Ninevites to be his enemies. He
did not want to go. Instead, He went in the opposite
direction. You can't hide from God. Instead of getting
away by ship as he had planned, Jonah found himself in
the belly of a big fish. But when he cried out to God, the
Lord delivered him. He will deliver you from all your
troubles. Even if you make a mess, God is merciful and
will hear your pleas if call on Him.

Today's readings:
Jonah 1; Judges 3:7-10,12-15; Psalm 34:4-5; John 2:1-5

December 1
You Can Do It

Walk out your faith by believing God to help you achieve your goals. Esther found herself in a seemingly impossible situation, as a Jewish orphan married to the king of Persia. She had been raised by her uncle Mordecai. When her uncle learned of a plot developed by the king's servant to destroy the Jews, he sent a message to Esther. He implored her to go see the king to ask him to intervene on her people's behalf. Esther was reluctant. She understandably feared for her life. Everyone knew entering the king's presence uninvited could result in decapitation. It was not something to be taken lightly. Yet, God had postured her to do what her uncle was encouraging her to do. So she asked others to join her in fasting and praying, then she went in to see the king. Perhaps you are facing what seems like impossible odds against your efforts to accomplish something. Maybe it is not a goal you chose but one that has been thrust upon you or simply a task you believe you should achieve. Know that you are well able to reach whatever ends God has allowed you to be faced with achieving. Know that God has created and postured you for such a time as this.

Today's readings:
Jonah 1; Judges 3:7-10,12-15; Psalm 34:4-5; John 2:1-5

December 2
Power Of Unity

When I was younger, I did not understand the purpose of participating in team sports beyond just having fun. Now I see they are so much more. They parallel life to provide valuable lessons. Just like in life, each team member has a role to play. They all depend on one another to fulfill their given assignment so the whole team can succeed. When one person fails to do their part, it puts strain on the others. Yet, there will be times when a team member is hurt or simply not able to perform at their highest level. The other team members must step up and bear one another's weight for the team to achieve success. In the best of times, when they are all flowing together on one accord, they can be victorious. God has made the church to be a body; like a team each of us has a function. When we each operate in our gifts while maintaining lifestyles that please God, we can fulfill His mandate to occupy until He returns. We can be fruitful, multiply, and fill the earth with godly offspring, by raising our children to know the Lord. The power of unity is key to our impact as Christ's body.

Today's readings:
Psalm 133:1,3; Genesis 11:1-7; 1 Corinthians 12:1-7

December 3
Don't Touch This

There is a principle expressed in scripture about how you should treat God's children. There are multiple examples of how those who come against God's people end up having undesirable experiences. Even those who He used were punished if they did harm to those called of God. I am reminded of King Saul. He chased David for years trying to kill him so David would not succeed him as king. One night he was sleeping in a cave surrounded by his men. David found him and crept into the cave, but he dared not touch someone God had elevated. God promotes and brings down. Instead, David cut a piece of Saul's robe off and then snuck away. The next morning when Saul arose, David stood afar and called out to him. He showed him the piece he had cut from his robe. Saul recognized David was a better man than he was because he chose not to harm him. You are called of God, imbued with His righteousness, and favored by Him. Therefore, whoever tries to harm you must give an account to Him. This is why you never have to seek vengeance. God will repay.

Today's readings:
Esther 7:3-10; Psalm34:21,105:13-15; Romans 8:29-30
2 Corinthians 5:21

December 3
He's A Keeper

We are bombarded with messages on social media that can influence our hearts and minds to live outside of God's will. Social norms are shifting. Dress codes have changed so dramatically it seems the less you wear the more fashionable you are deemed to be. The visual images that cascade across the television have reached a new depth in immorality, with sexual scenes and foul language deemed to acceptable even in shows geared towards families. As you seek to live a godly lifestyle you can find yourself swimming against a tide of unwholesome social norms. You may be tempted to compromise to fit in with the world. Rather than stress about making bad choices, meditate on God's promises. Keep your mind renewed by reading God's Word, praying in agreement with the scripture and making every effort to obey Him. Search for verses specific to your need. Yield to the Holy Spirit's guidance to avoid temptation and being trapped by the schemes of the devil. The power of God in you can resist the devil and he will flee. As you feed your spirit, you will be strengthened by the power of His Might.

Today's readings:
Deuteronomy 7:15; Psalm 121:7; 1 Corinthians 1:8
1 Peter 1:3-5 Jude 1:24-25

December 4
The Prerequisite To Knowing God's Will

There is a prerequisite to knowing God's will. Unlike some classes that say you need a prerequisite, but can still be passed without it, you must have this condition met before you can fully grasp God's perfect will for your life. You must have His Spirit. You need Him to help you grasp the true meaning of the Word. He is like your spiritual interpreter. He will translate the Word to help you understand it and apply it to your life. The Holy Spirit is not only like having an interpreter; He is also like a personal tour guide. He will guide you into all truth. Like a prophet, He will show you things that are yet to come. There is no need to seek a psychic who tries to read the stars, when you have access to the One who made them both – the stars and the psychic! To receive the Holy Spirit, you must be born again by accepting Jesus as your Lord and Savior. To do that, believe in His virgin birth, death, and resurrection, then pray and ask Him to come into your heart. Whoever calls on the name of Jesus shall be saved, and you will immediately receive His Spirit.

Today's readings:
John 3:3; 14:16,17; 1 Corinthians 2:13,14

December 5
You Already Have What It Takes

How many of you are like the characters in the Wizard of Oz searching for what you think you want when you already have everything you need. The Cowardly Lion had courage, he just needed to exercise it. The Scarecrow was the one who figured out how to get the trees to throw their apples. Toto had come to show them the way to get to Dorothy. The Tin Man was so sentimental he was clearly loving. You, too, have been given everything you need for life and godliness. It's a promise from God. You may not see what others see in you, or more importantly what God has put in you. Each of you have been uniquely equipped to fulfill the purpose He has for your life. That is why you can celebrate when others are successful in doing what God has purposed for them to do. You aren't in a competition with others. What God has for you is for you! When you walk with Him, you can be assured you have all the gifts, skills, resources you need to be successful in what He has called you to do. He will never set you up for failure. The world may doubt your ability, but God will see to it that you are victorious when you follow His path. You are fully equipped. You have what it takes to be victorious!

Today's readings:
Psalm 23:1,138:8; Philippians 4:19; 1 Peter 1:3

December 6
Bitterness Poisons

When you feel wronged by another it's important to go to the person to seek reconciliation. At a minimum, you want to work on forgiveness in your heart so that you don't allow a bitter root to be planted. Bitterness you hold against another is like gangrene to your soul. It will poison other relationships and areas of your life. It knows no boundaries. In 2 Samuel 15, King David's son Absalom rose to overthrow his kingship. He sought the counsel of Ahithophel the Gilonite, David's counselor, who's words were like oracles of God according to the Bible. And when David learned he was with his son, David prayed Ahithophel's counsel would be turned to foolishness. When gave advice to Absalom he shared a perfect plan for him to overthrow his father. But David's friend was also present, and he convinced Absalom to reject the wise counsel of Ahithophel. When Ahithophel realized his advice was rejected he went home and hung himself. He may have switched allegiances to go against King David because he was the grandfather of Bathsheba, holding bitterness against David. Forgive. Let God avenge offences. Bitterness poisons your heart.

Today's readings:
2 Samuel 2:26; Jeremiah 4:14-18; Ephesians 4:31
Hebrews 12:15

December 7
Blameless

You're not perfect. I would bet you can think of countless times and ways you have made mistakes in your life. We all have our own laundry lists. Yet, when you are in Christ there is no record kept of these things. You need to let them go and stop looking back. God has greater things ahead for you. This does not prevent people from keeping track of your shortcomings. Nor does it mean you cannot be held accountable to earthly laws and regulations. Still, many can testify how God's mercy intervened to lessen the consequences. God sees you differently when you are born again. In His eyes, you are a new creation. The old you, and its failures, are gone. God has cast them into the sea of forgetfulness. All too often we beat ourselves up and walk in condemnation over our past mistakes. It plays into the enemy's plan to keep you walking in defeat. You must reject every assault launched upon your psyche that keeps you walking in shame. Your self-assessment should be the same as God's view of you. He sees you as blameless. Your sins are covered by the Blood of Jesus. You are blameless in God's sight.

Today's readings:
Psalm 32:1-2,103:12; John 10:10; Micah 7:19
Romans 8:1,33-34; 2 Corinthians 5:17,21

December 8
Think On This

What are you thinking about? Your thoughts determine your mindset and actions. If you are constantly thinking negatively, you are likely living the same way. Examine every thought. According to Philippians 4:8-9, think about whatever is true, admirable, lovely, pure, or right. Otherwise, shift your thoughts to think about something that agrees with one of these attributes. You have the power to take every thought captive if it is not in agreement with God's Word. Imagine if your front door was ajar, some strangers entered, and made themselves at home. I'm pretty sure you would show them to the door. I challenge you to filter every thought through the Philippians 4:8 sifter. If it does not pass, then take it captive and replace it with a different thought that agrees with the Word of God. Pay special attention to how you think about yourself. Do not linger on negative thoughts about yourself. Remind yourself, if what you think about yourself is not in alignment with what the Bible says about you, it is a lie. Replace it with a thought that agrees with what God says. Your mind is the compass for your life. You are what you think you are...

Today's readings:
John 10:10; Micah 7:19; Romans 8:1,33-34
2 Corinthians 5:17,21; Revelation 12:10

December 9
Show He's Really Real

Many people have written to share their testimony of coming to Christ. One gentleman's testimony truly blessed me. He had never been to church and did not pray but there was "something about this God" that he could not ignore. That "something" is the power of God. Just like him, others can experience this truth through your witness. Your witness can come through several ways. One way is when you walk in unity in the body of Christ. Jesus said when we are one, we show the world that He is really the Son of God that was sent to save us from our sinful ways. Our oneness is a testimony to the world of the power of God. And we know this pleases God because where there is unity, God commands the blessing. You can also show He is real by your personal testimony. As you share what God has done in your life, you can encourage others. When you lift Him up, Jesus will draw all men to Himself. He will demonstrate His power through you with signs and wonders, miracles, and gifts of the Holy Spirit. By all these testimonies the world will know He is really real!

Today's readings:
Psalm 32:1-2,103:12; John 10:10; Micah 7:19
Romans 8:1,33-34; 2 Corinthians 5:17,21

December 10
God Of Restoration

God can restore everything the enemy has stolen. You may have years of poor health or financial woes. You may have seasons of great loss and heartache. You may have had times when you were walking outside of God's perfect will for your life, which resulted in you losing your peace. But God has the capacity to turn your circumstances around. The story of Job is a classic example of how God can restore. Job's righteous life made him a target for the devil. He lost everything. But because of his obedience, God gave him double for the many troubles he endured. Even David was able to recover everything that was stolen by men who had raided his camp. Just like Job, he had not sinned, yet he suffered loss. He prayed and God led him to recover all that had been taken. The enemy is always seeking someone to devour. And sometimes it is your sin that leads to loss. Like Paul, who was persecuting the church, you can choose a way that opposes God. Yet, also like Paul, you can still experience complete restoration if you are willing to repent. God is able to restore everything you've lost. Ask Him to do it.

Today's readings:
1 Samuel 30:16-20; Job 42:10-17; Joel 2:25
Acts 9:17-19; 1 Peter 5:8

December 11
Still Got A Praise

You have a choice to make each day and in every circumstance in your life. You determine how you will respond to the things you experience. You can be like Job's wife, who suggested he just curse God and die because of all the hardships he endured. Or you can be like the psalmist and declare, "I will bless the Lord at all times." Psalm 34:1. You don't have a choice about what happens to you, but you do have a choice of how you respond. When you choose to praise the Lord and give thanks to God in all circumstances you can walk in God's will. He inhabits the praises of His people. I can recall being in labor with my daughter. My nurse was clearly worried. She explained how my baby's heart rate dropped with every contraction. Immediately I began to shift the atmosphere by singing praise songs. Instead of responding to the nurse's news with fear, I proclaimed the promises of God with every song of praise that filled the room. As the atmosphere shifted, my baby's heart rate settled, and she was born healthy and whole. Whether or not you are in a crisis or simply choose to give God some praise. Let everything that has breath praise the Lord!

Today's readings:
Job 2:9,10,13:15a; Psalm 22:3,34:1-6,150:1-6
Acts 16:22-27; Philippians 4:6

December 12
Look To The Hills

When life seems overwhelming it can feel like you are drowning in despair. How do you escape such sorrow? Look up! The psalmist said he would look to the hills from which comes his help. He realized all his help comes from the Lord, the Maker of heaven and earth. Like with David, things can go so awry in your life. Also, like David, you can choose to strengthen yourself in the Lord. When families and property were taken into enemy territory, many chose to blame David and wanted to attack him. David didn't get wearied, though. Instead, he strengthened himself in the Lord. First, he had a good cry. It is not a sign of weakness. It is a mechanism of relief God put inside of each of us. Then, David looked to God. He focused on all His promises. He remembered what God had done in the past. Lastly, he used positive self-talk. Remind yourself who you are in Christ. You can do all things through Him that strengthens you. Remind yourself of the times God brought you out of a situation that seemed so hopeless at the time. Be encouraged. If He did it before, He can do it again. Look up!

Today's readings:
1 Samuel 30:1-6; Psalms 121:1,2, 138:7

December 13
Impossible To Forget

You may have days when you feel abandoned or forsaken by God. In those moments it is important to separate fact from fiction and feelings from faith. We walk by faith and not by sight. You can believe your feelings, or you can choose to believe the report of the Lord. His Word makes it abundantly clear you are impossible to forget. He loves you with an everlasting love. You are the apple of His eye. He demonstrated His love for you in the most tangible way possible. He died for you. Like a mother cherishes and never forgets her child, you are His beloved child. You are His own. Because God created you, He is concerned about you and will perfect everything in your life. Consider the fact that the Maker of heaven and earth is your Father. Even when things are seemingly not going your way, we know from Romans 8:28 that He is working all things together for your good. He has promised to never leave you nor forsake you. He has inscribed your name in the palm of His hand. Unlike a tattoo etched in indelible ink, His inscription can never be reversed. You are etched in His hand and on His heart forever. You are impossible to forget.

Today's readings:
Psalm 17:7,8, 138:8; Isaiah 49:14-16; John 15:13
2 Corinthians 5:7

December 14
Mind Your Business

I read a story about when D.L. Moody encountered a man who was leaning against a lamppost. He asked him if he was Christian. The man angrily told Mr. Moody to mind his own business. All who profess to be followers of Christ have been called to be Christ's ambassador. You are to tell everyone you encounter that God is reconciling Himself to the world and no longer counting sins against them. Let me put it to you another way. If your dad owned a used car business and you knew the only way your family could be successful was if your father's business was successful, I bet you would use every opportunity you could to let people know about your father's business. Well, your Father's business is saving souls. Weeks after Mr. Moody spoke to the man on the street, in the wee hours of the night, he was awakened by pounding on his door. He jumped up thinking there was an emergency only to find the man he had spoken to earlier at his door. The man shared how he hadn't slept a wink since Mr. Moody asked him that question. He wanted to know what He must do to be saved. Notice how he asked, and God dealt with the man's heart. Will you be about your Father's business today?

Today's readings:
Luke 2:41-49; Acts 17:30; 2 Corinthians 5:17-20

December 15
Give Them Me

Has anyone ever asked your opinion and you gave it to them? My guess is you have had this experience at some point in your life. When it happens, you have an opportunity to share your personal point of view, or you can give them something far better. As a child of the Most High you have the mind of Christ. You have the capacity to share God's perspective. You can give them Jesus. I recall once being asked by a friend how she should handle an opportunity to take a job. The job had been offered but her husband didn't want her to take it. I responded with what I believed to be consistent with the Biblical declaration that God has made them one, as husband and wife. I couldn't imagine God bringing her an opportunity that would cause a rift in her household. I don't recall my exact words, but I do remember hers. She said she could have asked others, but she chose to ask me because she trusted I would tell her what she needed to hear, rather than simply what she wanted to hear. You can give others your opinion or you can share with them the Lord's will. The Lord is calling out to us all, "Give them Me".

Today's readings:
Numbers 22:35,38; Isaiah 50:4; 1 Corinthians 2:16
Colossians 4:6; 1 Peter 4:11

December 16
Establish A Written Record

Studies have shown that when you write something down you are more likely to retain it in your memory. God told the prophet Jeremiah to write down all the things He had spoken to him. When you study the Word of God, you too should take notes. They will become your personal reference and resource on the promises of God. Over time you will be able to see how God speaks to you personally and how He has guided you throughout your walk with Him. In addition, it will help you to guide others in their relationship with God. When you seek to share what God has spoken, you will have a reference to turn to as a resource for where to find different passages in the Bible. If you create a system to index the things you discover in the Word, it will be an invaluable tool for you to use for years to come. Taking notes during Bible study or while listening to sermons will help you to build your library of information about God's will. Record what you have heard and read, and over time you will find you have a phenomenal written record that can be a blessing in your life and the lives of others.

Today's readings:
Proverbs 3:3; Isaiah 43:26; Jeremiah 30:2
Habakkuk 2:2; Luke 1:3; Revelations 2:8

December 17
You Don't Know Who You're Talking To

When Samuel came to anoint the second king of Israel, his father bought all his other sons out to meet the prophet, but God rejected all of them. He asked David's father Jesse if he had any other sons. He indicated he had one other who was out tending the sheep. The prophet insisted they should not begin their meal together until David arrived. After it was all said and done, it was David who was anointed by the prophet to be the next king. When Saul, who later became the Apostle Paul, was struck with blindness by the Lord, he was feared by Christians because he had been putting them in jail. But God had great plans for him. When He told Ananias to go anoint Saul, he objected because he knew how much he was persecuting the church. However, God assured him He had called Paul to be His servant. Just because someone's lifestyle may seem contrary to God's will, it doesn't mean He won't change them for His glory. Without David becoming king, we wouldn't have a Savior. Without Saul being converted, we wouldn't have the majority of the New Testament. God is not a respecter of person, neither should you be.

Today's readings:
Genesis 18:1,2; 1 Samuel 16:11; John 4:1-4
Acts 9:10-16; Hebrews 13:2

December 18
A New Home

When I was a child, the saints would sing about having "a building not made by hands." They were singing of the day when they would shed their earthly bodies and be clothed in their heavenly ones. The Bible says flesh and blood cannot inherit the kingdom of God. Your corruptible body you live in now is decaying. Your mortal body will be replaced by an immortal body. You will live in your new body in your new home forever. This is our temporary abode. Therefore, do not stress out over this which is temporary. Jesus said, "In my Father's house are many mansions; If it were not so I would have told you. I go to prepare a place for you...that where I am, there you may be also." God has new home for you. It is a place preserved for you in heaven, where Jesus sits at the right hand of the Father. A place where there will be no more suffering or sorrows, where God will wipe away every tear from your eyes. In your new house you will praise God and walk on streets of gold. So, whenever you feel like life is overwhelming look up. Remind yourself this will not last forever. And there is no place (on earth) like (your new) home.

Today's readings:
Psalm 23:6; John 14:2-6; 1 Corinthians 15:42-45
2 Corinthians 5:1-6

December 19
Just Like God

You can be a pacesetter or respond to the pace set by others. In some high-level long-distance track events, the organizers bring in a strong athlete to set the pace for the race. They start out leading the first leg of the race and eventually fade out of the way. The top contenders will keep the pace or even exceed it for the remainder of the event. God has set the pace for you to follow Him in how He treats those least deserving of His love. Jesus said if you only show love to those who love you back, it's no different from what unbelievers do. Walk in love towards those you may think deserve it the least. As a prison chaplain, all too often I heard others suggest the prisoners did not deserve my kindness. Consider, however, it is when you are at your worst that you need others to show you the most compassion. Extend the same kindness to others that you want someone to show to you. When the Pharisees asked Jesus about the greatest commandment, He responded, "You shall love the Lord your God with all your heart, with all your soul, and with all your mind." This is the first and greatest commandment. And the second is like it: "You shall love your neighbor as yourself."

Today's readings:
Matthew 5:44-46, 22:37-39; Luke 6:35; Romans 5:5

December 20
Your Past Can Make Some Wonder

When people know your story, they may find it hard to believe you have changed. They may assume your newfound faith is fake. This is what happened to the Apostle Paul. Before Paul surrendered his life to the Lord, he had been persecuting the church. It was Paul, formerly named Saul, who held the cloaks of those who stoned Stephen to death. Therefore, no one could believe he was truly saved. This often happens when prisoners give their hearts to Christ. They are ridiculed and accused of only having jailhouse religion when they profess their faith. Some only seek God while they are locked up just to bide their time while serving their sentences. Yet, many others have authentic conversions and continue their walk with the Lord during their incarceration and after their release. Some become pastors, evangelists and serve in other ministries. They may have been murders or thieves, drug addicts or dealers, prostitutes or even pimps. But God can change anyone. He can change you, your friends, your family members. You do not need to be ashamed of your past. Just give God the glory for how He changed you.

Today's readings:
Luke 8:26-39; John 4: 39-42; Acts 9:1-31

December 21
Fully Persuaded

The biggest obstacle to your faith is doubt. It will hinder your prayers. When you read your Bible make every effort to be like Abraham. Even though he had reached 100 years old and Sarah was well past her childbearing years, he believed what God had told him. He believed his body would still produce seed to impregnate her. He didn't doubt God's promises. He believed God was able to do exactly what He said He would. Every promise in God is yes and amen! He doesn't speak and not act. He does not promise and not fulfill His Word. He is a rewarder of those who diligently seek Him. He is not pleased with those who doubt His Word. You can increase your faith by hearing His word. Read it. Speak it out loud. Listen to others preach it and teach it. Are you doubting God in some area of your life? If so, find a verse or passage that speaks to your situation then memorize it. Meditate on it day and night until you become fully persuaded God will do what He said He will do in your life.

Today's readings:
Romans 4:20,21; Hebrews 11:1,6; James 1:5-7
1 Peter 5:7

December 22
Lowly

He left His place in Glory for your sake and mine. He was clothed in Majesty. He could have appeared to mankind in a palace but instead He entered through a peasant girl who gave birth to Him in a manger. No doubt it smelled unpleasant as it was the living quarters of animals. It was not fit for any baby's birth, much less the King of kings. But He was lowly in heart, even though not in stature. He not only had a lowly disposition, but He also showed regard for those of a lowly estate. One example was His cousins Zacharius and Elizabeth who were unable to have children. They lived in a time when the inability to bear a child bought great shame. They were well past childbearing age. Yet, it was them who God chose to be the parents of John the Baptist. He sent the angel Gabriel to let Zacharius know He had heard his prayers. As Elizabeth declared, God had looked upon her, His lowly maidservant. Perhaps you have felt insignificant, been marginalized, or overlooked. Perhaps to the world, your plight and prayers are not of great importance. But they are to God. You are important to Him. Remember, God cares about everything concerning you.

Today's readings:
Job 5:11; Zechariah 9:9; Matthew 11:29; Luke 1:5-17,48
Ephesians 4:1-2; Philippians 2:3; 1 Peter 5:6

December 23
Your Peace

Jesus is not only the Lord of peace; He is your peace. He can always give you peace in every circumstance. Through the suffering He endured for your sins, He purchased your peace, satisfying the law's demand for the payment of sin: death. And because of His sacrifice, you are now justified. God views you as holy. He treats you just as if you had never sinned. Otherwise, your sin created a barrier between you and God. He sent Jesus to be the propitiation for your transgressions, the payment of the wages of sin. Therefore, you have peace with God. Jesus had a forerunner. His first cousin, John, was sent before Him to guide people into the way of peace. He told them to prepare their hearts by repentance. He prepared the people's hearts, making the way for the Lord's arrival. As the God of peace, the Lord will command your peace, even making your enemies live at peace with you as you live in a way pleasing to Him. God's ability to give you peace is not limited to times when there is a lack of trouble. Rather, He can grant you His supernatural, incomprehensible peace that supersedes your understanding.

Today's readings:
Isaiah 26:3,12,53:5; Luke 1:79; John 14:27
Ephesians 2:14; Romans 5:11; 1 Thessalonians 5:23

December 24
Commends And Promotes

Solomon was endowed with great wisdom. He suggested you should not praise yourself but let others do it. God will commend you and cause others to do the same. Even if they don't, they will still have to honor you when God's favor is bestowed upon you. Likewise, though you may do all you can to be promoted, it is God who exalts. Promotion comes from the Lord. When God appointed king Saul as the first king of Israel he was immediately received by the people. But as time went on, he was so focused on pleasing the people he took his focus off obeying God. People pleasing is never a good thing. When you are led by His Spirit, God will handle how much people honor you. And remember, if God is for you, it does not matter who is against you. Focus on pleasing God and leave the concerns about being celebrated to Him. Remember, anyone who has influence can be influenced by God. Their heart is in His hand. He can and will turn it in your favor if you keep your focus on pleasing Him.

Today's readings:
1 Samuel 13:14, 28:17; Psalms 75:6-7; Isaiah 22:22
Jeremiah 29:26; 2 Corinthians 3:1,4-6, 10:18

December 25
For My Own Sake

There are some principles in God's Word that will simply bring joy to your heart when you grasp its true meaning. For those who are in Christ, it is a blessed assurance to know you are associated with God. When you encounter difficulties that are opposite to God's will for your life, you can call out to the Lord and ask for His intervention. Your plea can be based on something greater than your need, more important than your desires, and even far more impactful than your faith. God will intervene not just because you asked, but because your request aligns with His character. It's for the sake of His own purposes and plans. Like when He spoke to the prophet Isaiah, the reason He was going to act was for His honor. Once He makes a promise, He honors it for the sake of His reputation. Hence, if you petition the Lord to move because it is consistent with what He has already committed to do, then you can be assured He will answer. When He told Abraham all nations would be blessed through him, Abraham could call out to God with confidence to provide him with an heir, even at the age of 99 years old. God honors what He says.

Today's readings:
Ezekiel 36:22–32; Jeremiah 14:7–9; Daniel 9:15–19
Malachi 3:10; Romans 4:13-25

December 26
Between Good and Great!

When you have a choice between things that are ungodly and those that are not, it can be easy to discern which way to go. Yet, there will be times in your life where you may have to choose between alternatives that aren't so diametrically opposed. It is not always so black and white to know God's perfect will. Sure, you can choose either and perhaps experience a good outcome. On the other hand, choosing the right one may be crucial to your destiny in the Lord. When my girlfriend learned about a new church being founded, she sensed the pull of the Holy Spirit guiding her to join. When her future husband learned of the new church, he too felt led to investigate. He attended one of the meetings where the new pastor was casting his vision to potential members. For some reason during the discussion, he decided to leave. He was having second thoughts about joining. As he rose to walk away, the new pastor suggested that if he left, he might miss his future wife. The man returned to his seat and is now happily married to my friend. Develop your ear to hear what the Spirit is saying.

Today's readings:
Deuteronomy12:28; Joshua 24:15; Psalm 102:7
John 13:17; Hebrews 5:12-14; James 1:22-25; 2:14

December 27
Kept From Dangers Seen and Unseen

When the Israelites came out of Egypt, they had to fight for the land the Lord had promised them. When the nations began to hear about them, they became anxious. One of the kings decided to take the offense by having them cursed. He tried to hire the prophet Balaam to speak against them. But God intervened. He told Balaam not to go with them. When Balaam tried to do so God sent an angel to oppose him. Balaam couldn't see the angel, but his donkey could. God allowed the donkey to turn away from the angel's drawn sword. Balaam was beating the donkey because she kept turning away. Finally, God allowed the donkey to tell Balaam. It was her actions that saved him. God will use supernatural intervention to keep you from dangers you can see and those you cannot. He saved Daniel when king Darius was creating an edict to punish anyone who prayed to any god other than him. Daniel was put in a den filled with lions, but an angel shut the lions' mouths and he was well. God can and will protect you.

Today's readings:
Numbers 22:22-35; Daniel 6:16-23; Matthew 4:11

December 28
Thankful For Not

People have shared their gratitude for what God didn't allow in their lives. Sometimes you can ask God for something, but He doesn't let it come to pass. Once, when I really wanted a job, I was interviewed and given an offer. I had made preparations to leave the job I had at the time, but the Lord did not allow me to have any peace about it. At the last second, I declined the new position. A year or so later the whole office shut down. I would have been laid off too. When Barnabas and Paul were on a missionary journey, they had planned to go to Asia to preach. But the Holy Spirit hindered them. Paul dreamed people were calling for them to Macedonia. They went and led many to Christ, including a jailor who witnessed God's power when the Lord shook the entire prison and caused all the jailed to be freed of their shackles. He came asking Paul, "what must I do to be saved?" The Lord's hindrance led to many souls being saved. The greatest **no** of all was the Father's response to Jesus's multiple pleas in the Garden of Gethsemane. Sometimes "no" is the best answer you can receive.

Today's readings:
Matthew 26:39; Acts 16:6-10,25-34; 1Thessalonians 5:18

December 29
Are You the One?

When Jesus encountered 10 lepers, they all cried out to Him for mercy. Lepers tend to hang around with others who have common conditions. Much like you may hang around those with similar habits or struggles as you. Alcoholics hang with others who drink heavily. Those who indulge in fornication cleave together. People who sell drugs befriend others in that line of work. Lepers were shunned by others and forbidden to be out in public under Mosaic law. So, it wasn't surprising to find 10 together. When Jesus heard their cries, He told them to go show themselves to a priest to be declared clean. This would permit them to rejoin society. No doubt they were ecstatic having experienced the Lord's life altering power. The scripture tells us one of the ten went back to Jesus, gave glory to God for being healed, and expressed his thankfulness. Jesus commented how not only was it bothersome that only one gave thanks, the one who came back was a foreigner. It was the non-Jewish, Samaritan who expressed thanks. You may not come from a church-going family or be one that others include in their circle. But God can still heal you if you cry out to him.

Today's readings:
Psalm 75:1; Luke 17:11-19: Philippians 4:6-7; James 1:17

December 30
Be Still

What should you do when you do not hear from God? You can be like Sarah. She wanted a child so badly she told her husband Abraham to go sleep with her maid Hagar. At first, she thought it was a great idea. She was so focused on what she wanted, she was blinded to the impact it would have on her marriage and relationship with Hagar. She ignored the effects of how she was going about achieving her goal. You can likewise want something so badly you disregard whether it negatively impacts others or even consider whether it is something God wants you to have. Sarah took matters into her own hands instead of waiting on God. Have you ever done this? God had a plan for Sarah to have a son. She simply chose not to wait on Him. And because she did not wait for Him to answer her prayers, she orchestrated a set of circumstances destined to create pain in her life as well as those she involved in her scheme. You can come up with your own way, which often leads to destruction of peace and relationships, or you can wait for God to reveal to you His perfect will. Remember when God blesses you, He adds no sorrow to it.

Today's readings:
Genesis 16:1-7; Exodus 14:13-14 NIV; Nehemiah 8:1-11
Psalm 46:10-11; Proverbs 10:22,16:25; Matthew 7:7

December 31
Increase For What?

The prayer of Jabez has become widely known for his bold prayer to God. He was more honorable than his brothers, according to scripture. We don't know much about his brothers. But we know his actions were more godly than theirs. It reminds me of the scriptural principle related to prayer. When you come to God seeking Him to make sure you're treated fairly, you should come with clean hands. Meaning, you should present yourself as one who honors God's Word. How can you ask God to make others treat you according to His Word if you don't honor His Word? Jabez's mother gave him this name because he caused her pain. With little exception, childbirth is painful so it is curious that his mother would be moved to call him a name that literally means "he caused me to be sorrowful." Despite this he obviously had a relationship with the Lord. He cried out for God to bless him. He asked God to enlarge his territory, to let His hand be with him and to keep him from pain. God granted his request because it was in line with God's will. As you pray, remember to make God's will the goal for your every request.

Today's readings:
1 Chronicles 4:9-10; Psalm 24:4-5; Matthew 6:10
Revelations 5:10

ABOUT THE AUTHOR

Rev. Lettie Moses Carr. Esq. was born again as a pre-teen. After graduating from T.C. Williams High School, Alexandria, Virginia of Remember the Titans fame, she obtained her Bachelor of Arts from Smith College, Northampton, Massachusetts, and a Juris Doctorate from the University of Michigan Law School. She served as the Elder over Evangelism at the Church of the Great Commission.

Rev. Carr walked away from her law firm's partnership in response to the call of God to serve as the Administrative Chaplain of the Maryland Correctional Institution for Women, Jessup, Maryland where she ministered full-time for nearly 22 years. Her innovative ministry led to a full-fledged church developed inside of the prison walls with banner, dance, drama, mime, music and youth ministries which were highly celebrated by many who visited the worship services.

God continues to use Rev. Carr to reach the lost and encourage the His saints throughout the world through her daily 3:16 pm Prayer Line and the WhosoeverBelieves.org platform. She now serves on the staff of First Baptist Church of Glenarden, Landover, Maryland under the leadership of Pastor John K. Jenkins, Sr. as an Associate Pastor.

The Word of the Day

Made in the USA
Middletown, DE
05 November 2023

41894205R00209